UNITE THE TRIBES

Ending Turf Wars for Career and Business Success

Christopher Duncan

apress™

Unite the Tribes: Ending Turf Wars for Career and Business Success

Copyright © 2004 by Christopher Duncan

ISBN: 1-59059-240-9

Printed and bound in Canada 12345678910

Editorial Board: Dan Appleman, Craig Berry, Gary Cornell, Tony Davis, Steven Rycroft, Julian Skinner, Martin Streicher, Jim Sumser, Karen Watterson, Gavin Wray, John Zukowski

Assistant Publisher: Grace Wong

Project Manager: Kylie Johnston

Copy Editor: Tom Gillen

Production Manager: Kari Brooks

Production Editor: Kelly Winquist

Proofreader: Thistle Hill Publishing Services, LLC

Compositor: Kinetic Publishing Services, LLC

Indexer: Odessa&Cie

Interior and Cover Designer: Kurt Krames

Manufacturing Manager: Tom Debolski

Distributed to the book trade in the United States by Springer-Verlag New York, Inc., 175 Fifth Avenue, New York, NY 10010 and outside the United States by Springer-Verlag GmbH & Co. KG, Tiergartenstr. 17, 69112 Heidelberg, Germany.

In the United States: phone 1-800-SPRINGER, email orders@springer-ny.com, or visit http://www.springer-ny.com. Outside the United States: fax +49 6221 345229, email orders@springer.de, or visit http://www.springer.de.

For information on translations, please contact Apress directly at 2560 Ninth Street, Suite 219, Berkeley, CA 94710. Phone 510-549-5930, fax 510-549-5939, email info@apress.com, or visit http://www.apress.com.

Dedicated with humility, gratitude, and respect to Wayne Van Horne.

Some things should be spoken more often.
Some things are best left unsaid.
The hardest is to do both.

*To the fearless, the passionate, the true believers
who know in their hearts that within them is the power
to create a better world, I raise my sword in salute.*

Unite, and be invincible!

Contents

Foreword

I first met Christopher Duncan more than ten years ago when I interviewed him for a senior-level position at a large software company. I had already decided before the interviewing process that I would be interested only in someone with a predefined skill set and level of experience. When I saw Christopher's resume, I immediately recognized that, although he didn't possess these prerequisites, there was something that intrigued me enough to at least meet with him for a few minutes. I was so sure that he wouldn't be what I needed that I arranged the time of our meeting to start about half an hour before lunch. Three hours into our interview, my supervisor poked his head in the door and asked if I was going to hire the man or just keep him locked up all day.

This anecdote leads me to the first thing I learned about Christopher: he has a keen ability to convince others of something—even something that they might at first be diametrically opposed to—while at the same time doing it in such a tactful manner that the person thinks it was their idea to begin with. With regards to the interview, I had been rather adamant regarding the prerequisites that the successful candidate must possess. I came out of my meeting with Christopher fully believing that I had stumbled upon a revolutionary hiring concept: that, of course, talent trumps skill and experience! It was so obvious to me now, and I had figured it out on my own.

It wasn't until a few years later that I realized that Christopher's intention all along had been to get me to realize this. Now, he could have come in with both guns blazing, told me how my process was flawed and that any idiot could see that he was right for the company. My response would have been to yell "Next!" and that would have been the end of it. Just two more business people unable to get over their differing views and parting ways as a result. However, his approach was to answer my queries and pose his own questions in a quid pro quo conversation that ultimately resulted in us combining our strengths such that we both benefited.

My point to all this is that people wander in and out of our professional lives with varying levels of success. Sometimes the success seems to go so much against the odds that we chalk it up to luck or call it a fluke. However, at some point when someone seems to continually enjoy success, even the most doubting person has to step back and ask, "Is this person really lucky at being good or really good at being lucky?" After watching Christopher walk into firestorm after firestorm and end up being carried out on the shoulders of the CEOs and CTOs as the savior of product after product—and in one case, even an entire small company—I began to realize that, in his case, it was definitely the latter.

I then began to converse in earnest with Christopher about just what makes one person—or one company—successful as opposed to another. Was there some magic formula to the seeming randomness associated with this thing we call success? What he explained to me, and what you'll learn throughout this book, shocked me. It shocked me because, just like our initial interview, it seems so obvious once it's been explained and understood. If you want to see it for yourself, just look around you. Look at the captains of industry, the leaders of Fortune 500 companies, the manager of the team that always seems to hit the deadline and win the accolades of the company. Look at these individuals and what do you see? *Differences!* The first similarity is the obvious dissimilarity between them all. They come from varied socioeconomic backgrounds. They have different political and religious views. They're of different races and genders. The list goes on. However, look a little deeper than the superficial and you will discover the one common trait that all successful people share. They're not afraid to break the rules and try the unconventional to succeed. It's as simple as that.

At one time or another, every one of these successful people had to make a choice: do I go with everyone else on this or do I break from the norm, take a chance, and reap the rewards if my ideas are as successful as I know they will be? Most people take the easy route and, if they get a little lucky, enjoy a moderately successful life. However, by virtue of the fact that you're holding this book, you've already proven that your exterior is not made of wool and people don't count you when they can't sleep.

That just leaves one obvious question. If these concepts and techniques are so great, why isn't everyone using them? To answer that, let's look at "everyone." According to the United States Small Business Administration, nine out of ten companies fail during the first five years.

That's four-paws up. Bankrupt. When you start talking about how many of the remaining companies actually thrive and excel in their industry, the numbers are even bleaker. The simple fact is that most companies barely make it from year to year despite what they tell their employees and stockholders. The obvious point is that, when you follow the rules of the masses, how can you expect to rise above the masses?

This is exactly why—seemingly out of nowhere—a previously unknown comes to the forefront of a given industry and makes a name for both himself and his company. Read between the lines of the interviews with these people and you'll find out that they didn't possess any magical skill above the fact that they saw very clearly that coloring within the lines wasn't getting them or their company where they wanted to go. So they changed the rules. They stopped thinking about how their predecessor did things, and they decided to forge new trails. In short, they employed much of what you'll discover in these pages.

I don't want to go into any more detail than that because Christopher is the master at presenting this material in exactly the right order and pace. Besides nobody likes the guy that ruins the movie by telling you the ending. However, I will tell you what Christopher's unparalleled knowledge in the area of business and career management has personally done for me. Before I met Christopher I was the definition of a "moderate success" that I spoke of earlier. Don't get me wrong. I made good money and had a secure job. However, like many of you, I knew deep down that there was something better just around the corner . . . something that would allow me to use many of my ideas that I felt were basically being neglected.

That's when, at Christopher's urging, I personally started using many of the techniques you'll discover throughout this book. Tangible results? In recent years, I've helped build a Web site that sold for over $3 million, been the team lead on three award-winning software applications and enjoyed success as a best-selling author with ten books to my credit. In picking up this book, you've taken the first step toward your own success stories. Now let's see what you can accomplish. I have a feeling you'll surprise even yourself.

Tom Archer
President
Archer Consulting Group, Inc.
www.ArcherConsultingGroup.com

Acknowledgments

A book seems like a very simple thing when you pick it up. It presents the illusion that the author, and the author alone, is speaking to you. Of course, in reality, the process is quite complex, and it takes the talents of countless people to bring an idea to life. In fact, it's hard to appreciate just how many people until you try to name them all.

That was my original goal, but eventually I came to understand why the credits at the end of a movie go on for such a long time. It takes a *lot* of very cool, very talented folks to make it happen. Some of the jobs are obvious and some aren't, but, without each person contributing their expertise, this book simply wouldn't exist. If I tried to list every one of them individually, I'd doubtless leave someone out, which to me would be a crime. And so, my first and most heartfelt thanks go to all of my friends at Apress, who worked tirelessly, in good spirit, and moved mountains you'll never hear about. You guys rock. Every last one of you.

The picture on the dust jacket was yet another last-minute adventure due to the insanities of my schedule. However, once again, people make all the difference. JuDeane and Chan Garrett, my friends at Chan Garrett Photography, are my favorite photographers. (They're in the Atlanta suburb of Kennesaw if you happen to be in the neighborhood.) Not only did they do their normal excellent work, they always seem to make me feel comfortable and right at home. Thanks, guys. It's always fun working with you.

I also had help with the companion CD in a couple of areas. Although I composed and sequenced a great deal of the background music, on the tracks where you hear a live bass player it's the talented fingers of my old friend Jeff Patnaude. Digital music is a powerful tool, but sometimes there's just no substitute for the real thing. It's nice to have friends who are also great players. The wings and beer are on me next time, man. Thanks for hanging out and making music with me.

The wonderful voice of the announcer that you'll hear throughout the CD belongs to the talented Deirdre Smathers. In addition to being the consummate professional in the recording studio, she's also worked tirelessly behind the scenes with my company, Show Programming of Atlanta, Inc., for the past couple of years. If you're interested in hiring her for studio work on your own recording projects, you can reach her at Dee@ShowProgramming.com. Most importantly, though, she's been a close friend for many, many years. Thanks, Dee. I'll keep the cappuccino machine warmed up.

Although the last group of people didn't participate directly in the creation of the book or CD, I nonetheless would have accomplished little without their continual friendship, support, and encouragement. We sweat together, laugh together, and sometimes even sing together when our families gather for burgers and fun. They are the cornerstone of my life, urging me on as I work to become a better human being. Once again, there are simply too many of you to name individually. And so I will just say in plain English, both to you and your families, thank you very much. It is my tremendous good fortune to have you as friends.

When they put this book on the shelves in your local bookstore, my name will be on the cover. As you can see, however, I'm just one person among a large and talented group of very cool people. These pages come to you from all of us. I hope you have as much fun reading them as we did in bringing them to you.

Christopher Duncan
November 2003

{ Who Should Read
{ This Book

If you work for a living, or plan on doing so at some point in the future, this book is full of the things they didn't teach you in school. It doesn't matter if you're a high-level executive of a rich and powerful international corporation or you're the guy who happens to cook the fries when I order a burger. The information and techniques we're going to cover in the following pages speak directly to you both. If that seems a little strange to you, that's exactly the point.

People are used to drawing distinct lines between workers and management. This may look tidy on an organizational chart, but the effect it has both on company profits and on the people who do the work is devastating. Trying to separate business and productivity concepts into the two categories is guaranteed to divide your company's workforce. And that's a really bad idea. Ever hear the phrase *divide and conquer*? Your competition is hoping that you haven't.

WHAT'S THE PROBLEM?

Whether you're a worker or a manager, stop for just a moment and think like a consumer. Every day, you see the results of these divided and dysfunctional companies. Here are just a few of the countless examples that you probably see every day.

You call customer service in a major corporation and are greeted by unmotivated workers who have neither the training nor the authority to solve your problem. All they can do is pass you around to other departments while you spend enough time on hold to memorize every word in all the bad music they're playing for you.

You get the wrong food, cold at that, along with overwhelming apathy from the people who serve you at your favorite taco joint. Your meal is a mess, and they couldn't be less concerned about it. You complain to the shift supervisor only to discover that they're not that thrilled to be helping you, either. The only person who seems motivated to ensure that your meal is a pleasant experience is you.

You spend hundreds of dollars on software. The installation corrupts your system. After you fight your way through that battle, you find that the program is even less stable than the people who wrote it. You call tech support. They tell you an upgrade is coming out "real soon now." You pay for the upgrade when it arrives, and the cycle repeats itself.

You go to your local retail store, buy a product from a well-known manufacturer, get it home, and find that it doesn't work. You take it back and exchange it for another unit. This one works, but only for a week. Once more, you return it for a new unit. This time, it keeps functioning but little cosmetic pieces break or fall off. You give up and just live with it, all the while wondering if the company you bought it from has ever heard of quality control.

In each of these cases, what are you tempted to do as a consumer? Probably the same thing the rest of us do: you simply quit doing business with that company. Do you at least call the company and tell them why you stopped doing business with it or buying its products? Neither does anybody else. What you probably will do, however, is tell all of your friends, and maybe even a few strangers on the street, what a terrible experience you had with this company. You might even go so far as to suggest that they avoid this company at all cost.

WHY SHOULD YOU CARE?

You will likely be familiar with stories such as these, but you may not have made the connection just yet as to how this affects your company, your career, and your personal life. Consider this. All of these scenarios are the result of internal company problems. If, because of these problems, customers silently turn away and start dealing with your competitors—and I can assure you that they do just that every day without your knowledge—what effect do you think this will have on overall company profits?

Those of you in management will probably be quick to grasp the obvious implications. However, if you're just a regular working-class person, you may not really care whether the company makes a profit or not. Before you become too comfortable, however, you need to think about just exactly what does happen when company income and profits suffer. That's right: people start losing their jobs. Maybe even you. Layoffs, downsizing, rightsizing . . . pick whatever euphemism you're most comfortable with, but, at the end of the day, when a company suffers financial decline, people get fired. Of course, *fired* is an ugly term, which is precisely why I used it. When people lose their jobs, there's nothing pretty about it. And if your company doesn't get its act together, it could very easily happen to *you*. Unfortunately, this is a fate all too frequently suffered by workers and management alike.

Even if you're one of the lucky ones who survive the bloodbath when your company has to start cutting costs, your life won't be that much better. Who do you think gets to pick up the slack and do all the work of the people who just got the axe? That's right: you do. Your workload will double. Your pay won't.

This is not a dark and gloomy book. On the contrary, it's a book that shows you how to prosper when you thought there was no hope. However, it's imperative that you understand, right here and now, that—whether worker or manager—you're all in the same boat. And that boat is often an extremely bureaucratic and ineffective company that is just a couple of boneheaded management decisions and a few careless fry cooks away from dumping you into the cold waters of corporate distress. The sooner you realize that your personal fate is tied inextricably to that of your company, no matter how large the company or how disconnected you may feel from the people at the top, the sooner you have a fighting chance to steer clear of the rocks and keep your ship from going straight to the bottom.

Furthermore, you must understand one very critical, fundamental point: regardless of whether you're wearing a five-thousand dollar suit or a pair of jeans and sneakers, you're all in this together. United you stand. Divided you fall. That's a very old phrase, but, like most such things, it's still around because it's true. Ignore this at your peril.

HOW WILL THIS BOOK HELP YOU?

So, is this a management book that will help the people who are running the company devise more-effective corporate strategies, or is it a book to help workers improve their careers, make more money, and have an increasingly satisfying job?

It's both. It *has* to be.

But how, you may ask, can a book be about giving the workers more and yet enabling the company to increase profits? That's a very valid question, and the answer lies in an equation that would surely make your old algebra teacher twitch: 1 plus 1 is greater than 2.

This is something that the greatest conquerors in world history have always known. You don't build huge and long-lasting empires with only a handful of clever generals. They would spend all their time planning, and nobody would actually get up from the table to *do* anything. You can't do it with a large mass of people, either. They'd spend more time squabbling with each other than they would acquiring new territory. No, the way the great empires have been established throughout human history has been through the efforts of visionary leaders who understood that they could prevail only when united, workers and leaders together.

The old business model has a myth, as old as commerce itself, that divides people into two groups: management and those being managed. These lines separate your people, and a divided people cannot endure forever. In the pages that follow, we're going to erase these lines, as well as the boundaries between all other tribes in your company. That doesn't mean that managers will lose their authority or that workers will declare freedom and anarchy. Both scenarios are impractical and unprofitable for all concerned.

Instead, you'll see that every manager is also a worker, learn how every worker can lead by example, and realize how building alliances and a spirit of unity across all boundaries leads to higher morale, higher profits, and bigger paychecks. Along the way, we'll explore practical, down-to-earth approaches to problem solving and productivity, techniques that make sense to people who have to do real work in the real world. Instead of mindless platitudes, you'll be shown how to take time-honored principles and apply them to the work that you do on a day-to-day basis. And you won't be given simple answers; you'll be taught to think for yourself and how to arrive at a plan that works when faced with your daily reality of politics, maneuvering, ambition, incompetence, and short-term thinking.

No matter what your position in the company, you will have a clear path to a better career and a better life. That's because rich and powerful empires have the most rewards to share with their people. By the time we're through, your managers will be superior and inspirational leaders, your workers will be motivated to pursue brilliance, and you will all come to realize a simple but crucial truth. Alone, you are weak and vulnerable. Together, you are invincible.

*Business is war. You are surrounded each day by countless competitors who want your territory and your resources. And they will take them from you any way that they can. If they succeed, your company will lose its customers. Its bank accounts will go dry, and you will lose your job. You will have no money. You will lose your home. Your children will go hungry. **And your competitors will not care.***

No matter what your job is specifically, your group is far too small to stand alone. Your only hope for protection from these predators is to unite the tribes within your company and work together as one. To survive, you must rally beneath a single banner. You must become an invincible empire.

Only you can build this empire because its greatest power is its people—their passion, their productive strength, their ingenious creativity, and their fierce devotion both to the cause and to each other. Without the people, from the inspirational leaders to the workers who toil on the front lines, there is no empire. There is no protection from the predators.

No matter which tribe you call home, your loyalty must be to the greater good of this empire. Your members must stand together. No matter what part you play, you work not in isolation, but side by side with others. Strive for excellence, and you will inspire those around you to reach for greater heights themselves. Whether you are a leader or a worker, bring people together, reward their efforts, and give them a reason to care about the cause. Do this, and you will know only victory and prosperity. Do this, and no predator can harm you. For at the end of the day it is you, the people, who are the true strength of the empire.

Unite, and be invincible!

THE LAY OF
THE LAND

The Problem

Companies and people actually have the same goals and desires. Whether you're building a small home business or a huge international corporation, or just trying to make a living, you want money, security, and all the good things that come with success. You also face the same basic challenges in life, as you must cope with competition, changing economic conditions, and a host of unexpected events that can interfere with your goals.

Another thing that companies and people have in common is that gnawing, ever-present feeling that things could, and should, be a lot better than they are today. If you're building an enterprise, you have a vision. You look into the future and imagine how successful and profitable your company could be, and then you go about the business of creating and marketing your products to make those dreams a reality.

However, no matter how reasonable your plans seem, along with your accomplishments come frustration after frustration. Very often it comes down to people who just don't seem to behave the way you think they should. Sometimes it's the customer, and sometimes it's the people who work for you. These people, of course, interfere with your plans.

It's no different from the individual perspective. Regardless of how ambitious you may be and how great your ideas are to improve both your personal career and the department you work for, you run into enough brick walls to cause some rather impressive bruises. The structure of the company you work for and the politics of the people involved all seem to block your efforts to create new and better ways of doing things. This then limits your career and tests your patience.

In both cases, whether you're building a company or a career, you typically find yourself spending more time in conflict with the people and structures that inhibit your vision than you do making great things happen. This amounts to a lot of wasted time and energy that should instead be producing the stuff of success stories.

It doesn't matter what the industry is either. If you talk to enough people, from high-level corporate executives to middle managers to the people who do the daily frontline jobs of producing the products and servicing the customers, you'll continually hear the same stories. Unmotivated or uncooperative people coupled with restrictive organizations and structures create nothing but frustrations, tensions, and severely diminished results, both personal and corporate. It seems we spend more time struggling with each other than we do producing the results we care about. Because companies and individuals have the same goals and desires, why do we waste so much of our time in pointless and counterproductive conflicts?

THE BATTLE LINES

The dilemma predates the industrial revolution itself. For as long as we can remember, businesses worldwide can be characterized by an unspoken and pervasive culture that draws very distinct battle lines between the two major tribes in every company: workers and management. It's rarely verbalized or acknowledged in so many words, but the implicit assumption is that workers are little more than property, owned by the company and treated as such by management. Not surprisingly, this creates an incredibly confrontational environment. Sometimes it's a quiet and subtle undercurrent that never boils over but instead fosters continual grumbling and dissatisfaction on both sides. Other times, it's an overtly hostile atmosphere wherein management overworks and underpays the workers, who for their part spend more time complaining than actually producing. Usually, however, it's somewhere in between, and the result is never satisfactory for either party.

From management's perspective, workers are typically "the little people," who don't understand, appreciate, or care about the larger vision and well-being of the company. Employees are seen as selfish and undependable. Those dedicated souls in management who work countless hours of overtime for the good of the company often come to resent the attitude of rank-and-file workers who just put in their time and leave it all at the office when they go home, concerned with nothing more than their paycheck. In many environments, this scenario encourages management to treat workers as little more than stupid and lazy children who are disposable and must be herded and prodded like cattle to be productive.

Workers, of course, see things quite differently. They see their managers as political and self-serving creatures who are more interested in climbing the corporate ladder than they are in putting in an honest day's work. Additionally, the general consensus among the workers on the front lines is that managers are typically clueless about the realities that are faced by the people who do the real work. Additionally, high-level corporate policies are extremely impersonal, and all too often take little heed of the daily realities that employees encounter on the job. Bureaucracy is so prevalent—and thick—that it's almost impossible to change anything that doesn't seem to be working, and the result is that many employees simply give up trying. In short, managers are seen as shallow, inept, and ineffective, and the corporation is often considered an evil entity that manipulates and takes advantage of workers at every opportunity.

No matter what position you hold in your company, from the CEO down to the custodian who empties the trash, there's sure to be something in the descriptions of the preceding paragraphs to offend you. But consider this: if you find some of these characterizations and stereotypes offensive in a book that's trying to help you, just imagine how people in every company react when these observations are made by real, live people that they work with. The responses are often emotional, fueling the conflict between these two powerful tribes. Back and forth the battles go, with people arguing, resisting, withdrawing, and in general doing everything but moving forward with the common goals of companies and individuals. In short, we waste far more time and energy fighting with each other than we ever spend being productive. It's a wonder anything gets done at all.

THE OLD BUSINESS MODEL

There's no shortage of books and seminars to improve businesses, and an equal number exist to help people with their careers. Each and every one of them has merit, for there's always something new to learn. However, for all the different philosophies and methodologies on both sides of the fence, life in the average company still goes on much the same as it always has. More time is spent in conflict than in being productive. With all the brilliant minds out there trying to help us succeed, how can this possibly be?

Business and career strategies come and go, leaving our professional lives largely unchanged. This owes more to the problems being solved than the solutions themselves. Whether it's a business book or a career book, by definition it's speaking to only half of the problem—either managers or workers. Furthermore, without intending to do so, categorizing solutions and strategies into one or the other of these two camps helps further reinforce the Us vs. Them mentality that is continually tearing at the seams of even the healthiest companies.

The problem is simple. The old model of business—a worldview that draws dividing lines between workers and managers—doesn't work anymore. The company as an authoritarian group of rulers dictating to the indentured peasants of the working class is an outdated way of thinking. Maybe it worked once upon a time, and perhaps it never really worked. But it matters little. Today, it is no longer a productive or profitable business philosophy—not for the company, and not for the individual. When there are no winners in a game, the only logical course of action is to reconsider the rules.

It doesn't really take much intelligence or perception to pierce the stereotypes we've explored. Management is not a group of selfish, inept, and evil dictators. And workers are not a herd of lazy and stupid peasants. We're all, each and every one of us, the same. We're simply people trying to make a living. What we do for that living may differ, but that matters little. We have much more in common than any of us realize.

We all serve different functions in the company. Some of us are entrepreneurs who create businesses. Others manage and organize the various details that need attention. Still others perform the hands-on work that must be done. At the end of the day, however, we all collect our pay and go home to our personal lives. The next day, we get up, put on our work clothes, and do it again.

So, where is this magical dividing line, this demilitarized zone between the evil management and the poor, oppressed workers? Well, it simply doesn't exist . . . because the distinction is false. We are not separate races. We are one people. Attempting to divide us into these artificial tribes does nothing beyond causing trouble for all concerned. Anyone who actively seeks to define and promote these divisions has an agenda of their own, and you should be wary of them. *Divide and conquer* is a phrase that should be printed out and taped to your bathroom mirror so that each day you will be reminded of how dangerous this conflict is to us all.

A FRESH APPROACH

It's time for a new business model. We don't need to change the organizational chart, alter the rules of financial management, or attempt to subvert the market laws of supply and demand. It's not necessary (or even beneficial) for companies to eliminate management, pay all people the exact same amount of money regardless of the job performed, or reorganize the physical architecture of the typical corporation. These structures all exist for a logical and productive reason. Instead, and far more importantly, we need a new model for the way in which we think, for it's our professional philosophy that limits our benefits.

The classic business view of workers and management defines just two of the tribes that exist within your company. There are many, many more tribes, and people often belong to several at once. Just look around you. Everywhere that you see a group of people who feel they must compete in some way against any other group, you have a tribe. Beneath the surface of the major battles that happen daily between the tribes of workers and management are countless other skirmishes going on as departments and political cliques fight it out for internal power and control. Your company is a collection of warring tribes. And it's not getting you anywhere.

Solutions that are founded on the underlying assumption of Us vs. Them don't work. The only successful solution to the problems faced by companies and individuals alike is one that takes all people, at every level of the organization, into consideration. Just as it was in the days of old, your corporate environment of warring feudal states could instead be a vast and powerful empire. To succeed, to become powerful, your internal conflicts must give way to a group effort toward the common good. You must think and act as one. You must unite the tribes.

For your company to become a strong and cohesive force that not only succeeds profitably as a business but also brings personal wealth and success to its people, everyone must realize that the enemy is not *within*. Your true enemies are your company's competitors in the marketplace. *They* are the ones who will decrease your sales and reduce the amount of money available in the payroll account for raises and bonuses. It is the competition that will gleefully put your company out of business and cause you to lose your job. Therefore, all of the time and energy spent on petty internal struggles is wasted and would be far better utilized in building a stronger empire that can survive the continual threats from the competition and provide wealth and security for all of its people.

But, for this kind of success to happen, the artificial battle lines between management and workers must vanish, as must the lines between all other warring tribes. When there are no more tribes, when people instead view themselves as proud members of a single empire, all of the energy that was once wasted in internal conflict will instead be combined, focused, amplified, and directed toward increased productivity—leading to benefits for all. Your competition will be kept at bay, unable to harm you, and your company and your career will move forward from success to success.

Because your empire becomes ever stronger, no matter what your job or position is today, it will be better with each year than it was the year before. Furthermore, because you aren't constantly fighting with coworkers, managers, and other departments, you'll find that it's much more enjoyable to go to work each day. And, in the end, from the production workers to the board of directors, isn't that what we're all after?

The Empire

Corporate culture divides more than it unites. The prevailing wisdom of businesses everywhere is that larger structures should be broken down into smaller ones and managed as groups. If you draw such an organizational chart, it looks very clean and efficient on paper. In fact, it is in just such a way that many companies are born—on paper. However, unbeknownst to those at the top, they're creating more than just logical groups and divisions. Once an enterprise moves from the conceptual stage to a working reality in which people are hired and brought together, human nature comes into play and exerts a creative force of its own. From within the boundaries of business divisions and departments, ambitions and politics arise. They breathe life into organizational units, and these units begin to take on a personality all their own. No longer are they merely divisions of labor. As people bond from a common sense of purpose, these conceptual groups become very real. They become small villages or even nations unto themselves. They become tribes.

If only one tribe existed within your company, it wouldn't be a matter of any great concern. The very need to organize a business into smaller groups, however, guarantees that there will be many. Furthermore, because of basic human nature, there will always be competition where there is more than one group. The fact that your people are now caught in a struggle between tribes means that they're not directing the full force of their abilities toward the real enemy, your competition. They're fighting the wrong people, and it will bring your company to its knees.

As years go by, these separate groups become deeply entrenched. Constantly maneuvering for position and power, always struggling to obtain resources before another tribe can claim them, they begin to focus more on their internal status than on the work for which they were created. Animosity and bitterness arise among groups, and competition erupts into full-scale tribal warfare. People begin to focus on what divides them rather than what should unite them—the common good—until you no longer have a single company. Instead, you merely preside over a loose federation of warring states.

This internecine warfare reduces the output, diminishes the quality, and saps the creative force of your business. The experience of individuals within the competing factions is no better. Stress and frustration rise, fulfillment and rewards decrease, and people begin to dread coming in to work each day. And, all the while, your competitors never sleep, always watching for the slightest signs of weakness in your defenses. Is it any wonder that your company is such a mess?

No matter what part you play in your organization, stop for a moment and take a look around you. The signs are everywhere, too obvious to ignore. The walls built to protect your livelihood from the threats of the competition are slowly crumbling. You don't need a loose stone falling on your head to make you realize this, although it would certainly get your attention a little more quickly.

Whether you work for the company or run the company, you spend half of your waking life involved with your career. If it's a bad experience, then at least half of your life will be unpleasant. If you're the owner of a company or a high-level executive whose compensation relies on the profitability of the business, everyone else's problems suddenly also become your own. If your people are unhappy and spending more time fighting each other than engaging in productive efforts, your livelihood is at risk.

Therefore, no matter what level of the enterprise you work at, you're faced with a simple choice: you can ignore these dangers and suffer the inevitable consequences, or you can stand up and make a difference. If you choose to work for change, the task before you is simple and straightforward. You must unite.

THE COMPANY AS AN EMPIRE

To better illustrate the incredible potential of the people within your organization and to show how you can achieve personal success by helping to build a strong and powerful corporation, we're going to view your company as an empire because it truly is a modern-day version of one. Even if it's small today, it's still an empire in the making. Enormous or tiny, we're going to strengthen it and make it invincible so that it can stave off the marauding hordes and be capable of protecting and benefiting all its people. To do this, you're going to have to recognize the tribes within your organization and learn how to make them work together instead of against each other. If you think about it, the parallels really aren't that hard to see.

Just as when Genghis Khan united the scattered and warring Mongol tribes into the huge and powerful Mongolian empire, each corporate empire also has many tribes. Let's look at just a few examples:

◎ companies under the corporate umbrella

◎ divisions within the companies

◎ departments within the divisions

◎ workgroups within the departments

◎ different classes of job

◎ different groups within the classes

◎ social and political cliques everywhere

Some of the higher levels, such as different departments within divisions of a company, will make sense to those of you who work in management because you're trained to operate at a strategic level. Others may relate more readily to workgroups within a department. Such workgroups could be as large as different production units in a factory or different project teams in a software development shop, and even as small as the divided responsibilities you see in a restaurant, where one group prepares the food, another serves it, and yet another cleans up.

No matter how you look at it though, your company is composed of multiple groups performing specialized functions. Indeed, more often than not, one tribe has very little idea of what goes on within another, and, furthermore, it usually doesn't care. Each tribe will lean by default toward a self-centered perspective, thinking only of what benefits it and frequently fostering an isolationist attitude. Such is the nature of a tribe after all.

In addition to the similarities between businesses in terms of tribal organization and the social classes that the people fall into, all companies, regardless of industry, operate internally on the same fundamental business principles and perform many of the same actions. This is just as true of the local restaurant where you had lunch today as it is in the huge corporations that build multimillion-dollar aircraft.

All companies create products and services. They produce them, market them, and then sell them, interacting with customers so that they can charge and collect money. Every company must administer to daily details, and all are affected by external competition and are subject to market conditions. And every company, whether it realizes it or not, presents an image to its potential customers.

Unfortunately, it's not always the image it had in mind. When your company works with a tribal consciousness, the face presented to the outside world depends upon the attitudes and motivations of the individual tribes that interface with the public. If these people are thinking of their own little world and agenda rather than the good of the company, your enterprise will appear quite differently to the general public than you might have envisioned.

Regardless of whether your business is a chaotic land of warring factions or is a single, united people, it is a nation in the making. Embracing this concept allows you to become a part of something larger and more beneficial, improving your own career and building the stability and security that can be ensured only by the power of an invincible empire.

THE GOAL OF BUSINESS IS CONQUEST.

Thinking of your company as many tribes united into a single nation doesn't really require much imagination. After all, working in the corporate world often feels as though we're living in ancient times. You know that your tribe is part of a greater kingdom, but that's not really your daily perspective. The only things that are truly real to you are your neighbors and friends, the people you see and work with each day.

And so, tucked away in a remote corner and far removed from the rich and powerful rulers, you live in your own little village, oblivious to all other tribes. You do your work, you go home and eat dinner with your family, and life is good. That is, until the day when you look to the horizon and see your competitors, thousands of heavily armed horsemen bearing down on you, intent on taking everything you have of value and burning the rest. At that point, the personal ambitions and petty tribal politics don't really matter much, nor does your social standing. You're all about to have a very bad day.

What I've just described is not a scene out of the history books or faintly remembered childhood tales of knights and barbarians, swords and shields. This picture I've painted is only a loosely veiled metaphor for the corporate reality that is home to us all. Those unruly, predatory barbarians coming over the horizon are not extras from a Hollywood set. They're your competitors, and they're quite real. Even though they're not swinging swords and shooting flaming arrows, their intent, without a doubt, is very much the same: they want your territory, your customers, your money, and even your people. And they're not terribly concerned with how that affects you in the process.

We all get so caught up in the day-to-day details of our jobs that we tend to lose sight of the big picture. If we're to improve our lot in life and protect ourselves from these predators, it's important to get a better understanding of the world in which we live. We all work for companies, but why do these businesses exist? What makes entrepreneurs endeavor to open the doors of a new commercial enterprise?

Many of us get caught up in the goals and ideals of our given industry, perhaps to the point that we might think that companies exist for the noble purpose of improving society through our particular products and services. This kind of altruistic vision may be noble and inspiring, but it doesn't have any basis in reality. Companies don't exist to make the world a better place. They exist to make a profit. Regardless of industry, the first and most fundamental purpose of each and every business in the world is to acquire and profitably manage new resources and territory. In other words, the goal of business is conquest. Understanding this is a crucial step toward improving your situation.

This means that business, by its very nature, is a highly competitive pursuit. Your company dreams of controlling all of the market and all of the money. But then so does every other company in your industry. And they're all willing to fight you for it. Just as in warfare, then, your competitors are the enemy. They want your turf and your resources, and they'll take them from you any way they can. They will attempt to conquer and subjugate you, and if that fails they will strive to eliminate you altogether. Of course, from their perspective this is obviously necessary. Your company is a threat to their well-being and their very existence. That's because, given the chance, your company would do exactly the same thing to them. That's the nature of conquest.

DIVISIVENESS IS THE GREATEST ENEMY.

It doesn't matter if you're the top executive in the company or a production worker at the bottom of the food chain. Every week, everyone in your company shares a very powerful experience: you get up each day and go to work. The nature of your job, the hours you work, and even the clothes you wear will vary, of course, but each and every one of you, leader and worker alike, are members of the same community. And there is a power in that unity beyond your wildest dreams.

And yet, most people feel a constant sense of separation, perhaps even alienation. *The Company* is just some abstract concept, much like the air. You know that it's all around you, but you can't see it. You can't reach out and touch it. You're simply aware of the fact that you're employed by some vague and intangible entity. This odd phenomenon leaves many of us feeling completely disconnected, both from the company and from the customers and clients who are ultimately served by the products and services we provide. This disconnectedness spells disaster.

Even so, deep in the heart of almost every person is a burning desire to excel, to reach for greater things, to be a part of something larger and more powerful than they are as an individual. Unfortunately, bureaucracy and petty politics have all but extinguished this fire in many who would otherwise set new standards of excellence. This not only often deals a fatal blow to morale but also fans the flames of divisiveness, as people lash out and express their frustrations at what they cannot seem to change.

Lest you think that I've merely described the plight of the working class, it's important to realize that this feeling is experienced by people at every level of the organization, and in companies both large and small. Chances are good that your managers feel just as disconnected as you do. Remember, although your superiors may be nothing more than "the management" to you, from their perspective they're just people getting up and going to work each day, and they're employed by that same vague and abstract notion of a company as you are. Their job just happens to be different from yours. The basic stress and frustration experienced, however, are very much the same.

Divisiveness and class-consciousness can be more harmful to companies than all of their competitors combined. Nonetheless, this atmosphere of separation between workers and management is the norm. Some consultants specialize in teaching management skills—which implicitly exclude the nonmanagement worker. Other consultants focus on teaching career improvement, which subtly promotes the good of the worker over the good of the company. I cannot stress enough how strongly I oppose the artificial boundaries that such approaches create.

In the divided land of workers and managers, each side of the fence offers truly valuable skills and perspective, and neither recognizes that the fence itself is the first and most formidable enemy.

In fact, workers and managers have far more in common than they ever realize. Consequently, this is neither a career improvement book nor a management book. It's both, as it must be to make a difference. If the people of the company have rewarding careers, motivated by a deep sense that they truly have the fate of the business in their hands, the company will succeed. Successful companies are in turn capable of providing the very best in compensation, benefits, working conditions, and security to their people. Who are the people? They are the leaders and workers alike, at every level of the organization. Notice that the word *manager* has suddenly been replaced with *leader*. Workers can show leadership without being managers. Leaders are always workers, people employed by the company, even if they're managers.

Are the traditional distinctions getting blurry for you? Good. That is my intent. Through unity, you will build a stronger empire than you ever thought possible and through that strength enjoy a higher standard of living as an individual. Consequently, throughout these pages I will intentionally weave back and forth between the perspectives of leaders and workers, often with no warning or clarification of which point of view I'm speaking from. In fact, for each concept, there will always be relevance to both leaders and workers, depending upon how you apply it to your personal situation. Furthermore, no matter what your job, there will always be opportunities for you to lead others by example and through inspiration, making you a leader as well as a worker. No matter what your position in the company, I challenge you to look for this personal application in each and every sentence. It will make the empire—and, as a result, your career—much stronger.

UNDERSTANDING THE PROBLEMS

More important than anything else, however, is one simple but powerful realization: a company is nothing but a collection of people working toward common goals. Every single resource your company has—whether buildings, furniture, bank accounts, stock, customers, or anything else you care to think of—didn't just magically appear. Real, live people created or acquired those resources. No matter how vague and detached the concept of the company may be to you, it is not a separate entity with a mind and will of its own.

Neither does a company perform any function or engage in activities. Rather, it is the people who compose the company who make things happen. Real people. Just like you. Company productivity and innovation are simply aspects of how well your people interact.

Companies are neither productive nor creative. People are.

What are the implications, then, if it's flesh-and-blood people who do the actual work and bring the resources into being, rather than some abstract concept of a corporate entity? It means that the true power of a company—its very heart and soul, all that it is capable of accomplishing—is defined by its people. People, therefore, are power.

However, in almost every corporation in the world, this power lies largely untapped. This is in part because no one knows how to inspire the people to unleash their full potentials. Although they work in separate villages, within these tribes there is no esprit de corps, nor any inspirational leaders to rally them to action.

An even larger problem, though, is the fact that the people, those tangible, living resources who actually *are* the company, are constrained and limited by the rules and structures of the company itself. As a result, this tremendous power lies dormant, a victim of internal strife, bureaucracy, and inefficiency.

Another thing that is often forgotten by the upper strata of management is that it is not the high-level leaders but rather the rank-and-file workers who are the face of the company to the outside world. Your thousands of customers don't call the president of the corporation to place an order. When someone comes for service, it's not the board of directors who walks them through the solution to their problem. The quality of your products and services have much, much more to do with the attitude of your production-level workers than it does the vision of upper management. If this is kept in mind at every level, strategies will be practical and realistic, which they must be to succeed.

Any plan to expand or strengthen the empire lives
or dies by the efforts of its frontline workers.

Unfortunately, although the people are truly the power and potential of the empire, they are also its greatest vulnerability. The people are the company. By definition, this means that the company is therefore completely susceptible to every single aspect of human nature.

Regardless of how great their potential, people are frequently a royal pain in the posterior to deal with. They can be self-centered, emotional, possessive, and reactionary. They're often inconsistent, shortsighted, unmotivated, apathetic, and just plain lazy. Many people are also easily distracted and preoccupied with selfish and personal matters. The fact that some are willing to settle for less and are afraid of the unknown also makes them resistant to change. As a result, the average person will deal with these fears by becoming political, cliquish, and driven by a petty desire for power. Alternatively, they can become completely isolationist, preferring to bury their heads in the sand and hoping that the problems they face will just go away on their own. None of these attributes are going to help you build a better tomorrow. In fact, sometimes it's hard enough just getting someone to make a fresh pot of coffee when they take the last cup.

Unmanaged, these negative aspects will create divisiveness and destroy a company's productivity and profitability. One of the most common examples of this is corporate turf wars. An example of this might be a clash between the accounting and customer service departments over the control of internal software projects. The programmer tribe that manages the accounting and billing system wants ownership of the customer service software, arguing that, because customer information is part of the billing process, it therefore falls under its domain. However, the programmers in customer service take the stance that, although there is common information between the two departments, billing and service are distinctly different jobs and therefore they should have the autonomy to design software that best serves the needs of the service staff. And so, tribal warfare erupts as the struggle for control of projects begins.

The result is that every new project that might increase either department's efficiency or productivity gets stalled and often completely derailed as the two tribes fight it out, withholding information from each other, obscuring the lines of responsibility, creating intentionally vague or misleading communications, pulling political strings, duplicating effort, dragging their feet, and in general making such a mess of things that nothing truly productive ever gets done.

When the projects fail, as they all too often do, what ensues is a round of finger pointing and attempts to assign blame for the failure, both to prevent personal career liability and to make the other side look bad, thereby gaining an advantage in the next inevitable conflict. Animosity and bitterness between the departments grow, which has a negative effect on all other areas where the two should cooperate.

If you ask either tribe what the fight is about, you'll hear detailed and often emotional accounts justifying why each should have control for the good of the company. An example of human nature at its most predictable, all that each side is truly interested in is personal power and profit. The good of the individual tribe is the limit of their vision. The good of the empire is the last thing on their minds. In short, they think small. Therefore, their gains will be little more than petty successes, for one simple reason.

Limited vision brings limited rewards.

As we've already seen, the pursuit of power and profit is not in and of itself a bad thing in the business world, as your company must do battle with other empires in hopes of gaining market dominance and increased profitability. Without the struggle for power and profit, your company would not make any money, it would quickly go out of business, and you would be on the streets.

So why is it a good thing when your company wages war against others for a greater share of the gold but a bad thing when your internal departments do the exact same thing? Because the people involved in your internal turf wars are fighting the wrong enemy. They waste precious effort and resources grappling with each other. The conflict does not make the empire one bit richer nor stronger. In fact, it does just the opposite. These petty skirmishes cost the company money. Because you, the workers and leaders, in fact *are* the company, this means that it's money out of your own pocket in the long run. Think about that the next time you consider getting involved in these petty little battles.

Furthermore, while your company gnaws away at itself, you live in a paralyzed state of limbo. You're so busy fighting amongst yourselves that you have no time to repair the breaches in your outer walls. While you're busy arguing with each other, your competitors will take your market share. After they've done that, they will demolish you with their newfound strength. Chances are good that you won't even resist because you'll still be locked in pointless arguments trying to blame each other for what's gone wrong. You don't have to be an acute student of human history to understand the obvious implications.

An empire at war with itself cannot
survive attacks from external predators.

So how could otherwise intelligent and capable people let something like this happen? Why wouldn't people focus on the obvious goals of building a stronger empire instead of fighting amongst themselves? Once again, human nature provides the answer. In most enterprises, decisions are made based not on what's best for the company but rather on what will make an immediate and obvious improvement in the career path of the decision maker. This is an aspect of what will be a recurring theme throughout our explorations—short-term thinking. People frequently get caught up in immediate gratification and overlook the long-term consequences of their actions.

If you build your home before you build the castle walls, the enemy will simply overrun you. They'll also burn your home while they're at it, just for the sport of it—which won't do much for your insurance rates. Nonetheless, self-centered thinking poses a continual threat to the empire even after people have suffered the consequences and should know better. Another aspect of human nature is that we don't always learn from our mistakes as quickly as we should.

Yet another example of the vulnerabilities presented by human nature shows up once again as a lack of long-term thinking. Regardless of the industry, the quality of goods and service is more and more becoming a secondary consideration. People who succumb to laziness and apathy will tend to do no more than is necessary to get by, and, for those companies for which quality is not a high-profile priority, this diminished quality quickly becomes the standard.

Your competition absolutely loves this. If you build poor weapons and armor, I can assure you that you won't enjoy the results of your next encounter with them. Of course, not everyone is a warrior . . . even in the business world. It doesn't matter. If instead you work on providing the infrastructure for your company, it's no different than being responsible for the castle walls. You'll soon discover the problems that present themselves when the enemy breaches your defenses as though they were little more than castles made of sand.

Regardless of which department you're considering, in every aspect of your company you must realize that quality and the motivation of your people to deliver it are extremely critical considerations. Even if you have an excellent marketing department, your revenues will not survive poor workmanship forever, for one very simple and oft-overlooked reason.

Your customers are not as stupid as you think they are.

Your ex-customers won't tell you why they quit doing business with your company. They'll just silently disappear and start giving their money to your competition. If you sell boats that frequently sink, all the high-tech and glitzy advertising in the world won't help you. Wet customers are rarely repeat customers.

I've given but a few of the countless examples of the dangers that human nature presents to your business. Ultimately, if these weaknesses are allowed to continue and grow, your company will begin to falter. Perhaps it already has. On top of the problems that led you to this point, the limited and shrinking resources that result will create even more. Internal chaos and civil war will erupt as people scramble to claim any budgets, furniture, and livestock that happen to be up for grabs. Lethargy and complacency will contribute to weak defenses and ineffective offensive initiatives. In short, you will be in disarray, and your productivity will be significantly reduced. An unproductive empire cannot feed its people. A weak empire cannot defend its people. Does it really matter which way you perish?

WHY SHOULD YOU CARE?

There are some very important implications for you as an individual in all of this. As you can see, if your business is weak, disorganized, or dysfunctional, your competitors will hurt your company. That doesn't seem so bad when we think of the company as that vague and impersonal entity with which we feel no connection. Unfortunately, the damage that your competitors do is not vague or abstract at all, and it will not only hurt your business, it will hurt you personally. Even if you're not running the company, it is imperative that you understand the connection between the company's well-being and your own if you wish to ensure a stable and beneficial lifestyle for yourself.

Consider this: stronger companies frequently acquire weaker ones. In such an acquisition, you far too often lose benefits and pay, authority, and control over how you do your job. You often lose good people for no reason other than the fact that their jobs are duplicated in the conquering company. Everything changes, and, although change in and of itself is not a bad thing, changes of this sort usually lead to chaos, displaced people, and a lot of bad experiences. If you've ever been through one of these corporate mergers, you know in a very personal way what people have known throughout human history: life as a conquered people is unpleasant.

Another fate that befalls weak empires is that of being plundered and burned. (If you happen to be the conqueror, do remember to plunder *before* you burn.) Corporate raiders and venture capitalists will sometimes acquire a company, strip it of all its physical and monetary resources, and then, once they've bled it dry, simply close the doors—leaving everyone suddenly unemployed. Life without a paycheck is even more unpleasant.

Even if you're not the victim of pillaging, if your company's revenue suffers or its profitability is compromised, it will simply have less money to work with. This means that it's going to have to cut expenses, and payroll costs are typically the first to go. Because of slashed budgets, you may very well lose your job and find yourself without a way to feed your family. Spontaneous loss of income is not something that just happens to the unproductive. It often happens for no reason beyond being in the wrong place at the wrong time. Highly skilled and qualified people who have been loyal to their company for years lose their jobs all the time. The people who fire you will assure you that it's nothing personal. However, when you're the expense that gets cut, it becomes personal in very short order.

If you do weather the storm and manage to keep your job but the people sitting next to you lose theirs, don't think that you got lucky and managed to escape unscathed. Who do you think is going to have to do their work? It still has to be done. You just have fewer people to do it now, which means that those who survive the cuts will have to take up the slack. Your responsibilities, pressures, hours, and workload will increase. Your pay will not.

All of this is brought upon you when your company isn't strong enough to fight off the predators. By now, you should be starting to see the first threads of connection between the fate of that vague and impersonal entity called *The Company* and the personal well-being of you and the people you love. The two are intertwined in a much more intimate manner than you ever imagined.

Although it may not be obvious, this is actually wonderful news. If your fate is inextricably bound to that of your business, if the company is truly nothing more than the actions of the people it employs, then this gives you unprecedented power to change your quality of life. By improving the stability and profitability of the company that provides your paycheck, you build a stronger and more secure future for yourself. Unlike management philosophies that promote the company well-being at the expense of the worker, or career-building strategies that encourage a selfish agenda over that of the employer, in this equation there are no losers. That makes for a very long-term solution: when everybody wins, nobody wants to break the cycle.

THE DANGERS ARE NOT ALWAYS APPARENT.

Long about now, you might be thinking that I'm overdramatizing the situation with such extreme, life-and-death metaphors. In fact, you might be tempted to glance around your workplace and come to the conclusion that your company isn't really in any danger of suffering such dire consequences. From where you sit, it may well appear that your company is quite healthy. Although it's not perfect, you might view your business as stable and facing no real threats.

However, unless your job happens to be that of CEO, president, or some other high-level executive, it's worth noting that the view from where you sit is not likely to be comprehensive. If you're sweating away deep inside the blacksmith's shop, you're not going to have much opportunity to see the marauding hordes massing on the horizon. In a similar manner, although the people who work in the production department are a critical part of the process, chances are good that they have no idea what's going on at the highest levels of the company, in terms of both planning and financial stability. Furthermore, even if they were privy to this information, because they're trained in production work rather than finance or corporate strategy, they couldn't realistically be expected to interpret or understand the implications of the facts. It has nothing to do with intelligence or capability; they simply have no training or experience in this area. As a result, from where they sit, they have no way of truly knowing what state the empire is in.

But what if you *are* the head of the company? Surely from this vantage point you should have a clear picture of the dangers that lie ahead, right? Although it's true that you have a better overview of your business as a whole than do your production-level workers, your visibility is not unlimited. The daily output of your people as well as the face they put on your business to the outside world has an extremely significant effect on the health and stability of your venture.

If you are a top-level executive, especially in a large corporation, chances are good that you have absolutely no idea what truly goes on in the day-to-day life of the people upon whom your entire company depends. Ask yourself this simple question: could you put this book down right now, walk, drive, or fly to, say, your customer service department, ask someone to stand up so you could take their position and then actually have a clue as to what was going on and how to handle it? I didn't think so. Generals who lead from the rear rarely can. This is not an insult. It is, however, a vulnerability, and one that a good general will recognize.

Many executives may think that this is a preposterous notion because they were trained in management and therefore couldn't possibly be expected to understand the intimate details of the day-to-day struggles that their workers encounter. Perhaps they're right, but that doesn't help you see where the danger lies, either. Lack of knowledge is lack of knowledge, and, even if you shouldn't be expected to understand, that won't shield you from the consequences. At this point, some leaders may contest this assessment because the workers report to their management and those at the top get the summaries accordingly. I do appreciate the orderliness of a hierarchical structure, but, at the end of the day, it's still not going to give you the true picture of what goes on in the daily struggles of your people. This means that you're going to make critical decisions that affect the growth and future of your company based on limited or incorrect information—which is extremely dangerous.

When we were children, many of us played a game called Telephone. We sat in a circle, and one person started by whispering a statement into the ear of the person to their right. This continued all the way around the circle until it came back to the person who initiated it, who then shared with the group the original statement and what was finally told to them. The ensuing laughter was the point of the game. Particularly with large groups, the information can become so distorted that it ends up bearing no resemblance whatsoever to the original fact.

Now let's apply that to your corporate structure. This time, however, instead of a game in which no one has any reason to distort the truth, you have multiple levels of management, each represented by a real, live human being who has a personal agenda and ambitions all their own. By the time a very real and practical problem travels from a frontline worker to their immediate superior and then up the chain of command to the top, it will have not only have been distorted by the general nature of the Telephone game, it will also have been intentionally manipulated by each person along the way so that it helps to bolster their personal plans.

The information then lands on your desk, having also been massaged and altered to conform to what people perceive that you want to hear. As you sit comfortably at the highest level of your company looking at this report, you will have absolutely no idea what's happening downstairs in the real world. Unfortunately for you and contrary to the egotistical assessments of some of history's greatest generals, it is not the commander who fights and wins the battle. It's the people on the battlefield. It doesn't matter how rosy the picture looks at the top; if they're having a rough go of it on the front lines, you're in for big trouble, which is all further compounded by the fact that you'll never see it coming.

If the differences in perspective relative to your position in the company weren't enough to obscure your vision of reality, you're also subject to the dangers of isolationism. It's only reasonable for you to see things from the worldview of your occupation. However, within your tribe will always be a tendency to indulge in tunnel vision, thinking only in terms of what affects your unit personally and ignoring everything else. Uncomfortable or untidy details are often glossed over because it feels easier and safer to concentrate on your own little world than to consider the complexities of the empire as a whole, and how your tribe fits into the overall scheme of things.

Without a doubt, it's a complicated business to build a strong empire. On top of that, what's best for the empire may not be what's best for your tribe at this given moment. However, instead of realizing that what's good for the empire will ultimately be good for the tribes, many tend to resist, either passively or openly. Focusing only on their personal short-term goals, they fail to see the benefits that come from a larger worldview. If you work within such a group, it's hard to avoid getting caught up in the prevalent way of thinking. Without conscious effort on your part, your focus will become more and more narrow, and, once again, you will not see the dangers to the empire until they are upon you. Of course, there's a fundamental problem with that.

> *Once the enemy has attacked, it's a little late*
> *to sharpen your sword.*

People also tend to consciously overlook any difficulty that could ultimately affect the health of their company because the issue doesn't seem to be very large or threatening at the moment. Therefore, a small problem is often ignored, and, in silence and obscurity, it is therefore free to grow and spread. A tiny hole in a dam will slowly get larger and larger. At a certain point, however, big chunks of the wall start breaking away and things begin to deteriorate much more rapidly. So too is it with the little problem that was ignored. Once again, the dangers to an empire that you assume to be healthy are not always obvious. That will be of little comfort to you as you're looking for a life raft.

~~~~~~~~~~~~~~~~~~~ ((⊙)) ~~~~~~~~~~~~~~~~~~~

AN EMPIRE DOES NOT HAVE TO BE EVIL.

O f course, to some, the entire concept of an empire invokes thoughts of an overbearing and oppressive nation. Consequently, they may have reservations about viewing their company as a conquering empire. Like most reactions and instincts, this has some foundation in reality. It is true, without a doubt, that, in both nations and companies, large-scale abuse of power can follow large-scale success. Furthermore, poor behavior in this regard is, in and of itself, a weakness that can be exploited by your enemies. How the conqueror treats the vanquished says much about the character and vulnerabilities of the nation.

Do I promote the notion that you should build your company into an invincible empire that conquers all others in your field? Absolutely! If you don't, someone will certainly do it to you. It's as much a matter of self-defense as it is acquisitive, remembering the old adage that the best defense is a good offense. However, what I do not promote, and openly oppose, is abuse of power by any person or company, at any level. This is not a matter of morality, and my stance on this issue is purely strategic and practical. At the end of the day, no matter what your endeavor, it is unwise to forget the human factor.

People who are treated poorly will do everything in their power to resist your plans, and they will attempt to seek vengeance at a later and more convenient date.

From a tactical perspective this is an unnecessary liability, and one that can be avoided by simply treating all with whom you come in contact, both allies and vanquished alike, with as much respect, kindness, and consideration as possible. Do this and you will find that those who once dedicated their very lives to opposing you will suddenly decide that yours is now a noble cause to flock to. Instead of seeing themselves as conquered, they will instead consider themselves to be liberated. As a result, your ranks will swell with people who are suddenly among the most passionate supporters of your cause.

Good and *evil* are also relative terms. Ask any ancient Europeans about the Mongols who rode under Genghis Khan, and, as they're sharpening their swords, they'll describe them as evil barbarians who must be destroyed. Ask any Mongols enjoying the benefits of life in a powerful empire, and, as they're sharpening *their* swords, they'll tell you that, without a doubt, the empire is good and must be expanded. Of course, neither camp is shy about using that sword to get what they want, and both are quite sure that they're right.

Although both empires describe themselves as good and their enemies as evil, in truth there's just not that much difference between them. Each is attempting to build a stronger empire to provide for their people. Failure to do so would simply result in another nation conquering them. In this regard, the business world is no different than human history. If you don't build a strong company, you'll ultimately be put out of business by someone else who does. That means you're out of a job, and so is everyone else you work with.

However, the way you go about expanding the empire is just as important as the result. It's true that you can achieve short-term gains by lying, cheating, stealing, and abusing others. Nonetheless, this sort of behavior invariably comes back to haunt you. People who have been treated poorly become future adversaries, not future allies. If you approach all of your strategies and initiatives with a goal of treating everyone fairly, and quickly embrace as friends those adversaries who now wish to join you, the results your efforts bring will stand the test of time. Treat people well, and they will work hard to strengthen what you've done rather than tear it down. Be fierce in battle, but, in all other ways, strive for benevolence. In this way, your empire will stand the test of time.

The { People

I f the empire is nothing but a collection of people working toward a common goal, then no matter how many buildings, desks, and bank accounts a company acquires, there is no single resource that is as precious or valuable as the people whom the company comprises. We've explored the concept of your company as an empire. However, when you look to the strength of an enterprise, you need not look far to find it. Possessing the power to build, innovate, strengthen, and transform, the people truly *are* the empire.

No matter what your goals, no matter what problems you're trying to solve, and before you can take your first step toward improving and expanding the empire, you must understand just what a business is. The fact that a business is a collection of people may seem obvious, but, like many such things, tremendous and profound implications lie just beneath the surface of this initial observation. If you, the people, literally *are* the face of your company, then by definition there is not a single, solitary aspect of your organization that you cannot change. A company is not an abstract collection of resources, paperwork, and procedures. Rather, it's a collection of human beings who manipulate those resources to achieve their goals. Don't like your logo? Need a new product? Want more customers? Large or small, no matter what it is today, your company can be completely different tomorrow through the efforts and talents of you and your people, the most remarkable of all your organization's resources.

THE INVISIBLE COMPANY

A nd yet, many still view businesses as paper entities, expressed by balance sheets, stock prices, procedures, and policies. High-level executives shuffle bits of paper around as though they were maneuvering pieces on a game board. Mission statements, press releases, marketing, and advertising . . . all of these things serve to abstract the company, to create an entity that's talked about in the third person, even among the people who created it. It's as if a corporation were one of the ancient mythological gods, invisible yet omnipotent, intangible but still somehow permeating the corners of every office on each floor. A soul without a body and with legal perpetuity, most corporations present the visage of a deity, a consciousness and will to which we must be sub-servient and over which we have no control.

Although many corporations are born with a big bang and an even bigger investment, a great many large and successful businesses start life as small and humble companies. Through the vision, innovation, and hard work of a handful of people, these startups can be grown and transformed into huge, international conglomerates that eventually be-come worth staggering amounts of money. Along the way, too, what was once real and personal is transformed and mutated into something large, vague, and intangible. The small, excited, and motivated group of friends and associates who dreamed together and perspired together to bring a new idea to life no longer exist. In the place of inspiring inter-personal relationships are now titles and divisions, policies and procedures, guidelines and constraints. And, worse, no single individual is accountable for the actions of this corporate behemoth, much to the dismay of customers everywhere.

In fact, the growing trend of consumers becoming alienated with large business entities is very much due to this latter point. Corporations have learned, through technology and bureaucracy, to erect a barrier be-tween them and the people who pay for their services. It is often literally impossible for a customer to contact a decision maker who can actually change the way in which things are done. Instead, consumers must deal with the many and varied layers of abstraction that the company pres-ents, each with the power to say no but none able to say yes. The modern-day corporation has reached a point at which it is unaccount-able to the people who pay its bills.

That's bad enough in terms of alienating your source of revenue. What's worse is that these very same scenarios erect barriers between the company—that virtual and nonexistent entity turned deity—and the people who fill the halls and perform the actual work. For the people employed by modern companies, both workers and leaders, it is no longer personal. It is not possible to speak directly to the decision mak-ers. You must fill out forms, expect delays, wait for resources to be allocated, weather continual reorganizations, and suffer many other such indignities until the initial fire and passion of creating change and making a positive difference is lost forever.

Off in the distance, a rumbling sound signals yet another of the em-pire's protecting walls collapsing to the ground. A lone scout from the enemy turns and rides silently away to report his findings.

When your operation grows so large that the very weight of bureaucracy is enough to crush the innovation and passion out of your people, you have reached the beginning of the end. Sell your stock. Quickly. Alternatively, you can fall back on the one true resource that the company has always possessed. Somewhere, just around the corner, across the street in the warehouse, or perhaps even in a cubicle down the hall, you'll find people. They can help you.

HUMAN NATURE

Although human shortcomings are without a doubt a significant vulnerability to the company, the reverse is happily also true. It may seem a cliché, but the people truly are the heart and soul of the empire. In fact, it is the seemingly limitless potential of the human race that is the hope of every venture, regardless of industry, size, or scope.

At their finest, people can be selfless, passionate, and generous. When you need something you can really count on, you'll find people who are dependable, hard working, motivated, and enthusiastic about what they can accomplish. They can be visionary, idealistic, adventurous, and innovative—the very spark of creativity. Most people are also far more adaptable than even they realize and are capable of making the best of any situation, even when stoic endurance is temporarily called for. Best of all, when you're trying to build a group endeavor, you'll appreciate the social nature of humanity, for they are cooperative and team oriented by instinct. That's just the sort of thing you need when building an empire.

Of course, this is but a short list of the many wonderful aspects that every single person in your company possesses to one degree or another. Without a doubt, certain qualities are more developed in some people compared with others. However, each person possesses tremendous potential, awaiting only the inspirational team member or leader to ignite the fire within. In short, people got you into this mess, and people can bail you out.

But why *should* they? If you've allowed your company to become a maze of such massive proportions that it's sucked the very life out of them, what makes you think that they'll suddenly spring to action, rally to your banner, and pump new health and vigor back into your business? Excellent question. Truth is, they won't. Well, at least not without a darned good reason.

EVERY JOB IS A CAREER.

If you wish to call upon the passionate spirit of the people who compose your company, it is of critical importance to understand the link between the quality of their careers and the well-being of the empire. A great many business people attempt to improve their bottom line by shaving costs wherever possible. Employee benefits and payroll can be considered as targets that are frequently attacked, whether it's pay cuts, putting a freeze on raises, or even such seemingly innocent things as no longer providing free soft drinks in the kitchen. If your company is in enough trouble to necessitate cost cutting to begin with, you're only shooting yourself in the foot by alienating the one resource that could help you turn things around: the people.

On the other hand, many employees feel that simply increasing salaries could be the solution to every problem in the organization. Blindly throwing money at the problem can be just as disastrous as neglecting the careers of your people. If the money spent on increased payroll doesn't bring you tangible results, then you've only made a bad cash flow situation even worse.

The solution, of course, begins with understanding what a career is, and what aspects of it the workers and leaders in your group deem to be critical. It is only with this information that you can come up with meaningful incentives to motivate the ones who can turn your disasters into success stories. Like many such endeavors, if you truly want to find out what's important to someone else, the first thing you should do is to try to think from their perspective.

Oddly enough, however, a great many workers and leaders don't really understand for themselves what their career is. In fact, many would tell you that they don't have a career, just a job. Simply put, for the purpose of building an invincible empire, a career is your present occupation. A more correct definition may be that a career is your *chosen* occupation, but that's not going to help us right now. It may be correct on paper, but it's more valuable to you in your professional life to realize that whatever it is you're doing for a living today *is* your career. Sorry.

Do you have dreams of becoming a rock star? Groovy. When you're paying the rent with a guitar in your hands, then it's your career. At present, though, the dining room floor needs mopping and that, not rock and roll, is your career. Of course, you're free to change careers as often as you like, and there's nothing wrong with having dreams provided that you're willing to do the necessary work to make them a reality. Nonetheless, if you get up and go to work each day, even though the dictionary may disagree on the finer aspects of the point, you must approach it as your lifelong pursuit. In other words, whether it's managing thousands of people, answering a telephone in the customer service department, or flipping burgers until your dreams come true, it's not just a job. For the present moment, no matter what you want to do with your life in the future, it's your career. Strange as it may seem, no matter how menial the job, understanding this is the first step to freedom and power.

Another way of looking at the picture is that a career is the general progression of all your professional achievements. Of course, the minute we use the word *professional*, it immediately brings to mind visions of briefcases and conservative business apparel. In other words, *professional* seems to imply a white-collar job. This means that the guys sweating in the back of the warehouse are left out of professional circles and, by implication, are less important. This is a dangerous attitude and one you should work to avoid, particularly if you ever want that fancy new desk to make it off the warehouse floor and into your office.

> *Tell someone for long enough that they're not important, and they will eventually believe you. So how does that help your cause?*

Unfortunately, we're going to once again redefine the popular notion of a word. If a career is what you're doing for a living today regardless of what you want to be doing tomorrow, then it is also your current profession. Consequently, if driving a forklift and loading trucks is your profession, then the general progression of your achievements in this area, as we've just phrased it, describes your career.

Let's say, for example, that you started your job as a minimum-wage busboy, cleaning tables in your local burger joint. You did a good enough job that your pay was increased and you were promoted to waiting tables. Having demonstrated above-average people skills and a good work ethic, you were eventually promoted to part-time shift manager. Even if you quit tomorrow to go on the road with a rock and roll band, you could correctly describe your job in the hamburger business as a brief career, and a successful one at that.

Why is it important that—from both the management and the worker's point of view—we consider each and every job in the empire, no matter how menial or low paying, as a career? The importance lies in the psychological effect that it has both on you as a worker and on how you interact with the people who work with you or for you. We usually think of our occupation as "just a job" when it is low paying, uninteresting, temporary, or unpleasant. Furthermore, the implicit categorization of employment as being "just a job" immediately communicates that we don't really care that much about it. It's merely something that we hope is short term until we find something better, or, worse still, it's something that we've just resigned ourselves to endure because of the lack of opportunity. We come to work, put in our eight hours, go home, and try to forget about it until the next day.

WHAT'S IN IT FOR YOU?

Now stop and think about this for a moment. Whether you're the owner of the company trying to increase profits, a leader trying to turn a bad situation around, or a worker with a desire to see your group do better, just how much enthusiasm do you think you're going to get from a bunch of people who consider their employment to be "just a job," a period of unpleasant or uninteresting time that must simply be endured? You can talk about the good of the company, their obligation to you because you're the boss, or good old-fashioned team spirit, but all of your words will fall on deaf ears. They couldn't possibly care less. Why? Because there's nothing in it for them if they do.

Does that sound selfish to you? Before you get too judgmental, take some time and reflect on your own motives for the things you do in life. Although you may in fact do some things purely out of the kindness of your heart for the noble purpose of helping others, if you're honest with yourself you'll find that most of those take place after you've come home from the office and that they are rarely work related. We fight rush hour traffic and sit in cubicles because they pay us to do so. If we're lucky, we may also do something for a living that we're passionate about. However, even in that case, we wouldn't do it for someone else if they didn't pay us to show up. We'd be doing it at home, in our own way and on our own time. And probably in our robe and bunny slippers.

There is no experience in the world as powerful as staring out at ten thousand armored horsemen, seeing them raise their spears to the sky, and feeling the vibration in your chest as they clash them into their shields as one, with a shout so resounding that the very ground shakes. This is a power that changes lives and shapes nations. No one can witness such a sight and not be moved. The next time you watch a movie with a bunch of warriors on horseback, turn up the volume really loud and try to imagine what it must have felt like to be there. If all your household pets frantically scurry off to the back bedroom, don't worry. They'll be back when it's dinnertime.

Now fast-forward to the present day. The people in your company who perform the day-to-day production work, those people who feel that their employment is just a job—*these* are your horsemen. Turn their jobs into careers! Show them that they're important, that they can make a difference, give them a sense of unity and purpose, and the power of their enthusiasm will straighten the backs and raise the spirits of people at every level in the empire.

Unskilled or moderately skilled workers are typically the least financially rewarded. Although there may be some economic sense to this, it is both senseless and inexcusable for these people to be the least rewarded in terms of career satisfaction. Whether you're trying to motivate your coworkers or your employees, if you want people to give it all they've got and go that extra mile for you, you're going to have to give them a reason to do it. And, for this reason to be effective, it also has to be a reason that *they* care about. If you can't offer them more money due to budget limitations or the fact that you're their peer rather than their manager, you're just going to have to get creative.

However, it's not as hard as it may seem to find meaningful rewards. One of the biggest problems that people have with their work is that it's a large block of hours out of each day that they don't enjoy at all. The quality of your daily workplace reality defines the quality of your career. Furthermore, to a certain extent, the quality of your career defines the quality of your life, if for no other reason than the fact that most people spend more than half of their waking hours each week at work. Consequently, it doesn't take much imagination to realize that, if your everyday experience is unpleasant, you're going to be unhappy and therefore not at your creative and productive peak. Do you want to be surrounded by excited and productive people? Then keep the following simple fact in mind.

All other things being equal, happy people are
much more productive than unhappy people.

If your workplace environment is stifling, you're not going to be very innovative. If you've encountered enough repression, you may eventually lose hope for positive change altogether. If that's the case, you most certainly will not bring any about! People have to feel valued and important. It's a basic human need. They also require hope for the future. Without that, they will sink into the pits of the most unproductive and profound depression that you can imagine. Worst of all, depression is an extremely contagious disease, and one you certainly don't want to spread in your organization. It can be fatal to an empire.

Therefore, no matter what you're trying to achieve, if you want to enlist the support of other people, find a way to make their working hours happy ones. Give them a sincere and meaningful way to feel that they're important and that what they're doing truly makes a difference. Create this environment, even if it's in small incremental steps, and give them hope for the future that it will continue to improve.

Do this, and they will move mountains for you. They will take on the hardest, most impossible tasks—the very jobs that they would have complained bitterly about doing before—and they will instead take pride in the fact that, not only did they do a job well, they did a *difficult* job well. You will have transformed your group from a depressed and defeated bunch of people to a proud and highly motivated team that now feels that they are the elite, the best of the best at what they do.

When you reach your people on a personal level, the difference that their resulting attitude will make in the company is profound, for these are the people who work at the most fundamental levels of your business. The people in the field, in the office cubicles, in the factories and warehouses, in the customer service areas—such people are your foundation. Without them, the company is nothing but pipe dreams on a drawing board. Turning their jobs into careers by giving them a reason to care about the future and the quality of their work will light a fire that can blaze throughout your entire business.

We've spoken in terms of the least-rewarded workers, but the same rules apply all the way to the top. More money is always a good thing from the perspective of the person receiving it. However, you can improve many other aspects of their careers that, with little to no expense, will yield tremendous rewards. The basic human needs don't change just because you happen to be an executive or middle manager, and you're still just as responsive to basic human needs if your job also happens to be your passion.

Find the frustrations that your people encounter, and help them change their days from a period to be endured to a time of passionate expression. Give them true hope for the future and a sense that they're important, that they really do make a difference, both as an individual and as a group. When people look at their watches and comment with surprise and disappointment that they can't believe it's quitting time already, you'll know you're making their lives and their jobs a better experience. Time truly does fly when you're having fun, and people having fun do the best work.

MAKING THE CHOICE

If the people are the empire, if a career is what they're doing at the present moment to contribute to the company, then the only difference between a successful business and one that's failing is the quality of the people's careers. People who are passionate about their careers will be the problem solvers, the consistently high producers, the role models and inspirations for others.

Some give up and give in to the frustrations and limitations of the structures that have been created over time. Others take a look at what the company has become and shout, "No! We want something better, and we're good enough to make it happen!" They've discovered the true secret to building a better tomorrow.

> *The crucial difference between a good career and a*
> *bad one is nothing more mysterious than personal choice.*

No matter what level of the organization you work at, the day you finally stand up and declare that you've had enough and are going to fight like crazy until you can make a difference, take a quick peek over your shoulder. You'll find that many others are suddenly standing up behind you, silent, but determined and ready. You are not alone in your sense of frustration, and you never were. You have many, many kindred spirits in your company. All they need is the inspiration and example of one person to give them the strength and confidence to stand up themselves. It doesn't matter if you're a worker or in management. You can be that person, and the changes you spark will become legendary.

But how, you may ask, can you make a difference in an environment that is inflexible by nature, stifles innovation, and is hostile to change? Remember, your career is the foundation upon which the empire is built. Improve your career, and you will improve the empire. Oddly enough, the first step in this process is one that a large number of people never take. You must decide that you want to improve your career and will do whatever work is required to make it happen. Without that strong personal commitment, nothing else matters. This is why so many people at all levels are heard to grouse on a daily basis about how bad things are, and yet a year later they're still complaining about the very same things. They never took that first step. If you don't decide to improve your career, it's not going to happen by itself.

One of the first things you'll find is that the decision to take responsibility for your own fate and your own actions is empowering in and of itself, and that feels good. Right off the bat, before you've done anything else, you've already improved your daily work experience. You have a new feeling of hope, and you see opportunity where before you saw nothing but a dead-end street. This decision alone will make subtle changes, in you and the quality of your work. It may also spark interest in the more perceptive of your peers when they see that new gleam in your eye and wonder how they can experience it for themselves. Share your decision with them, and you may find that, before you've even started doing the actual tasks required to create change, you now not only have hope, but *allies*. You're already way ahead of the game, and you're just getting started.

One of the first practical steps you might take is choosing to become better at what you do. In my time as a factory worker, I saw production people grab unused machines and repeat the moves of their task slowly and repeatedly, as if they were practicing some deep secret of the martial arts, trying first this way and then that in search of the most efficient motion. I've also seen the satisfaction radiating from them when, weeks later, they'd made massive increases in their productivity because they were simply better, more practiced, and efficient at their task. It feels good to be the best at what you do.

Cubicle workers often do work that could be enhanced by corporate training programs. Most companies, however, don't allocate the funds for this purpose. For example, if you're an office worker, you probably use specific software to do your job. It's very common today for commercial, off-the-shelf programs such as word processors and spreadsheets to be extremely powerful, and therefore extremely complex. Most people use only about 10% of the functionality that's available to them in a given program. However, if you learn all the shortcuts, features, and power-user tricks that it offers, this software could help you become massively productive and make your work easier and more pleasant at the same time.

If your company won't foot the bill for training classes, your decision to improve your career may lead you to the local bookstore, where you spend your own money on books to help you get that other 90% out of your tools. Like our friend who improved his factory production skills, you too will experience tremendous satisfaction over the increases in productivity, not to mention making your life more pleasant by turning tedious tasks into simple operations through the power of fully utilized software. Of course, this doesn't just apply to computers; it applies to any tool you use in your job. Surprisingly, all that's usually required to master your tools is the decision to take some time and work at it. It's really that simple.

In our first example, our factory worker's increased performance on the job elevated more than just his job satisfaction. When it came time for raises, his improvements were noted and rewarded. However, in his case, it didn't cost him any money to improve this skill. Why should the office worker in our next example spend personal money on books or training materials? Where's the payoff, the return on their investment? In this case, given the difference in work environments, it occurs in many ways.

Factory workers are much like enlisted soldiers: once a grunt, always a grunt. If you didn't go to officer's school, you don't become an officer. Therefore, promotion into management based merely on increased performance, although not impossible, is at best unlikely.

In the office, however, the rules are a bit different. Become an obvious guru with important software, and soon you'll find you have the opportunity to mentor others in a casual, unofficial capacity. You won't get paid for this. However, as time goes on, you'll be demonstrating not only personal initiative, but also leadership skills that may very well result in promotion to a leadership position. Of course, you may also get a raise or two as well for the same reason as our factory worker did. Both of these make you a profit on the cost of your books with the very first increased paycheck.

You'll also find that, by helping your peers, you gain allies and respect. By improving the overall production and efficiency of your group, you make your management look good, gaining you even more powerful allies. By taking the lead and improving matters on your own, you've also justified with tangible results the cost of additional training, which may be all the ammunition your manager needs to get training courses authorized for the entire group.

Thus, your status will grow, your power will grow through your increasing network of allies, and your job satisfaction will improve from seeing in no uncertain terms that you have made a difference. In the process, you'll probably inspire several others to start becoming more involved in improving their own careers. Leading by example, particularly when you're not in an official leadership position, and then seeing the positive effect you're having on the lives of others are incredibly gratifying experiences. And, of course, throughout all of this, you're increasing your income and perks. All because you made a conscious decision to stop waiting for others to change your world for you.

But what of the empire in all of this? To be sure, we've witnessed a few individuals improving their personal stations in life. But what about the company? How does it benefit?

Even a small increase in productivity and efficiency is a gain. However, just as a tiny spark in dry grass can start a huge brushfire, so too will such individuals have an effect on the good of the empire far beyond their personal reach or responsibilities. People everywhere, whether they realize it or not, are always looking for the next source of inspiration, for a better reason to get out of bed in the morning, for someone to show them that, yes, in fact, the impossible truly can be accomplished. The herd instinct is not always a bad thing. Let just one person stand up and initiate change, and, before you know it, you will have an epidemic of positive change as it spreads first within their tribe, and then throughout their entire organization. If those of you who are in management are perceptive enough, you'll see what's happening and immediately get behind it, thereby augmenting the process and taking it to yet a higher level. This is all nothing more complicated than simple grassroots change. The results, however, are extremely powerful.

WHO ARE THE PEOPLE?

Without a doubt, then, the people are a powerful force in any endeavor. But who, exactly, are the people? As previously noted, instead of referencing workers and management, we've been thinking in largely in terms of workers and leaders. Your initial reaction might be that there's no substantial difference between the terms *manager* and *leader*, and hence wonder why I'm bothering to make the distinction. In fact, *leader* and *manager* are not synonymous, at least not in the real world. It's not uncommon to find managers who are really little more than bureaucrats, organizing paperwork as it passes from one level of administration to another. Managers of this sort often deal with their people in a similar manner. Instead of becoming a motivating factor in their department, they simply pass along orders or parse out and distribute a given set of tasks, once again operating in little more than an organizational capacity. To be sure, such skills are necessary in the process of managing a group of any size. However, this does not inspire people to rally behind you.

People don't follow managers. They follow leaders.

A manager who is truly a leader does much, much more than just shuffle paper. Leadership is all about inspiring, motivating, supporting, and directing your people, and knowing how to bring out the best in each individual. It's also about understanding when it's a good time to get out of their way so that they can do their job for you.

Leaders are also protectors, shielding their people from petty politics, mindless bureaucracy, and pointless busy work so that they can be truly productive. They also know how to gain the respect of their people. Respect that is sincere cannot be demanded from someone; it can only be given. And there's only one way that can happen: you have to earn it. We'll talk about many aspects of leadership as we go along, but the most important thing to remember for now is that a leader is someone who becomes a part of their group, understands the needs of their people, inspires them to greatness, and then supports them so that they can achieve that greatness. Some managers are leaders and some are not, although they can all become leaders if they so choose.

Having painted a little clearer picture of what I mean when I talk about leaders, let's consider the workers. You'll often hear me talk about the real people who do the real work in the real world. That's what I mean by a worker: someone who produces a tangible result for the company, rather than those who oversee or organize that productivity. It could be a welder in a shipyard, someone on a construction site, or a person packing boxes and loading trucks in a warehouse. They may require different specific skills, but these are all examples of manual labor.

A worker can also be the person who does your company payroll each week, someone who fills a technical support hotline position, the sales rep who brings in customers, or the person who designs your advertising layouts for the daily paper. Although this is not manual labor, these people all still clearly produce tangible results. Even creative people, such as those who write the manuals for your software, musicians who record the music for your television ads, or the designers who visualize and create the new clothing fashions each year, do real work in the real world. Therefore, they all qualify as workers.

However, our perspective must be a bit more complex, because the real world is not black and white, particularly when it comes to leaders and workers. You may find leaders who are also a contributing part of their team, such as a lead design engineer for an automobile company who helps do the design work but is also in charge of that department.

That is a leader who is also a worker. Above and beyond the leadership, real work is also being produced. Therefore, he qualifies as both.

Along those lines, workers can also be leaders. We're conditioned to think of managers and authority figures as the only leaders and then draw the dividing lines between them and everyone else. This, too, is false and wrong.

> *A leader does not need explicit authority to lead;*
> *neither does the lack of that authority invalidate*
> *any of the benefits that result.*

Very often you'll find situations in which a group of workers are all peers, with no one person having any greater or lesser position or authority than another. Yet, within this group, a clear leader can be seen. This person may possess a bit of charisma or extra drive, or might be something of an inspirational visionary. He may have the gift of keeping morale high or knowing how to encourage people to give their very best. Additionally, this person may be the one whom people naturally come to with problems. Although having no official title or capacity, such a person can have a huge effect on the productivity of the group. Everyone is familiar with the concepts of leading from the front or leading from the rear. When a person in a group takes on a leadership role that benefits the group, that's leading from the middle, and it is an extremely powerful notion.

Why, though, you might ask, go to the trouble of creating a more complex way of looking at leaders and workers when everyone is already familiar and comfortable with the concept of managers and workers? One of the biggest killers of corporate productivity is the implicit state of Us vs. Them. Talking about workers and management draws immediate battle lines between two separate, distinct, and confrontational forces. It is the definition of the two largest tribes, to which all other tribes in the empire belong. Fostering this sense of separation is incredibly divisive, and, if it gets out of hand, it will rip your company apart.

Furthermore, no good purpose is served by making this artificial distinction. As we've seen, leaders can also be workers, and it's also common for workers to be leaders. Maybe that's a little less tidy than you care for, but it's the first significant step to uniting a divided empire. Leaders and workers often encounter very similar difficulties. I see no reason to support this notion of separation that so often exists in the business world. Let go of the illusion. Forget about the defensive posturing you instinctively do to protect your isolated tribe, and start thinking as a single, unified, and powerful people. Start thinking as part of an empire.

Remember, a nation at war with itself is going to be very ineffective in dealing with the outside world. If you want to put an end to unproductive tribal warfare and internal strife, start by removing the false distinctions that foster such an environment. Forget about dividing people into managers and workers. Instead, cultivate and support leaders wherever you can find them.

In turn, leaders must inspire and support workers, providing the support and encouragement they need to do work of the highest caliber. To do so is to bring out the very best in all of your people.

By eliminating the false barriers between them, you will also unite your many small and weak tribes into one huge, focused force that's capable of defeating any enemy and moving your company to a position of dominance. Many battles must be fought before your empire can stand tall and proud, and stronger and more glorious than all others. To win these battles, you must be united, leaders and workers shouting with one voice. When you let go of your tribes and join together to form a single people, you will be an irresistible force. Remember: the people—leaders who are workers, workers who are leaders, and all those in between— are the heart and soul of the empire. Cast aside your petty differences, and look ahead to the successes that you can achieve together. When you are united and strong, none can stand against you.

The ⁝ Solution

No situation is ever truly beyond repair until the last person throws in the towel and gives up. As long as one person is still willing to try, there is always hope. This means that no matter how discouraged you may be, no matter how many times you've tried to change things for the better and failed, you are not beaten. Remember, tribes are made of people, and the people are the empire. Because people can always change, this means that your company can change as well. Even if you're the only person left in your group who still wants to create a better tomorrow, even if everyone else has been beaten down by the system to the point at which they've lost hope, all it takes is one person to change the face of the entire organization. This one person is you.

When you're trying to start a fire at your campsite, you can have all the kindling and wood in the world, which by itself will do you little good. What starts the roaring fire is not the straw and twigs, but the single, effective, and dedicated spark. So too is it with people. Although it's easy to become overwhelmed by stress, frustration, or hopelessness, it's also a basic feature of human nature that everyone wants to be on a winning team. People love the feeling of power that comes from being a part of something larger than themselves, something that's moving forward and generating excitement. All it takes is the single spark to get this fire burning.

By not giving up and giving in to the status quo, you will continue to reach for solutions to the problems that face you. Even though some solutions may escape you, some of your efforts will also succeed. As you build on these small, incremental successes, others will notice and express an interest in getting involved. Embrace their offer, allow them to share in your growing stream of small successes, and you will find that your spark has grown into a small flame. Every roaring bonfire that has warmed the fingers and toes on a cold winter's night has begun in just such a fashion.

> *Consistent effort creates momentum, which brings hope.*
> *And hope is the first step toward becoming invincible.*

Throughout the course of human history, great nations have often arisen out of chaos, isolation, and turmoil. In matters of life and death, smaller tribes have banded together, overcome famine and foe alike, and worked one step at a time to build a strong, unified nation that's capable of sustaining them. If this can happen when the currency is human life, it can certainly happen when the currency is, well, *currency*. Individuals and groups passionate and dedicated to creating a better life are always the harbingers of new and great things. No matter what shape your company is in today, regardless of how large or small it may be, amazing things happen when people become excited and join to realize a common vision.

Some in your tribe, usually the weak or the tired, will tend to do nothing but complain that the times they are a-changing: the market is more difficult, the competition more plentiful, and the grass in general is just not as green as it was in the more profitable days of old. What's worse is that all of this may even be true. Nonetheless, it is nothing more than an observation of today's perceived reality. It does not dictate the state of tomorrow.

For hundreds of years, the horse was the primary means of transportation. Consequently, in every country, many merchants made a very good living as horse traders. They spent their entire lives learning as much as possible about their four-legged merchandise and the people who needed them, and this knowledge enabled them to trade wisely and profitably.

Then, one day, the automobile became the new standard for transportation, and the horse was relegated to the domain of recreation, although those ponies smart enough to snag a good agent managed to land roles in the movies. For the people who had dedicated their entire lives to becoming experts in equestrian matters, however, the introduction of the automobile was a disaster. Almost nothing about the horse applied to the car. How were these people to survive now that their entire set of professional skills had been rendered obsolete? For many, it was the beginning of hard times as they struggled to get by on what meager sales they could still make to lovers of these great and proud beasts.

However, in the local tavern where horse traders often gathered to drink and commiserate with each other about how bad the times were, tucked away in the back corner quietly minding their own business were individuals completely absorbed in books. A closer inspection would reveal that these were not books on the finer points of horse breeding, but rather the intricate details and concepts of the automobile. These same people could be seen in subsequent weeks trading cars from the same lots where they once traded horses, and making a handsome profit in the process. While others were busy crying in their beer about how tough times were and how hopeless the situation had become, these entrepreneurial souls were busy learning the skills needed for a new trade.

People adapt and prosper when they believe in the promise of the future, refuse to give up, and are willing to do whatever it takes to make the transition.

Of course, all of that study and adapting stuff sounds like a lot of work. In fact, it frequently is. So what happens if, instead of putting in the extra effort required to meet these new challenges, you simply do nothing? In the immediate moment, perhaps nothing. Life could very well go on tomorrow much as it did today, and as a result you may be lulled into a dangerous complacency.

Many people fall prey to this peril, assuming that, because they're drawing a paycheck today, they can just keep doing what they've always done and the paychecks will keep coming in. Anyone who gives this even passing consideration will immediately see the holes in this theory. What actually happens, often in a quiet and subtle manner, is a steady downward spiral. As anyone who has seen a whirlpool knows, the closer to the center you get, the stronger and faster the current. By the time you realize that the situation is deteriorating, things may be happening so fast that you're overwhelmed and caught completely unprepared. The paycheck that you assumed would always be around can vanish like a Ninja before your very eyes.

Without action on your part, your position will always become weaker, not stronger. This is the default.

No matter what aspect of life you may be considering, a few universal rules will always apply. One of them is that there are no actions without consequences. As we've seen, these consequences may be slow and subtle, but, sooner or later, the wheel always comes around. Initiating change requires hard work, and sometimes lots of it. If you're flipping a mental coin trying to decide whether it's worth the effort to get involved, you'll make better decisions from an informed point of view. So, let's take a look at what life's like in both a weak and a strong empire. Although situations may vary from tribe to tribe, the eventual results will be the same for all.

THE CONSEQUENCES
OF WEAKNESS

When your company is weak or stagnant, it affects more than just some mythical bottom line tended to by corporate accountants. It affects you personally. Each new perk or extra bonus, every increase in salary—even the extra patch of asphalt for your personal parking space—all cost money. Cold, hard cash. It doesn't matter how benevolent the owners of the company may be or how much they truly and sincerely care about the happiness and well-being of their employees. If they don't have the money, you're not going to get the raise. It's as simple as that.

Furthermore, not only does a company that is slipping in the marketplace have fewer funds with which to improve your compensation package, it could also drift the other direction. When times get hard, people start to lose jobs. However, the ones who don't get fired still suffer, as they typically have to endure much more Spartan working conditions. All of this translates to a distinctly diminished quality of life.

However, money is just the most obvious casualty of a stagnant company. When your organization starts falling prey to bureaucracy and slipping into a lethargic state, the work atmosphere begins to suffer as well, and in a tangible manner. People adopt a more pessimistic attitude. Apathy sets in. Peer pressure actually discourages excellence for fear that someone will upset the status quo and they'll be required to do more work. Tribal politics and needless procedures begin to stifle creativity and innovation.

The job you once loved can quickly turn into a dreadful way to spend a day. Although this may not take cash out of your pocket immediately, it will certainly drain the last ounce of enthusiasm from you, and seriously affect your overall quality of life. You spend a lot of hours at your job. If that occupation offers no satisfaction or sense of accomplishment, your overall happiness suffers accordingly.

Not only does your job become an unpleasant experience, it's likely that you will spend even more time experiencing the unpleasantness. When the business outlook is bad, many companies use the fear of unemployment as a tool to force people into large blocks of unpaid overtime. The threat, whether implicit or explicit, is that, if you don't put in all the extra time they desire, you'll simply be replaced with someone else who will. This, of course, increases your tension and wears you down further, which leads to an inevitable result that a surprising amount of managers never understand:

> *People suffering from fatigue and stress*
> *don't do their most spectacular work.*

This in and of itself may contribute to yet another twist in the downward spiral of the company when sales drop as a result of the poor quality of goods and service. Naturally, the unenlightened manager doesn't make this connection and instead insists on even more overtime to solve the problem. Putting out fire with gasoline is rarely an inspired move.

Another evil that increases its handhold when the company isn't moving forward is internal politics. When your tribe is fired up and working hard to achieve yet another brilliant success, nobody has the time or inclination to play petty power games. When things are slow, however, there's often little to do *but* scheme and manipulate. This isn't a particularly productive use of time, and it just gets in the way of those who would work to improve the situation were they given the chance. Politics are also a recurring factor in career advancement. The tougher things get, the more people scurry to curry favor rather than attempting to rise through the ranks on the merits of their labors.

If you find it depressing to read all this, then you've experienced first-hand the effect that the situation has on the people of every tribe in the empire. Hopelessness sets in. People start dreading the days they have to spend at work, becoming sluggish and apathetic, and doing only the bare minimum needed to get by. Should someone come along and try to do better, they get little help at best and active resistance at worst. When the spirit of a company dies, there's little left but an empty shell. If the workers are suffering, the company suffers.

When your people are unhappy, your company will feel the pinch in ways both obvious and subtle, for it is a point worth making over and over again until you can chant it as a mantra in your sleep: the people *are* the company. We've already seen that poor-quality products and services will eventually overwhelm your sales force, resulting in diminished revenues. However, discouraged people don't reach for new and creative solutions. As a result, your company will lack the innovation needed to keep pace with the times, and your competition will out-pace you. Additionally, because your people simply don't care any longer, waste and inefficiency will be rampant and demolish your bottom line. That doesn't leave any spare money for that raise you were hoping for.

But rarely does a company enter a state at which every single person in the entire organization becomes disheartened and apathetic. Although this may well become the fate of the majority, some will still work for improvement. In a deteriorating situation, these people will be scattered across the company. However, confusion and poor communications among the tribes will diminish their efforts. Even your successes, therefore, will be smaller.

Because the people are discouraged, they won't care about the good of the empire. In fact, they will even reach a point where they don't care about the good of their own tribe. They'll give far less than 100%, and the productivity of the company will be lessened as a result. On top of the diminished output, labor costs will be disproportionate to the results received, and these increased relative costs will once again diminish profits.

Worldwide, many managers operate daily on the assumption that their people don't have to be happy to be productive; they just have to shut up and do their job. In fact, there's often a kind of macho attitude among such people, a feeling that, if they were to consider the feelings of those they supervise, they'd be seen as too soft and consequently ineffective. It has always been a popular belief that, to get the most out of people, you have to be tough and unfeeling. That's not leading. That's managing. Badly.

People are not robots that operate exactly the same every day as long as voltage is applied. Especially if you try to apply that voltage in the form of a cattle prod. Abusing people does not win their loyalty, nor does it inspire them to do better. It only builds resentment and resistance to whatever goals you may have. Therefore, all morality aside, you should always think about the happiness and satisfaction of those in your tribe for some very practical and compelling reasons. Do it because it directly affects your company's bottom line, and the company's bottom line affects you personally.

THE BENEFITS OF STRENGTH

All this talk of higher expenses and diminished profits may be something that those of high standing in the tribes can relate to, but what of the common people, those who toil every day to generate these profits? Why should they care about the profits of the company? Indeed, each person in the tribe has every right to ask, "What's in it for me, personally?" If that question can't be answered satisfactorily, you're going to find that the size of your tribes continues to decrease as people defect to another empire, in search of one that will provide for them.

However, just as the good of the people has a direct relationship to the good of the empire, so too does the good of the company affect the good of the people. A stronger company means a more secure career because it has more money to reinforce its position and can therefore stave off competitors. Weaker companies cannot, and so they simply go out of business. Furthermore, a company that makes a lot of money has more to spend on you. This shows up not just in your paycheck, but also in perks and benefits such as better insurance programs, more vacation time, company discounts, and a host of other things that you enjoy.

Of course, the paycheck is the most important part of the job, and a stronger company will still be around this time next year to provide you with one. And, although not a monetary concern, caring about the success of your company has an additional benefit: it's actually fun to work on a winning team. When the empire does well, the morale within the tribes will be high. That's always a gratifying and uplifting experience.

In fact, there is a circular path of benefits between the company and the people. Benefits that flow to the company amplify those that the people receive. Happier people, consequently, amplify the benefits to the company, and each side therefore continually receives increasing benefits.

For the individual, increased compensation can take the form of better pay, more benefits and perks, and even greater power within the tribe. Greater job satisfaction comes from many factors, including more-creative input, more respect and recognition for your efforts, and even social considerations such as more friends and fun on the job. It all adds up to a day that's a more enjoyable experience.

Of course, life on the job has both a direct and indirect effect on the rest of your time. An enhanced personal life comes from better job security, thus eliminating stress and worry about unemployment. Additionally, a successful and well-managed company demands less overtime, so you actually have time to enjoy the benefits you've earned.

This leads to an overall better balance between work and home life. No one ever lies on their deathbed and regrets that they didn't spend more time at the office. At the end of the day, it is your home life that's truly important. A better balance between work and recreation means that both will be enhanced.

All of these benefits to the individual are amplified and eventually find their way back to the empire. For businesses, anything that improves the financial picture is highly beneficial. This shows up in ways such as greater cash flow, increased sales, and better profits. Increased productivity means greater innovation, better products and services, more efficiency, and less waste.

The goal of every empire, of course, is to have an ever-stronger position. Dominance in the market, an enhanced reputation, and greater visibility in turn lead to a more solid foundation upon which future successes can be built.

From this point forward, we will focus less and less on tribal considerations and turn our attention more to the greater good, for, as you can see, it is the empire that will nourish and protect you. It is perfectly acceptable for the company to have tribal structures to improve organization. However, it is not only unacceptable but highly disloyal for you to identify more with your tribe than with the empire, for one very pertinent reason:

The tribe doesn't write your paycheck. The empire does.

Furthermore, your village depends on other villages. No matter what part you play in the company, you cannot break your tribe away, put it in a separate building, get a business license, and start making money as a new company. Alone, your group simply does not perform all of the functions necessary for any ongoing business. Should you decide that your tribe is truly the heart and soul of the empire and you can go it alone, you will first have to hire other people to perform additional functions such as sales, accounting, maintenance, production, and so on. The moment you do this you've proven the point, for once again it is not one tribe that survives in isolation, but a collection of tribes that thrive as a united empire. So, let go of your petty tribal ambitions. Think big. Really big. See yourself as part of an invincible empire!

Does this mean that you should eliminate group consciousness from within your tribe? Absolutely not. For each tribe to function at its peak, it must be a highly unified and effective organization in and of itself, and esprit de corps is an important force. Every tribe can still proudly fly its banner, as long as that banner flies below the standard of the empire. Know where your loyalties lie.

Every time you increase the effectiveness of your group, don't think in terms of how much greater you've made your tribe, but instead of how much greater your tribe has made the empire. If this seems a small distinction to you at the moment, as time goes on you'll come to realize the tremendous power that such a perspective brings to the empire and all who reside within.

THE PILLARS OF THE EMPIRE

Understanding the need to unite is the first step toward a stronger future for you and your company. However, making this a reality requires a plan. Although they can sound exciting, simple platitudes and catchy buzzwords don't mean a thing in the real world unless there is a practical course of action to follow that will bring about positive change. We don't live in a textbook world where everyone follows the rules, and things always go as planned. The structure of the reality we need to change is large, complicated, and entrenched. Vague academic ideas are of little value. We need practical tactics that can survive in your normal business environment, where the unexpected occurs as often as the expected. It doesn't matter if these tactics are pretty. It only matters that they work.

Our goal is to erect a new philosophical structure, to build a new reality of a united and invincible empire. What we need for this endeavor is a solid foundation that will support people in their efforts to promote and strengthen their company. Our framework will be the Pillars of the Empire.

Every company across the planet, even within the same industry, is unique and different. The people, corporate culture, and a host of other dynamics will vary wildly. It is therefore impossible to write a detailed plan that addresses every scenario encountered by every person in every company. There is no magic potion that will work its charms in the same way for all who try it. Regardless of the strategy, every idea and tactic must, to some degree, be adapted to your individual situation and then applied accordingly. There is no silver bullet. That may not be what you want to hear, but anyone who tells you otherwise is blowing smoke.

Additionally, nothing will ever replace the ingenuity and adaptability of the motivated and creative human being. Only people can react and improvise so wonderfully. Therefore, instead of trying to saddle you with a set of strict and inflexible rules that may not make sense in your situation, each of the ten Pillars will address one of the fundamental concepts necessary for success at every level, from the boardroom to the front line.

However, even with the human talent for comprehension and interpretation, general concepts alone would be of minimal value. Therefore, just like the monumental pillars from the Roman empire still standing today, every Pillar of the Empire is built from a number of individual Stones. Each Stone describes a single task that you will perform, an attitude that you must adopt, or a strategy that you will employ under the conceptual heading of that Pillar. Because what we need are practical, streetwise tactics that work with real people and real situations, we'll then take these major tasks and discuss them in everyday terms, so that you can adapt and apply them in your specific environment.

A chapter is dedicated to each of the ten Pillars of the Empire. As you'll see, both the concepts embodied by the Pillars and the individual actions represented by their Stones can be applied at every level of your company, regardless of your industry or position. You don't have to be in a position of authority to put them to work. In fact, although those in powerful leadership jobs are in a position to effect tremendous change with them, they have been specifically designed to be effective for the people who work on the front lines of the business world, those creating the products, servicing the customers, and managing the groups. No matter where you reside, whether you're a person in charge or a worker on the front lines, you'll be able to take these Pillars and make a difference, both for yourself and your company.

MAKING IT WORK

No matter how difficult your environment or how large your problems, you have the power to build a better tomorrow. Like many things, however, the way you approach the effort will dictate your level of success. If you simply read this book, try to remember a few things from it, and then put it back on your bookshelf, you will have wasted your time and your money. Worse still, your world will not change. If you want to transform your company and your personal career, it's going to take more than just a little light reading on your coffee break. To change your environment from a collection of warring tribes into a powerful and united empire, you absolutely *must* follow through with these steps. It's the only way you will see tangible results.

First, it's critical to understand that this is not a book: it's a way of approaching your professional life, a path to follow. It's not enough to simply read the pages. You must embrace the philosophy and make it a part of your daily experience. All of the divisiveness in your company will not vanish overnight, nor will your personal career suddenly improve, just because you've absorbed more knowledge.

You must take action.

More importantly, you must make it your new passion and hobby to integrate these ideas into your job and your life, constantly looking for ways to apply the concepts and tactics in every situation you meet. Like artists perfecting their creations or athletes honing their skills, your mind should constantly drift back to these basics, even in your personal time, allowing you to continue to improve your expertise and effectiveness. This is not a quick fix. Quick fixes don't last. It's a lifestyle, an approach to your business and your career that grows stronger with the passing of time. Because much of any success is built on your ability to deal with people in a positive and productive manner, you'll also find yourself applying these techniques in your personal life. As you achieve more and more of your goals, you'll find that it's an enjoyable exercise, indeed.

As the last chapter mentions, this book is also your field manual. The Pillars will give you the foundation and framework that you need to effect change, but it's up to you to apply these to your real-life situations. Of course, these scenarios will constantly change, as nothing stays still for long in the business world.

Consequently, you'll use this book as your personal reference guide, constantly evaluating your environment, considering your challenges, and applying the principals of the Pillars to the problems you need to solve. This is not a treatise for the ivory tower, and you shouldn't worry about getting the cover dirty. It's your personal, living, working manual for success. In time, the pages should be dog-eared, the section provided for notes should be overflowing, selections that are relevant to your experience should be highlighted, and every page should have scribbling in the margins. Each person's book will look different, and, as time goes on, every copy should show considerable wear. If they do, you'll see it in your company and in your career. A pristine copy on your bookshelf won't help you in the slightest. So put this book to work.

It's also a textbook of strategies to help you turn philosophy into reality. Like any textbook, this means that there are exercises at the end. These exist to help you evaluate your specific situation and show you how to successfully apply the principals in the harsh light of your everyday reality. The actions taken by a high-level manager responsible for thousands of people will be much different than the steps followed by a frontline customer service rep. To make the Pillars work, you have to apply them to your own environment. Nobody likes homework, but, if you don't do the exercises, nothing in your company will change. Do your homework.

As mentioned, we've included an area for you to make note of your successes, typically just by jotting down a line to indicate what you accomplished. You're also strongly encouraged to keep a journal where you can list details of both your successes and those areas where you encountered difficulties. History tends to repeat itself, and you'll find it extremely useful to be able to reflect back on previous times when you faced similar obstacles and see in detail how you prevailed. Additionally, during those periods where you're stressed, fatigued, or just aren't winning the particular battle you're fighting, reviewing previous successes can be invigorating, reminding you of what you're capable of and often giving you the renewed strength you need to carry the day.

Most important of all, you have to understand that, strange as it may seem, the concept of unity in your professional life will be a bold new concept to many. The only way for it to change your world and bring all of you success and fortune is for it to spread like wildfire throughout your company. Remember, this isn't the way things are normally done, so you will naturally meet some initial resistance. Alone, you're isolated, weak, and vulnerable. However, there's strength and power in numbers. Share everything you learn, pass along every tip and trick, and tell people about your successes. This will rally others beneath your banner, which will increase everyone's ability to succeed.

Socializing is another powerful way to build alliances, share techniques, and improve morale. If you and your group get together with other groups in your company for lunch, dinner, coffee after work, a backyard cookout, or any other such gathering, it increases everyone's realization that, even though you work in different areas, you're all a part of the same empire. It's also exciting to hear about the successes that others are having, and it's very practical to hear how they've applied the Pillars in their own environments, as it will likely give you new ideas of your own. Additionally, the friendships you build in a social context with people you would rarely get the chance to talk to at work have strategic value to you both, expanding your network of powerful alliances that you can call upon to help you build a stronger empire.

You should also make use of all the support materials available to you from our company Web site at www.ShowProgramming.com. PDF files of the Pillars and many other useful reminders can be downloaded, printed out, and used as wall hangings to help reinforce the concepts you're trying to promote. Additionally, the audio CD available at the above Web site contains more information to help you along as you drive to and from work each day.

Lastly, I would love to hear from you so that I may share your success stories with others. You'll find an area dedicated to this on our company site. By making yourself a part of the larger community, you'll not only inspire others with your achievements, but you'll expand your network of allies beyond your own industry and into the world at large. I can't emphasize enough how powerful alliances can be in building companies and improving careers. You can never have too many, and variety is always a good thing.

As you can see, there's much more to success than simply reading a book and chanting a few magic words. But then, you always knew that. For people like you who are continually looking for ways to improve your professional and personal lives, doing the work required is never the difficult part; the only difficult thing is discerning what the most productive steps are to take. When you follow through with the actions I've just outlined, you're not only going to build a better world for yourself, but also for those around you. Although there's certainly a tactical benefit to helping others, it also has a pleasant side effect. It just feels good.

UNITE!

Creating a stronger and more prosperous empire and enjoying an excellent career as a result are goals that are within your grasp if you will simply dedicate yourself to the task. To do this, you must let go of your tribal limitations because in this freedom lies the power to effect tremendous change. Remember, tribes do not build empires. People do.

When you let go of your tribal consciousness and realize that individual people are the sparks from which the bonfires of success arise, then you have just admitted that you, personally, have the power to change your world. No longer must you succumb to hopelessness. Never again will you face a great obstacle against which you are powerless. Within your tribe, it is you, the individual, who will change the face of the empire.

As you do so, individuals from all other tribes will rise up to join you, shaking the very foundations of the company with their passion and enthusiasm. On that day, you will finally realize that the empire is not some vague paper concept or a loose federation of competing states, but rather a united people with whom you share the same goals. From border to border, each of us wants a better life. That is our common bond, and it is what will transform you from tiny squabbling bands into the rich inhabitants of a powerful nation.

You are not unimportant members of small and isolated villages. You are the unified people of a great and powerful empire. Alone, you are weak. Together, you are unstoppable.

Unite, and be invincible!

THE PILLARS
OF THE EMPIRE

I ⧘ Vision

Employ long-term thinking and build a long-lasting empire.

Nobody wants to look for a new job every year because his previous company went out of business. And nobody builds a business with a desire to see it fail. In both cases, people are looking for results and benefits that stand the test of time. One would think that, because of this, everyone would have their eyes on the big picture and be thinking in terms of the long-range plans and vision of their enterprise.

However, as anyone who has held a job for more than a month can attest, this is rarely the case. From the highest executive positions to the everyday production tasks of the average workers, people succumb to short-term thinking. They become focused exclusively on the issues of the day, and in the process are so busy putting out the fire at their feet that they don't realize the company itself is burning down. This becomes apparent only later, when the entire structure collapses and they find themselves once again in search of a job. They were successful in solving today's problems, but they failed to prepare for a secure tomorrow. The latter is a much more costly mistake.

The only way to ensure long-term benefits, security, and prosperity is through long-term thinking. In other words, you must plan, live, and work with vision, and you must integrate the efforts and minute details of each day into this grand scheme. Only thus will you guarantee that the prosperity you enjoy today will still be there for you tomorrow.

Vision is not the exclusive domain of the highly paid business executive. Each person, at every level of the empire, is capable of broader thinking. Indeed, every individual must make vision a high priority and a part of their daily tasks. If you are a leader, it is your duty to see the direction of the company and mold your efforts to support it. You are also charged with conveying this purpose to your people in a way that is realistic and meaningful to them so that they, too, may contribute to the greater good. If you are a worker, to you falls the task of making this vision a reality. In every action you take, you must keep one eye on what you're doing and the other on where it's taking your company. With leaders and workers joined together in a harmonious effort to build a better tomorrow, the results will be many times greater than your individual efforts, and you will all enjoy the fruits of your labors.

Contrary to what some may think, living with purpose and vision is not a difficult task. It merely takes a dedicated decision to make it a priority in your daily life. Once you've done that, it's often as simple as putting one foot after the other.

PICTURE THE END RESULT IN FINE DETAIL.

No matter what your task, regardless of how large or small the goal you wish to achieve, you simply cannot succeed in your efforts unless you know exactly what the finished result should look like. You must have a very firm and detailed understanding of what you're looking to accomplish before you take your first step. If you're an artist, how can you possibly paint a picture of a tree if you don't know exactly what a tree looks like? If you think you already know, let's test that assumption with a handful of pertinent questions.

What does the bark look like? What's the texture? What's the shape of the leaf? Exactly what shade of green? How do the branches grow? Is it rigid, or is it flexible enough to sway in the breeze?

Know what a tree looks like now? Great. What does it look like in the fall? Didn't think about that, did you? How about spring? Does it bear fruit? Does it flower? How does it seed? What about winter and summer? Each season brings a specific set of circumstances. Your tree will react in harmony with this.

Got a tree for all seasons now? Wonderful. But exactly where does it grow? What are the exact specifications of the climate? Have you considered the precise temperature range, acceptable humidity, annual rainfall, and highest winds that it can tolerate?

So now you know all there is to know about a tree, right? Well, not quite. You still don't have the complete picture. How does it interact with its environment? What animals does it attract? Does it have natural predators? Does it rise above the forest and get adequate sunlight, or do others overshadow it? What plants stifle its growth? With what plants does it have a symbiotic relationship?

You may contend that an artist with easel and paintbrush doesn't have to know all of these things to paint a tree, and this is true. However, what if you were involved in preparations for a new orchard? You would not only have to offer a rendition of what that orchard would ultimately look like, you'd better understand all the other issues involved, or you'll have a very dead bunch of trees before long. On the bright side, you can at least use them for paper, which you'll doubtless need because printing your résumé will quickly become a priority.

The important thing to glean from our exercise with the trees is to realize just how poorly lacking our concept of a tree is without making a concerted effort to fully visualize one. If someone asked you yesterday about trees, you might have replied that you knew all about them. Now, however, with just the briefest of examinations, it's clear that, when you get right down to it, there's still much to learn. That's the point, and it applies consistently, no matter what it is you're interested in accomplishing. You cannot achieve a high-quality result until you have a detailed picture in your mind of just exactly what that result is.

You can apply this lesson of the visualized tree to every single goal you encounter in your company. As more people understand the value of breaking down a vision into fine detail, your efforts will be increasingly more effective, no matter what they are. Because a stronger empire benefits you personally, you should make it a point to share this insight with everyone you work with. Then, together, you will move forward and achieve great things, because you'll all know exactly what it is that you're working toward. There's tremendous power in such understanding.

You can accomplish anything in life if you're truly willing to commit your mind, body, and spirit. The very first step in bringing your vision to life, however, is knowing *exactly* what that vision is. Sure, this is one of those statements that sound overly simplistic until you sit down and truly think about it. Therefore, for each new task, you must consider it well before taking your very first step.

PLAN LIKE YOU'RE GOING TO LIVE FOREVER.

Another aspect of short-term thinking is the tendency to make plans that look good for a finite period of time but have known difficulties that will arise after that. One would think that this would be an unacceptable approach, but very often the feeling is that the trouble of today is sufficient and that tomorrow will take care of itself. In fact, schemes are frequently concocted in the workplace with the personal benefits being the only consideration, and with an implicit underlying attitude that somebody else can deal with the consequent problems. That's not only unethical, it's just plain stupid. Why? The long-term prosperity of the individual depends upon the long-term prosperity of the empire.

You won't have to look very far in your own company to find examples of short-term thinking. In fact, you may have been in meetings during which someone proposed an obviously flawed solution to a problem at hand. If you were brave (or foolish) enough to point out that the quick fix was a long-term disaster just waiting to happen, you were probably confronted with some of the standard defenses for such tactics:

◎ By the time things go sour, it will be another department's problem. (Protect your tribe in the short term at another tribe's expense.)

◎ Perhaps by then a better solution will have arrived (denial and wishful thinking)

◎ We'll worry about that when the time comes (aversion)

◎ There is no problem (the ostrich syndrome)

◎ That's not your responsibility. Sit down and shut up. (They know it's a bad idea and don't want it publicized.)

These are just a few variations on a theme that's all too familiar. The common thread is that people focus, once again, on putting out the fire at their feet and actively avoid considering the long-term effects of their actions. Regardless of the reason for their avoidance of the consequences, there's one fundamental thing that is almost always overlooked. Even though it seems like they're off the hook because the long-term issues are now considered to be someone else's problem, these problems will damage the company in ways large or small. Because the prosperity of the individual ultimately depends upon the prosperity of the empire, they're actually shooting themselves in the foot; it's just a very slow bullet.

The solution to these problems is really quite simple. As is often the case, it comes down to nothing more mysterious than priorities and lines in the sand that you choose not to cross. No matter what you're trying to accomplish or what problem you're looking to solve, pretend that you're immortal and will be working for your company for the next five centuries. Assume that no matter what goes wrong, it will hurt you personally. Then move forward keeping that perspective in mind, refusing to shrug off the responsibilities that you owe to the future.

In and of itself, this perceptual trick will not solve your problems or make the perfect solution magically appear. However, what it will do is keep you working on the problem until a satisfactory approach is discovered—which is the next best thing to magic. You'd be surprised how often sloppy solutions and ill-conceived plans are put into place for no other reason than people being in too much of a hurry to come up with a better idea.

In general, humanity is full of brilliance and inspiration. To tap into that may take extra time, but it's time well spent. Once you realize that your own future is linked to the future of the empire, you'll no longer be willing to settle for short-term solutions that guarantee long-term disasters. You'll be motivated to reach for a better plan, and, being so driven, you will almost always find one.

Once you've come to this realization, the next step is to make sure that everyone you work with understands it as well. Many people live their lives on automatic pilot and simply don't think of changing their perspective. Therefore, you must show them how the consequences of tomorrow are always of the utmost importance to them personally, and start building alliances with like-minded people.

You'll often meet resistance when you try to hold out for a better solution, being pressured instead for the quick fix. This is why you must educate as many people as you can reach. There is strength in numbers, and, when you have the support of others, you'll be in a much better position to deliver the solid, long-term solution. Better still, with each success, you will be able to gather even more people to your banner, for they will see that you were right and that they have personal and tangible rewards to join with you.

You'll never realize how truly amazing you can be until you decide to claim the consequences of the future as your personal domain. When you own the future, you own the present. As others join you in this thinking, your combined power will make you a strong-enough force to build a better tomorrow through a smarter today, no matter what resistance you encounter.

ANTICIPATE HOW PEOPLE WILL REACT.

No matter how lofty your goals or how well you've mapped out the journey, you're going to depend on—and sometimes fall into conflict with—other people. It's a common scenario for people to devote days, weeks, or months to intricate strategies only to have them fall apart the first time the plan hits a snag. You'll often hear people, in the midst of their troubleshooting, muse that they simply didn't realize that this person or that department was going to react in such a way. Simply put, they didn't understand the personalities and perspectives of all the players involved, and they were consequently unprepared for resistance and adverse reactions. They never saw the trouble coming until it was too late.

Just like when playing a game of chess, you must always think several moves ahead. To do so in a productive manner, you have to be able to predict how others are going to respond. Your assumptions will never be 100% accurate, of course, but, if you make it a part of your normal thought process to consider not only the logistical aspects of any plan but also the human factor, you will be much more effective than anyone else. Your initial plans will be tailored to the individuals you'll be encountering rather than pursuing an impersonal or academic approach based on pages full of numbers, names, and departments.

Additionally, because you've taken the time to understand the nature of the people involved, you'll have contingency plans based on the various ways that you predict they may respond. Anticipating several possible reactions and having a plan for each will practically guarantee that a large portion of your planning efforts will end up in the trash can. That's okay. Don't think of the time you spent on the unused backup plans as time wasted. Instead, consider the fact that, *because* of the overall number of hours you spent in detailed planning, you were prepared and you succeeded. Those extra contingencies that you didn't use are just a cost of doing business successfully.

In any endeavor, people are the wild cards. No matter how brilliantly you strategize, if you fail to take this into account your plans will be disrupted time and again, leaving you spinning idly in the breeze wondering what just hit you. There's no need for that. Although it's impossible to predict with absolute certainty how any person or group of people will react, with attention and study you'll find that you're quickly able to predict and anticipate the responses of others with growing regularity. As with any other skill, you'll improve with practice. The simple fact that you've made the study of people and their reactions a priority in your planning gives you an incredible tactical advantage for one very simple reason: *most people don't.*

So how do you go about anticipating the way that people will respond to your ideas, proposals, initiatives, and plans? Study, and pay attention! Countless books have been written on human nature. Go to your local bookstore and read! Furthermore, don't limit your studies to human nature alone. Consider the culture in which you live. People are influenced not only by time-honored instincts, but also by local, regional, and national attitudes and norms.

While you're in the bookstore, make sure you also look at some books on human psychology, and specifically emotion. If you haven't discovered this already, it won't take much time in the business world to realize that, no matter how professional we're supposed to be in our endeavors, people still make emotional decisions. Are emotional decisions always the smartest or best? Obviously not. When you're reacting in the heat of the moment instead of acting on a well-conceived plan of action, you're extremely off balance and vulnerable. Nonetheless, a surprisingly large number of people do just this. If you understand the emotional hot buttons of the people you're dealing with, you'll have a much more accurate idea of how they will react to any situation you create. It's another advantage, and a big one at that.

You must also consider whether the reactions you encounter will be in pockets of isolated groups or if an overall snowball effect could create a larger problem than the sum of individual responses. Again, understanding the nature, motivations, and emotions of others will give you ample insight into just what sort of reactions you can expect.

Having prepared for as many contingencies as possible based on your observations of the people you're dealing with, you're in a very strong position to see that your vision not only survives but thrives. Does all this sound a bit manipulative? Good. That's exactly what it is. Business is war. I can assure you, if you don't prepare and control the battlefield to your advantage, someone else will come along and impose their own vision, and your dreams will suffer accordingly. Know who you're dealing with, how they're going to react, and be prepared for it. In this manner, you can protect your vision and continue to bring positive change to your organization.

KNOW THE CHARACTER OF YOUR LEADERS AND ALLIES.

As an extension of preparing for the reactions of others, you must have a firm grasp on the character and moral makeup of the people you're dealing with. If your fate is at the mercy of your leaders, understanding their character is critical. Are they ethical? Will they reward you for your efforts? Can you trust them? You should ask yourself questions like these on a regular basis, and make sure that you're comfortable with the validity of your conclusions before trying to promote your vision. Regardless of whether you work under a noble leader or the scum of the earth, you can still succeed. Your approach, however, will obviously be very different depending on whom you're dealing with.

In addition to your leaders, what about your allies? Within any organization, you'll find like-minded individuals and groups who will support you in your endeavors. Failing to understand the quality of their character is just as fatal as not understanding your leaders because both have the power to completely disrupt your plans.

It also works the other way. If you're a leader, you must understand the nature of the people who work with you. Can you count on them to follow through? Can you trust them? Will they do the right thing, or will they instead fall apart out of preoccupation with self-interest? If you don't know the morals and ethics of the people you count on to get the job done, your vision may spiral into complete disaster.

You must also look to the future. Will the person who agrees with you today support you further down the road, or will they bolt at the first sign of opposition? Can they be bought by the competition, whether internal or external? Do they have the personal strength and conviction to hold to their course no matter how rough the waters get, or will they simply drift in whichever direction the wind is blowing? Before you can count on them and make any kind of plans based on their participation and support, you must not only know where they are today, but where they will stand on the issues tomorrow.

People also react differently to the euphoria of success and the heartbreak of failure. Will the tides of fortune alter their judgment? Do they have oversized egos? Will they become cocky and overconfident when things are going well? Are they likely to become completely pessimistic when something goes wrong? No matter how sound their judgment may be in the calm stages of planning, it could be radically different under fire. You need to consider these things before—not after—you decide to count on them.

Loyalty is another critical consideration. Some people support a vision because they truly believe in it. Their motivations are pure: the simple and admirable desire to effect positive change. Other people are simply opportunistic. If your worldview suits their ambitions today, then they will serve as your staunchest supporters. However, when the tides change and they see better opportunities in another camp, they may abandon you with no warning whatsoever and even turn against you. So how do you protect yourself? Sometimes the best way to see the future is to look into the past.

How did they treat the people they interacted with before they met you, and how are they treating other people even now? Like many clichés, there's a certain amount of truth in the adage that a tiger doesn't change stripes. How someone treats others is quite likely how they'll treat you as well. If you see a wide gap between how they appear to you and how others view them, examine it carefully before trusting them with the care of your vision.

BE COMPLETELY PREPARED BEFORE UNVEILING YOUR IDEAS.

Many people, out of either impatience or the desire for personal attention, have a habit of talking about their plans and ideas to anyone who will listen, long before they're prepared to implement them. Although it may have been proper play when we were children to give "fair warning" in our competitive games, as an adult in the business world it's little more than political suicide. No matter what you're trying to accomplish, chances are good that there will be others within your company who are competing for the resources or control that you want for your own goal. If you give notice of your plans before you're prepared to act on them, you give the competition a chance to prepare for your tactics and beat you to the punch.

Rule number one is very simple: until you're completely prepared and ready to put your plan into action, keep your mouth shut! Discuss your vision on a need-to-know basis only. Other than stroking your own ego, no advantage can be gained by bragging about what you're going to do next week or next month. The disadvantages of premature announcement are numerous and often fatal.

Whether your vision is a large or small one, you must prepare exhaustively. Eventually, a time will come in the process when you need to act before you can move things ahead any further. You may also from time to time wish to release *disinformation* to throw your competitors off track, but this is once again just another form of action that's not to be taken until you're prepared to utilize the benefits that it brings. In the meantime, plan, prepare, and even drill and rehearse when possible, and make sure that you are in every way ready to strike with overwhelming firepower before anyone has even the slightest notion of what you're up to. If you keep things quiet until you're prepared to act, then, by the time any opposition to your plans can mount, you will have already achieved your victory.

If, however, you are greeted with immediate agreement and success when you do unveil your plans, you may feel that you went to all that trouble for nothing. Sometimes this will be true. But who cares? You prevailed! More often, though, your seemingly effortless success will be due to the fact that you were so thoroughly prepared for every contingency that any who might have opposed your ideas saw the futility of resistance, and therefore offered none. The greatest victory in battle is to win without a fight.

Furthermore, regardless of whether your victory is a lengthy or speedy one, all of the effort you put into preparations leaves you extremely well organized when it comes time to actually implement your plans. Many an endeavor has succeeded in the initial phases, won the support of all critical parties, and then fallen flat on its face due to a lack of adequate structure and organization in implementation. If you fail, it doesn't matter what stage of the game it happens in. You've still failed. As such, each and every bit of work that you put into the overall selling and implementation of your plan is of tremendous value. Get your act together and keep it quiet. Then, when you're ready, spring into action and seize the day.

GIVE PEOPLE A REASON TO CARE ABOUT YOUR VISION.

This is the most common mistake made in every company, worldwide. Leaders come up with great new ideas and expect that, by simply voicing them, people will rally beneath their banner. The very best example I can give in this regard is the common practice of corporations advertising their "mission," which is usually some vague and meaningless jumble of corporate-speak. So, with all due respect to whoever comes up with these ideas, let me say this as gently as possible. Nobody cares about your mission statement.

Shocking, isn't it? Many executives who were taught in business school that you must have one of these things when you start a company have difficulty grasping why they have absolutely no real value in the day-to-day affairs of their business. Above and beyond the fact that they're usually so vague as to convey no practical information, there's one critical piece missing, and this piece determines whether a mission statement will motivate anyone. A mission statement never gives people a real, practical, and tangible reason to care about it. It's nothing more than eye candy for the bureaucratically impressionable.

No matter how honest and hardworking they may be, all who work for your company from the president down to the custodians are—you guessed it—people. They come to work each day for one and only one reason: there's something in it for them. Typically, the paycheck is first and foremost on the list, but it's not the only motivating factor. Many people are lucky enough to love what they do for a living. Consequently, other factors that fall under the broad heading of job satisfaction also come into play. Ego ranks high on the list for many. Remember, we're dealing with people here. However, regardless of what the reasons may be, the simple fact is that people are there doing work for you because you've given them a reason to do so. Take away those reasons and they will trample you underfoot as they stampede to the exits.

Of course, the mission statement is just a convenient and obvious example of a useless vision, made so because the people have no reason to care about it. A business, however, is one continual stream of effort, and there will be many times when inspired workers and leaders come up with a new vision, large or small, to improve things. When you're that person, the most important thing you need to consider if you want any support is why people should care about what you're proposing.

Consequently, you need to be prepared to present the personal benefits of your vision to the people you wish to participate, and I do mean *personal* in the most literal way. Every individual will have unique desires, and groups of people will also have common goals and ambitions. You must appeal to individuals in terms of their personal well-being. It falls to you to explain why your vision, when successful, will bring them benefits that they can actually see and will care about. Do this, and you will have their immediate attention. Follow through on your promise of benefits, and you'll also have their most loyal and enthusiastic support.

Does it mean that people are selfish and bad because you have to appeal to their self-interest? No, of course not. We all have self-interest. It's an inescapable part of life. But, the bottom line for you is that you need support for your vision, and this is what it takes to get it. Furthermore, it meets my criteria for a good business deal, because everybody wins.

You get the support you need, and your supporters get benefits. That's not only good from an ethical point of view, but it's the best way to run a long-term business. As long as everybody gets what they want, the wheel keeps turning.

However, a piece is still missing here. It may seem obvious, but, before you can show someone how they can benefit from your inspirational new idea, they have to understand what it actually is. In fact, you should be prepared from the very beginning to spend significant time and effort on this. Don't expect others to see your vision.

If it were obvious, someone would have done it already. You must assume that you will not only have to go to great lengths to explain what your idea actually is and what its implications are, you also need to be ready for all the work involved in winning people over to your way of thinking. Sometimes, the reason nobody has done it before isn't that the idea didn't come up, but rather that whoever came up with the idea didn't take the time to win people over. An idea rarely sells itself. That might have something to do with why companies pay people commissions to go out and actively sell things.

Before you can begin preparations to garner the support of others, it helps to understand whom the pivotal people or groups are so that you can focus your persuasive efforts in the right direction. Not only do you need to know who these people are, you must also understand what's important to them, for the only way to sell your vision is from their point of view, not yours. They don't care about what's in it for you, only what's in it for them. Human nature is a wonderful thing, as there are very few aspects of life that you can count on to be so unfailingly predictable. This is an advantage.

One last thing to consider when giving people a reason to care is the possibility of competing visions. Just because you're inspired and motivated to change the world for the better, don't assume that you're the only one. Others have their own worldview, and, if they're any good at all, they're going to work just as hard as you at winning the hearts and minds of the influential people. The more you understand the details and implications of any competing visions, the better you can prepare your counter strategies. If they promise people the moon, find a way to promise the stars. Just make sure that you *always* deliver on your promises.

PRESENT LONG-TERM BENEFITS IN PRACTICAL TERMS.

Another problem people have with rallying behind a new initiative is that the results may seem too far away to have any real effect on their daily existence. It may be very true that your vision will improve the lives of every single person in your department, or perhaps even in the company itself. However, if people won't see any benefits for two years, it's unlikely that they'll get too excited about your efforts. Even if they do, after a few months with no tangible reward for their endeavors, they'll either lose interest or become disillusioned and negative. Either way, your support will fall away in the midst of your initiative, and you're dead in the water.

You can't blame people for this, nor belittle them for their lack of faith. In any group, there are very few true visionaries. The problem with many of them is that they believe that seeing the possibilities is all they're required to do. It is not. Yes, you must see a better future, but you must also be a great communicator and motivator to bring your dream to life. Part of this is showing the rest of the company just exactly how they will benefit, and some benefits had better be lurking just around the corner if you want to keep their attention. People, by nature, tend to have a short attention span. Ignore this at your peril.

In addition to breaking your plan down to show incremental benefits, you may also find yourself battling another proposal that is much more appealing because it's a short-term solution. As is often the case, a short-term proposal may fail miserably over the long haul, but the majority of people won't realize this in the beginning. Remember, they're not the visionaries. You are. It's up to you to do the math for them. Add up the numbers or tally the appropriate results for both approaches, spanning the entire duration. You must be able to demonstrate, in irrefutable terms, that the short-term solution comes up, well, short over the course of time. You must also show that your plan, although perhaps not as spectacular in the beginning, is unquestionably more beneficial when it's all said and done. If it's not, you should give serious consideration to discarding it and joining the team with the better plan. Remember, the long-term health of the empire affects you personally.

Additionally, you must be able to map intangibles into tangibles. Just as the mission statement is too vague to be relevant to most people, many visions suffer from the problem of living in the abstract rather than the concrete. Don't expect people to make this leap on their own. You have to map it out for them. That's your part of the deal as a visionary.

INTEGRATE SHORT-TERM SOLUTIONS INTO THE LARGER EFFORT.

Even though you have a long-term plan that will bring lasting benefits to your people, at times you simply must put out the fire at your feet. If you don't recognize and acknowledge this fact of life, you'll immediately lose all credibility. You'll also end up with crispy toes. Long-term solutions are all well and good, but many times, if you don't deal with the short-term problem, you won't be around to worry about the long term. So what's a visionary to do?

The first thing to clarify is what *not* to do. If you decide to eliminate the annoying short-term problem with a quick and dirty fix so that you can get back to the mountaintop and contemplate your grand scheme, you're doing no one a service, especially yourself. There's one very important reason for this. Every short-term action has a long-term effect.

The hallmark of quick fixes everywhere is that people don't consider the ramifications of the solution. All they care about, at least for the moment, is that the flames aren't scorching their shiny new shoes. From there, many people quickly fall into the old "tomorrow will take care of itself" way of thinking, which is little more than denial and irresponsibility. Whether it's a hack or a well-planned action, it will always have consequences. The critical difference between the two is that, for the well-planned action, the consequences have been considered and accounted for in the overall scheme of things. In other words, when you have a short-term problem, come up with a solution that eliminates the current symptoms without deviating from your overall long-term goals. This takes more effort and consideration, but it keeps you on track for your vision while giving you credibility for being a practical, here-and-now problem-solver. That pays big dividends when it comes to credibility and trust.

Alternatively, you may find that someone else has a perfectly good short-term solution to the problem that requires only minor modifications to keep the long-term consequences from being detrimental. By approaching this person, sincerely complimenting them on their ingenuity and giving them credit for being a visionary themselves, you open the door to cooperation. At that point, you'll have a much more receptive ear when you show how, working together and with just a few tweaks, their idea can coexist within the framework of your long-term plan. Make sure they understand that they'll still get the credit for the solution, not you, and that you'll be first in line to tell the world how brilliant they are.

Additionally, you can point out to them that, above and beyond solving short- and long-term problems, you've each gained yet another thing of inestimable value. By joining forces in this endeavor, you have acquired new and potentially powerful allies in each other. Not only have you solved the problem at hand, the two of you and all of your collective supporters are now united, much stronger together than you were individually.

SHOW HOW TO GET THERE FROM HERE.

Just as you'll encounter difficulties when people can't translate your dream into practical benefits that they can understand, you must also show people that there is a clear and logical path that leads to the long-term benefits you espouse. Many people come up with good and noble ideas. However, what separates the true visionary from the hopeless romantics and impractical dreamers is the ability to translate that dream into action in a sequence of clear and simple steps that everyone can follow. That's what gets things done. It also garners the respect of people higher and more powerful than you in the chain of command, earning you a reputation as a practical, results-oriented leader. And that's horsepower that you can always use.

Nobody will follow you in pursuit of your vision if there isn't a clear, believable path to get there from here. People are afraid of the dark and fearful of the unknown, and they will resist change with all four paws. If you can't show them a way to accomplish your goals that seems organized, well thought out, and at least reasonably safe, they'll clear the room before you get your next sentence out.

To demonstrate the validity of both your quest and the pot of gold at the end of the rainbow, show the sequence of events as you see them unfolding. People are always more comfortable with an incremental approach to things, as it's easier to grasp one small step and then the next than it is to get their minds around a huge concept all at once.

In doing so, employ cause and effect so that they can see that no leap of faith is involved. Many people have been burned enough times in the corporate world that they simply have no faith, and it's hard to blame them. You should be able to demonstrate that, after accomplishing one incremental step, it produces tangible results that set the stage for the next step. In this way, once again, a large campaign can be broken down into practical terms that even the least imaginative in the group can be comfortable with.

This incremental approach also allows others to come up with innovative ways to solve the problems that you'll encounter. You get the benefit of the group's creativity, and your group becomes more enthusiastic about your vision because they feel like an important part of the success rather than excess baggage. Once again, you've taken another step toward uniting the people, from which your group and the entire empire will benefit.

Understanding the path toward your vision also allows people to be prepared for the transitions and results. This enables them to carry forward their own plans in harmony with yours, so that neither is derailed and each supports and reinforces the other wherever possible. Joining other groups and their efforts together with yours, closely or loosely, broadens your scope yet again, for you now have several armies working in harmony on the same front. Not only does this bring more power to bear on the problems at hand, the momentum in and of itself helps the movement to grow. Everybody wants to be part of a winning team. As it becomes more and more obvious that you, your people, and your allies are moving forward to great things, you'll find that, instead of having to beg and plead for support, people will now come to you, individually and in groups, wanting to be a part of the vision. And this, of course, was always part of the vision.

WIN THE WAR, NOT THE BATTLE.

N o matter how well you prepare and how brilliantly you execute your plans, you will eventually encounter difficulties. At times, you may even lose a battle. It is extremely important that you always keep your perspective and focus on the vision itself. The moment you get caught up in tunnel vision, losing sight of everything except the task at hand, your dream is in great peril. Sure, it's nice to win every battle, but remember that all that's important is that you bring your vision to life. If you suffered failures along the way but still achieved your overall objective, no one will care. If, however, you become obsessive about winning every single engagement at any cost, then you may well find one day that you've won the current battle but lost the war. At that point, it will have all been for nothing.

Additionally, it's important to maintain momentum. Not only does it keep things moving forward, it's critical to morale. When you get caught up in the marshes and find yourself making no progress at all, people begin to falter and lose hope. Remember, *you're* the visionary, not *them*. The responsibility of maintaining hope and enthusiasm falls on your shoulders, and the easiest way to do that is to keep things rolling so that you see a stream of incremental successes and accomplishments, even if they're small ones sometimes. Don't get bogged down. Stay light on your feet.

If you insist on winning every single argument, you'll also eventually build animosity and resistance that would not have existed if you had been wise enough to yield lesser points on a strategic basis. By giving in to a smaller, less critical matter, you may indeed lose a minor battle. However, by showing yourself to be reasonable, approachable, flexible, and open to compromise, you'll often gain the respect and cooperation of those who previously opposed you. If you concede a point but gain an ally, did you really lose the battle?

You should also understand the importance of each battle long before you begin the campaign. In your earliest planning stages, you need to assess which objectives are absolutely critical to the success of your vision, which ones heavily influence the outcome, and which are clearly optional. Among other things, performing this triage allows you to manage your resources and plan your strategies accordingly.

Prioritizing your major efforts will also give you a sense of cause and effect. When studying the campaign to achieve your vision, consider the consequences of winning and losing for each battle. There will not only be some obvious implications in terms of the overall war, but also a sequential effect as the outcome of one endeavor invariably influences the next engagement. Knowing what objectives you must accomplish and comprehending the results of each success and failure will also help you make the quick battlefield decisions that will inevitably fall to you when a fight you never expected suddenly shows up on your front doorstep.

Taken individually, none of these steps are mysterious or novel. In fact, if I've done my job properly, they should all seem very, very obvious. What's important is that, when bringing a new vision to life, you consider each and every one of these points and act accordingly. More often than you might care to think, the gifted visionaries of humanity who accomplished great things did so not because of an intellect that far exceeded that of mere mortals, but rather because they had a good idea, took their time, and did their homework. Most importantly, they did the one critical thing that so few people take the time to do. Understanding that the most powerful and dynamic resource at their disposal was people, they gave their utmost attention to every aspect of human nature. They realized that they were dealing not with abstract plans and vague concepts, but rather with real people who had feelings and desires of their own. And they acted accordingly.

A vision begins with a dream, an inspiration rising from the hearts and minds of those who see things not only as they are, but as they could be. They dare to reach for the stars. The inspired visionary, that passionate soul who can bring those dreams to life, is the one who realizes that nothing can be accomplished until people are joined and dedicated to a common cause. Only together, each standing upon the shoulders of the one who came before, can they truly rise high enough to reach the stars and achieve the impossible.

VISION

Employ long-term thinking and build a long-lasting empire.

◎ Picture the end result in fine detail.

◎ Plan like you're going to live forever.

◎ Anticipate how people will react.

◎ Know the character of your leaders and allies.

◎ Be completely prepared before unveiling your ideas.

◎ Give people a reason to care about your vision.

◎ Present long-term benefits in practical terms.

◎ Integrate short-term solutions into the larger effort.

◎ Show how to get there from here.

◎ Win the war, not the battle.

II ⦚ Leadership

See a better life for your people,
and be passionate about making it happen.

You don't have to be a leader to lead. You just have to want something better and be dedicated to bringing that vision to life. Whether you're a trained executive or manager of many years or a frontline worker who's never had any desire to hold authority, you will nonetheless inspire others and lead simply by the example you set. That's the only kind of leadership that truly matters. Of course, when you dare to stand up and be seen working for a better tomorrow, like it or not, you become a leader. However, it is far better to perform the duties and have the title assigned to you afterward than it is to follow the path that so many have taken in their careers of lobbying to get themselves assigned to a position of authority without having first demonstrated the ability to lead.

People don't follow empty slogans, and they don't care about the buzzwords of the day. They follow leaders who reward them and increase their sense of self-worth. If you get caught up in thinking that people shouldn't be so self-centered, you'll waste valuable time that could be better spent getting things done. People are who they are. An honest look in the mirror will also remind you that you, too, are a member of the human race. We go to work each day because we're rewarded, financially and otherwise, for our efforts. If the announcement were made one evening that paychecks would no longer be handed out, your office would be empty the very next day. There's no dishonor in admitting this; we participate in a fair exchange of labor and compensation. Keep that in mind when you're dealing with people, and you'll always have an understanding of what will motivate them.

Desiring to change your company for the better is the mark of a dedicated worker. Possessing a passionate urge to improve the well-being of the people around you in the process is the mark of a great leader. If you set goals for the good of the empire, but make the well-being of your people an obvious priority, they will move mountains to guarantee that those goals are met. They may even whistle a little tune while they're doing it. When the work is done, the tasks accomplished, and the rewards distributed, they'll remember that, while many others in the company made empty speeches about strengthening the empire and improving the lives of the people, you actually did something about it, and they benefited. That alone will go a long way toward gaining their support when you come up with your next initiative.

SHOW HOW PERSONAL EFFORTS MAP TO TANGIBLE REWARDS.

One of the greatest challenges that leaders face is trying to motivate people. This is true at all levels, but, the grander your scheme for the company at large, the harder it is to communicate it to the everyday workers and leaders who have to carry out this vision.

Nowhere is this more apparent than in a huge corporate environment. The people in the company typically get memos, emails, flyers, and other such impersonal notifications of some new initiative that the company is embarking upon. This, of course, implies new tasks and goals for the people who do the work. However, because of the vague and impersonal nature of the large, bureaucratic environment, most people have little motivation to safeguard and improve the bottom-line profitability of the company. It's not because they're lazy or worthless people; it's just that they simply don't understand how their personal efforts will eventually come back around to them and translate into personal rewards.

If you, as a leader, issue an edict that the percentage of waste on a particular job is too high and must be reduced, you might expect that people will enthusiastically dedicate themselves to finding a creative solution to this problem. They will not. They realize that reducing waste in their department by 10%, which could translate literally into millions of dollars in a large company, will not bring them so much as a thank-you note, let alone any tangible financial rewards. Consequently, they'll do only the bare minimum that they must to avoid incurring the wrath of their management, and not one thing more. If you want people to do something for you, show them how they will be rewarded when they succeed.

In addition to announcing the task to be accomplished, to lead effectively you must have a plan in place that will not only track results but also link them to individual effort. Only with this information can you reward your people fairly, and only by rewarding your people can you ever hope to bring out the brilliance that they possess.

It's also important to realize that not everyone is a superstar. To motivate all of the people around you, it's necessary to create opportunities for achievement at many levels. Although this goes contrary to what many in the old model of management believe, it also means that you must set mediocre goals for mediocre performers, and make a big deal out of it when they succeed.

Once they realize that they can, in fact, succeed and do adequate-quality work to receive praise and recognition, they will be more enthusiastic about their work and will also feel better about themselves. Many people are poor producers not because they lack ability, but simply because they don't believe in themselves. If someone feels that they're a failure in life, then they will be a failure in all of their endeavors. By giving such people a chance to succeed, you help to break that cycle and allow them to gain self-confidence, perhaps for the first time in their lives. This alone can bring about profound change in the quality of their work.

Other times, however, it's much more difficult, particularly when, at the company level, you're addressing a problem that doesn't provide a clear cause-and-effect link between personal effort and paychecks. This is your time to come up with creative solutions. Every situation is different, but you can always follow one path: the good of the individual depends upon the good of the empire. Having this path to follow, you must then trace benefits received by the company at large all the way back to the people you're addressing and show, in no uncertain terms, how this translates to a clear benefit that lands on their very own desk. Remember that money isn't the only benefit that people work for and you'll have a much greater array of choices at your disposal. Above all, it has to be real to them. You have to make it personal.

BUILD A SENSE OF OWNERSHIP IN THE CAUSE.

Another reason people become demoralized is due to a feeling that they're just passengers in the overall ride. The company is just some vague concept, and whether tasks and initiatives succeed seems irrelevant to the individual. They're simply expected to do what they're told. Off in the distance, in some faraway corner of the empire that they never visit, somebody else sees the results of the work that they do.

To build pride in the empire, you must make each person truly believe that they are responsible for its rise or fall. And this is not some petty manipulative scheme. It's the truth. An empire is nothing but a collection of people. Therefore, the people, that mass of individuals who show up each day to do the work, are responsible for the fate of the nation. It is, in fact, *their* nation. A leader is someone who can communicate this to people in a way that is real to them.

Furthermore, when people feel a sense of ownership in both the empire at large and in the individual causes that you're currently moving forward, they get a sense that they are in control of their own destiny. That's a powerful feeling, and when they experience it you will suddenly see the weak stand up and become strong. Of course, they were strong all along, but, no matter what inherent capabilities you possess, you are nonetheless as weak as you believe yourself to be. Show them that they are in charge of their own lives, and watch them cast aside their preconceived notions of inability. It's wonderful to see your people make such a transformation, watching their eyes light up with a new sense of self-worth and control, and being there when they suddenly realize that they can accomplish difficult things.

No isolated individual will ever be able to solve the ills of the world. Great things happen only when you unite with your coworkers, with your leaders, and with those who are in your charge and approach your problems as a single, unstoppable force. Your peers, your managers, and the people who work for you all have the ability to achieve great things. However, this alone is not enough because your competitor's people possess the same innate talents. What makes the difference is inspiration, that ability to fire people up, encourage them, and motivate them to reach for the fabled brass ring. This is where the individual can truly shine, for one voice can raise the voices of a thousand.

Instead of leading by assigning tasks and demanding results, learn some new leadership skills. Experiment and explore. Discover how you can have conversations with people and show the need to be great, and where the solutions can be clearly seen, at least conceptually. As you do this, leave holes in the scenario you paint where the solutions should be. Furthermore, as you paint these scenes and intimate where creativity or effort is needed, with practice you'll be able to do so in such a way that it's obvious to a few people that they possess the exact skills needed to solve this critical problem. However, don't point it out. Let them come to this conclusion on their own. Instead, focus on the glory that would naturally fall to any who could make this happen.

One of the rewards you're offering for their efforts is status, and it's a powerful motivator. You'll find that people will be enthusiastic about taking on even the most unpleasant jobs when approached in this manner, because they *gave* the solution; it wasn't demanded of them. Furthermore, they'll feel good about themselves because not only are they giving, but they're solving an important problem and showing initiative. People who feel good about their work never fail to do great work. And, of course, as always, continually keep your eye out for any other rewards that you can bestow upon people who get the job done for your group.

REWARD EVERY SINGLE PERSON WHO CONTRIBUTES TO SUCCESS.

It's important to accomplish your tasks and achieve great things. However, all too often, a group of people gives heart, body, and soul to get a job done only to find that, in the end, only a couple of people are rewarded or even recognized as having been responsible. Transformed into electricity, the amount of resentment this generates could power a large city for decades. It is one of the single most stupid and divisive things that the old model of management continually does, year after year. If you want the power of a united empire, you must reward each and every person who plays a part in its success.

There is nothing wrong with giving greater rewards to those who made greater contributions. In fact, you absolutely must do this or you'll alienate your most productive and creative minds. The important thing, and what most companies miss, is that everyone who participated in the success must receive some tangible reward. What you're doing through this practice is training and conditioning their way of thinking. You're demonstrating to them, in a very real and practical manner, that the laws of physics do in fact exist in your group. Do a great job, contribute to the common good, and you'll be rewarded. It's the law of cause and effect.

Even though you give smaller rewards to those who made smaller contributions, they must get *some* reward. You must also make it a point to avoid downplaying the small contributors, but instead glorify them just as you do the big producers. Let people know that the hero at the head of the line braved a thousand arrows to achieve a critical objective, and should be cheered. Then make sure everyone also cheers the fact that, without the rank-and-file workers each firing a couple of arrows of their own, that hero never would have lived long enough to do great things. The hero is lauded. The people on the front lines are glorified. And everyone walks away feeling pumped up for the experience. Care to guess how effective they'll be in their next engagement?

It's important to reward the results that can be seen and understood by all, and that's the easy part. When someone contributes to the production needed for the group effort, those results are obvious, so it's easy to map effort to reward. The harder part, though no less critical, is to reward the efforts that are intangible. If your company had the best month of sales ever, it's easy to compensate the sales staff, but the custodian who cleans the offices at night may not immediately seem like a contributor to increased company revenues. The clever and inspired leader, however, will make sure that even the cleaning crew is put in the spotlight, for obviously the boost in morale that results from a neat and tidy office helped the sales staff reach their goals. In other words, if it weren't for the excellent job done by what you declare to be the absolutely best cleaning crew in the industry, which is clearly superior to all other crews worldwide, the sales goals would never have been met. As your cleaning people take their much-deserved bow, make sure nobody claps louder than the sales people who got paid the most.

Think that's silly and pointless? Apart from that fact that your office will now sparkle with a brilliance to rival Camelot for months to come, there's a not-so-obvious reward that the company receives from these newly motivated custodians. Enthusiasm is contagious.

Everywhere the cleaning crew goes, they'll be whistling a tune, slapping the workers they meet on the back, and reminding each person in every office that the empire they all share is truly superior to all other empires. You pay fair market value for the cleaning. The motivational services you now get from them are cheap at a hundred times the cost of the rewards you gave them. Whether it's the people who make the offices shine, the laborers sweating away in the warehouse, the service reps taking the heat from frustrated customers, or any other group in your company, when you make each individual feel like they were a part of the success, the fire of the motivated will ripple through your business in almost tangible waves. Reward everyone who participated. If the contribution isn't obviously tangible or relevant, find a way to make it so.

SWIFTLY REMOVE THOSE WHO WORK AGAINST THE COMMON GOOD.

It is not only my deep personal and ethical conviction that acting with benevolence and positive interaction is the best way to get things done, it's a matter of simple practicality. Happy and motivated people are the most productive people on the planet. So what do you do with people who are clearly negative, destructive malcontents, interested not in the good of the empire but only in spreading discontent and achieving personal gains regardless of the cost to others? More importantly, how do you deal with them in a way that doesn't destroy the goodwill of your productive people? It's a difficult and crucial question.

Just as enthusiasm is contagious, so too is negativity and discontent. If you allow it to exist in your environment, it will spread like a disease. Before you can stop it, your entire company will become a collection of unproductive, petty, and sniping little creatures, right up to the point at which your competition puts you out of business.

You must first try everything you can think of to turn such negative people around and make them a happy, contributing part of your group. However, if all of your efforts fail and the negativity continues, then you must simply eliminate this person from your group—swiftly, permanently, and without hesitation. There's more than one reason people have called me a corporate barbarian. I'm not about to sacrifice the happiness and prosperity of hundreds or thousands of people and their families all for the sake of one malcontent who consciously works against the common good and refuses to change.

So, with forewarning that we will now contemplate some of the more unpleasant aspects of building an empire, what's the first step to take? Before you're within a hundred miles of contemplating a surgical strike, you must explore a host of opportunities to avoid the conflict altogether. First and foremost is taking the time to distinguish between substandard effort that can simply be improved through positive means and the destructive malcontent who seeks only to complain, obstruct, and tear things down. With the former, you'll almost always find that what we discuss in the Pillars will show a way to encourage and motivate them, bringing out the best in their work. It would be not only a terrible injustice but also a loss to the empire if even one such person who could be turned around were instead simply discarded.

However, if you've done your best and it's clearly obvious that the malcontent will not be swayed from negative attitudes and pursuits, there's only one course of action. The person has to go. Don't argue with them, don't fight with them, and don't try to embarrass or harass them. Just get rid of them, creating as little fuss as possible. Although various state and federal laws protect the worker (and rightfully so), failure to perform the services for which one is hired is usually acceptable grounds for termination.

Additionally, you must eliminate not only *active* negativity but *passive* negativity as well. Any person who does not care about the cause, anyone who will just not get up off their posterior and at least try to build a better world for the common good must be banished from the empire immediately. Poor skills can be improved, and unmotivated people can often be motivated. However, the chronically apathetic can seek therapy on their own time, and in the service of someone else's company. Better that they be your competition's liability than your own.

It's not a pleasant experience, but it's worth noting that for most companies it's also not a very frequent experience. When such a problem does crop up, and you can't turn them around and make them part of the family, then do what you have to do. When you're done, you can wash away the distasteful memories by throwing yourself into yet another stunning success that benefits and brings happiness to all the people of your empire.

SHIELD YOUR PEOPLE SO THAT THEY CAN BE BRILLIANT.

Surprisingly, one of the prime factors in low productivity has nothing to do with the attitudes or skills of your people, but rather the myriad distractions that pull them away from the task at hand. Whether it's a stream of unproductive and unnecessary meetings or the push and pull of internal company politics, your people are being subjected to disruptive forces on a daily basis. While they're dealing with these things, they can't be doing what they were hired to do.

So, the very first duty of a leader is to act as a shield. Your people must be protected as much as possible from all the corporate noise so that they can be brilliant for you. Sometimes we must lead from the middle, without the authority to demand change. However, if you're a manager who therefore has power as a part of your position, the task is even clearer. Your people simply don't have the authority to say no to a distraction; you do. Think of yourself as a strong and high castle wall around your people. When they come to you with tales of ridiculous meetings that they really don't need to attend, support them. Get them out of the meeting, and do what you can to preempt future requests. Of course, meetings are just one example. If you work in a typical company, you'll have no shortage of others. If you do, ask around: your people will be happy to provide you with a list.

In fact, it's actually a good idea to ask them what their common distractions are. Another part of your job extends beyond the castle walls you build for them. You must be on constant reconnaissance, always probing the borders, always keeping your ear out for the latest political schemes that might affect them. When you discover new problems, strike preemptively and eliminate the distraction before it ever gets near your people. The result will be twofold: first, your people will be much, much more productive than they ever were before; second, they will enjoy a bit of a utopian existence—workdays where all they have to do is their job. Particularly in careers in which people do what they love, this will earn you the respect and loyalty of everyone under your command. You might even attain a bit of folk hero status. Your people will love you because now they're free to be ingenious, and you'll love them for being so brilliant. Once again, everybody wins.

In World War II, the U.S. Army's General Patton was an extremely conspicuous and controversial figure. While he never made any apologies for seeking personal glory, he went out of his way to see to it that his subordinates got the credit. More importantly, although he had the reputation of being an extremely tough disciplinarian, he had an almost devotional dedication to the well-being of every single soldier under his command.

For example, he issued orders that soldiers were always to be provided with dry socks no matter how difficult it may be logistically. The actual, strategic reason for this edict was to avoid the debilitating effects of trench foot. But it was practical as well as personal: true, the soldiers couldn't fight as effectively with trench foot, but Patton also didn't want them to suffer because of his sincere love for the common soldier. The result was that, no matter how hard he was on them, the soldiers who served under him had a distinctly different attitude. When asked where they served, soldiers of other American armies would recite the number of their army or division. However, soldiers who served under Patton's command would simply say, "I was with Patton." *This* is the attitude you want in your people, but there's only one way to get it. You have to earn it, and you can do that by consistently thinking of the well-being of your people.

KNOW THE WORK THAT YOU LEAD.

It's so commonplace as to be unremarkable: time after time, poor leaders are promoted to positions where they have absolutely no practical experience with the work being performed by their people. Sometimes they get there through politics, and sometimes by the decisions of higher-level leaders who are just as clueless. At times, the sheepskin factor comes into play. Contestant A has no experience, but possesses a college degree of the day's current flavor. Contestant B has no formal education, but has been performing the tasks to be managed for years and is considered an expert in the field. However, because it's a management position, Contestant A gets the nod because, according to the old business model, managers should always have degrees.

These are just a few of the reasons that we often find leaders who lack skill, experience, or understanding in the work that they're managing. It doesn't take a lot of imagination to predict what kind of results their departments will produce. No matter how capable the workers, they will repeatedly be given orders that result in less than desirable outcomes.

Lack of experience coming into a new leadership position is no excuse because we're all capable of learning new skills. The simple fact of the matter is that many leaders don't bother to learn new skills. Sometimes it's laziness, and sometimes it's an ego-driven perception that doing the actual work is somehow beneath the manager. Regardless of the reasons, the result is that the situation never improves, and the department is nowhere near as productive as it could be. This also fuels the fires of separatism. It's hard for workers to feel like uniting with a leader for whom they have no respect.

If you want to improve the situation, the first thing you have to do is give leaders an incentive to gain frontline experience. Once again, we encounter the recurring theme that, to get people to do what you want, you have to give them a reason that appeals to their personal self-interest. Leaders are no different than anyone else in this regard.

If you have the authority to promote or otherwise affect the jobs of management, you should be asking yourself the same kinds of questions that we considered earlier when talking about mapping effort to reward. Can you offer bonuses or financial compensation to those who are adept at the work they manage? If money isn't available, how about ego? This is particularly easy if you already have a leader who's highly skilled at the production work.

Of course, no matter how you get these leaders involved, your department will without a doubt begin to show results. As the leader receives more and more recognition for the successes, the motivation to improve job skills only grows.

In the U.S. Marines Corps, it doesn't matter whether you're an officer, a pilot, a soldier, or a clerk. In the beginning, you're trained to be a *grunt*, the universal nickname for the working-class soldier who has to do the dirty work of slogging through the swamps with a rifle. As you can imagine, if you later go to work as a pilot providing close air support to ground troops, you're going to be very, very effective because you know exactly what it's like to be a grunt. However, no matter what your eventual position, because you started as one and continue to think of your fellow soldiers as brothers, the grunts in the field are always going to claim you as one of their own. This brilliant management and training strategy should be applied to every business in the world. In the Marines, once a grunt, always a grunt. The resulting teamwork and pride in accomplishment are hardly surprising.

If you and your peers encourage and embrace your leader with every effort they make to learn the practical, frontline job skills, you'll go a long way toward giving them a good reason to improve. Make your leaders feel proud to be a grunt, and claim them as one of your own.

BE ONE OF YOUR PEOPLE.

This points to another aspect of command that should be adhered to by any skillful leader: don't stand apart from the people you lead. There are those who claim that familiarity breeds contempt, and so a leader should not become too casual with the workers. It's true that you must be able to maintain a command presence and a posture of leadership, but those who feel that they can't socialize or be one of the troops are far too insecure to be in charge in the first place. Being a leader is a matter of character as much as ability. If your character is threatened by the lack of an artificial pedestal upon which you can stand, then you never had any to begin with.

In battle, you can lead from the front lines or you can lead from comfort and isolation, far from the action. The latter is not only more convenient in terms of comfort, it's also safer. However, it should be obvious that this approach has numerous and overwhelming disadvantages as well. In a military operation, if you expected your people to march twenty miles a day, you might not realize the difficulty they had because it was twenty degrees below zero and their feet were frostbitten. After all, you were many miles away, had a nice fire going, and were wearing brand new boots. There's no possible way that you could understand their problems, let alone lead them in any kind of meaningful way.

It's no different in the corporate world. Where is your office? What kind of conditions do you work under? And how do these conditions compare to those of the people who are out there doing the real work in the real world? Some leaders contend that it's important to have impressive offices and expensive furniture because, after all, they're *leaders*. What if a client came in? It's important, they feel, to present the proper image and look important.

If there's any truth to that, then keep the fancy office, but by all means use your managerial power and influence to garner a standard cubicle in the thick of the fight that can serve as your field office. Then live there enough of the time to gain a true picture of the daily reality of your department. There's no way you can appreciate what your people contend with until you've experienced it yourself.

It's also been a common observation throughout history that a general should never dress more warmly than his troops do. People don't have much respect for someone who asks them to suffer hardships in the pursuit of a goal when it's clear that the leader isn't willing to suffer any hardships at all. Find ways to demonstrate to your people as a matter of course that you don't ask them to put up with anything that you wouldn't put up with yourself. You'll be amazed at how much of a bond that will create. Once again, you're tearing down the wall between workers and leaders and forging a single, effective group.

You must also never praise leaders more than workers, at least in public. It is very rare that the people in charge get their hands dirty doing the actual day-to-day work required to accomplish the goals. The workers do this, and therefore it is the worker who must be praised above all. The leaders' egos must be satisfied by the power of being in charge and by enjoying the larger share of the spoils that fairly come to them.

If you have leaders who require attention and ego stroking at the expense of those who did the actual work, you must remove them immediately. They will destroy the morale of their workers, who will rightfully resent doing all the work while the leader takes all the credit. In a proper relationship, the leader nonetheless gets plenty of credit from his own troops. As in the example of General Patton, when you're on a winning team and serving under a leader who clearly cares about you and gives you the credit, you're going to tell everyone you meet what a great leader you have. It's just the way it works.

LEAD THE CHARGE PERSONALLY.

Although you must at times take up a strategic and removed position to lead an effort, this usually happens only when you're leading on an extremely large scale. In such a case, the logistics and time constraints of keeping up with everything simply prohibit being at the front lines because there are too many fronts and not enough time to stay on top of them all personally.

However, for the most part, this Pillar addresses those who lead in organizations in which they can still make a difference personally. When you don't ask others to do what you wouldn't do yourself, it's often helpful to go out there and do it, just so they can see that you're sincere. Furthermore, when you're out in the midst of the day-to-day operations of your people, you earn your pay as much by being an inspirational role model as anything else. There's nothing that fires your people up quite so much as seeing you personally step into a production position, tackle the same problems that they encounter, and prevail. It shows them that the problems can be overcome, and it motivates them to try harder. If the exalted general isn't above busting his own tail on the tedious tasks of the day, can you imagine how sheepish everyone else will feel about slacking off?

You should also do everything within your power to take the work that you and your people do and make it personal. To a degree, everyone needs the ability to go home and leave it at the office just to maintain some kind of balance in their lives. However, when you make it personal, it brings out the very best in your motivational and problem-solving talents. If your group has a tough assignment or deadline, you may well encourage them to do whatever it takes to succeed. However, if you tell this to them at 4:59 and then leave for home at 5:00 while the rest of them are working until midnight, they're not going to have much respect for you.

I remember one time working into the wee small hours of the morning on a project with a critical deadline. My manager was sitting in a cubicle right next to mine, asking what he could do to help. At times, the honest answer was that there really wasn't much he could do until I finished what I was doing. Did he therefore decide that, because there was nothing to do, he may as well just go home? Most managers would have done exactly that. Instead, he got on the phone to his wife, who happened to work in a different department for the same company, and asked her to order pizza and bring it to the office for us. His wife then sat right there with us, and, whenever there was even the most menial spare task that could be done, they were both all over it. That project was delivered on time and under budget. I can assure you that if I'd needed to move a mountain to not let him down, I would have been driving around town trying to steal a dump truck.

In this particular example, it's also worth noting that the pizza came out of his personal wallet, because the corporation had no budget for such things. None of us would have died of malnutrition had he and his wife not bought us dinner. But that wasn't the point. The fact that he told us the deadline was important and then demonstrated that he took it personally in every possible way sent the message that it wasn't an environment of workers toiling and leaders observing. There was no Us and Them. It was just one big Us, and together we did what every other department in the company said was impossible. United, we were unstoppable. We came together because our manager inspired us by leading the charge personally.

GIVE THE CREDIT TO THOSE WHO DID THE WORK.

It's always easier to single out one person, put them in the spotlight, and tell the world how great they are than it is to do the same thing with a large group of people. It's easier logistically and financially, and it also offers a hero that people can focus on more readily. Consequently, after your people have done an absolutely brilliant job, you may find that, because you are the leader, everyone wants to make you the center of attention and heap praise upon you personally for doing such a great job. It's only natural on the part of others, and it's going to happen unless you personally do something about it.

At every opportunity, you must express sincere and public appreciation for the work your people are doing. Don't memorize some glib and phony phrases that you can quickly toss out to the masses. Take the time to think about it. When possible, mention your people by name. Instead of the one hero people want you to be, find the real heroes in the ranks, and tell stories of their exploits. And don't forget everyone else. People love tales of the regular working-class stiff and how they overcome adversity. Emphasize the tremendous spirit that your team has and how well they work together. Most importantly, make sure the world knows that your people are the real stars, and that for you it's truly an honor to be associated with such a winning group. And make *absolutely* certain that you're sincere. Phoniness in this regard will not only alienate your people, but everyone else will lose respect for you as well. Your people have done much to admire. Share it with the world.

In dealing with your people, whether your peers or those you lead, always live by your word. Nobody ever cares why you didn't follow through on a promise. They just remember that you lied. You must also be fiercely loyal to those you call your own if you ever wish to have that loyalty returned. One very significant and practical way you can do this is by looking after their job security as though it were your own. There are always times in the progress of a company when jobs may be at risk. When you have people who have delivered for you time and again, go to the ends of the earth if you must, but protect those people. When they realize what you've done, you'll be able to count on them even more.

Trust is another critical factor in leadership, and it's one of the easiest to manage. Simply do what you say, and never act in a manner that could be seen as unethical. It doesn't matter that you treat your people well if you treat people outside your group poorly. Everyone knows that what you do to someone else, you may do to them, and it will affect their trust in you. If you make it a point to do whatever is necessary to avoid letting your people down, and you do it on a regular basis, they'll notice. Particularly when they see you put yourself on the line personally to protect them and their interests, you'll garner the reputation of someone who can always be counted on when times get tough. There's no greater compliment in the world. Furthermore, once you have such a reputation, another interesting thing happens. The next time you decide to risk your job for the sake of protecting your people, look over your shoulder and don't be surprised to see every single one of them right there, ready to back you up and even quit themselves if necessary to protect you. Trust and loyalty go hand in hand.

When your people or your peers do things well, make sure they're the ones who are in the spotlight, even if you have to buy the spotlight yourself. Because of the resulting pride they take in their work, they will continue to amaze others by performing the impossible and joking about it afterward as just another normal day.

TAKE THE BLAME YOURSELF.

This last point needs very little elaboration. Your people will make mistakes, and sometimes you'll make a bad decision yourself. The result will be that the wrath of the gods will descend upon your department like something out of a bad movie.

When things go right, even if the department performed brilliantly because of your personal ideas and efforts, the glory goes to your people. When things go badly, however, no matter whose fault it is, the true leader is the one who stands up and says loudly, "No, things went wrong because I personally made that decision, even if Joe here performed the action. He was doing as I instructed and would have caught blazes from me had he done otherwise." You and Joe both know that it's a pack of lies, that Joe screwed things up all by himself, perhaps in direct contradiction to your orders. That doesn't matter. The two of you can talk about it later, in private. In public, it's your department, and your responsibility. Even if it means that you or your career suffer personally as a result of a reprimand, you absolutely must shield your people.

If you do end up bearing punishment for the actions of your workers, remember that Napoleon once observed that the first quality of a soldier is not to fight, but to endure. You're tough. You can take it. Furthermore, your people will see it. If you think they were loyal to you before, you can just imagine how much they'll stand behind you now.

There's a well-publicized story about the Normandy invasion in World War II. General Eisenhower was the one who had to make the call as to what day to launch the operation. History recalls it as being a difficult success. However, it could have gone the other way and been an unmitigated disaster. On top of that, weather for the landing was dicey at best. He had to make a call at the last minute to launch the invasion, knowing that the weather could easily turn the entire plan into a fiasco that wasted the lives of thousands and even altered the course of the war.

Because the professional soldier knows that any day in battle may be his last, Eisenhower had a note in his pocket. It simply said that if things went badly with the invasion, the fault was his and his alone. He was prepared to take full responsibility for the failure. In a similar manner, General Patton often told his commanders that, if a risky plan that he was demanding them to carry out succeeded, he would state that the idea was theirs, but if it failed they were to announce that they were ordered to do so by him.

A benefit that arises from you personally taking the blame is that your people will no longer be afraid to reach for the stars. As anyone who has ever tried to do something new and creative knows, you have to take chances to achieve great success. Sometimes, you fall flat on your face. However, if you're afraid to try, you will always be mediocre. Because your people know that you'll back them up, they'll reach for their very best in solving your problems, and they won't be afraid to launch bold new initiatives. Consequently, they truly will be the best of the best.

Leading isn't about giving orders. It's about inspiring confidence in your people, and earning their trust. The visionary leader is someone whose ego doesn't need that artificial wall of separation between worker and leader. After those boundaries are torn down, people are able to work as one highly motivated and extremely dedicated unit. Whether it's a small production group or the empire as a whole, leaders understand that it is the people who are the true heroes and the people who physically accomplish the great things. A leader may plan, organize, contribute to strategy, and offer tactics. However, the most important thing a leader can ever do is build a strong sense of identity in the people and inspire them to reach for their very best.

Some lead from the front, and some lead from the rear. However, it's important to realize that you, the worker, can always lead from the middle. You don't have to be a leader to lead.

Look around you, and realize the tremendous potential of your people. Realize, if they simply had a banner, a cause to rally to, that together they could achieve greatness. All they need is a leader. So hoist that banner. Give them a cause. Whether you're managing thousands in multiple divisions or you're a frontline worker with no explicit authority, you have within you the power to change your company forever. Reach out to your people. Show them that in unity there is strength. Inspire them with your vision and teach them all what you have learned about leading so that they can do the same. Strong empires are built by leaders at every level who inspire, encourage, and protect their people, so that they can in turn set new standards of excellence.

LEADERSHIP

S ee a better life for your people, and be passionate about making it happen.

◎ Show how personal efforts map to tangible rewards.

◎ Build a sense of ownership in the cause.

◎ Reward every single person who contributes to success.

◎ Remove swiftly those who work against the common good.

◎ Shield your people so that they can be brilliant.

◎ Know the work that you lead.

◎ Be one of your people.

◎ Lead the charge personally.

◎ Give the credit to those who did the work.

◎ Take the blame yourself.

III ⟩ Organization

*Build a structure that allows
your people to be ingenious.*

In the old business model, companies are often structured and designed "by the book." In other words, people go to school and are trained in the art of starting, organizing, and running companies, and that's the way it's done. However, in the real world, the organizational structures that look so good on paper are an absolute nightmare to the people trying to get the job done. Sure, all the boxes and lines look neat and tidy when printed out in a report, but these artificial boundaries severely impede the flow of information and ideas that could benefit the company at large.

There's no denying that this hierarchical structuring of companies offers obvious organizational benefits. People have been arranging countries, armies, and businesses in such a manner for thousands of years. Nonetheless, in the quest for productivity, sometimes the rules must be broken, or at least bent until they squeak. The proper solution is to take the best ideas from wherever you can find them, and apply them in a manner that suits the dynamics of your particular business needs. If it happens to look good on paper when the reports are printed up afterward, consider that an unintentional bonus.

MAKE IT EASY FOR GOOD IDEAS TO REACH DECISION MAKERS.

One of the biggest problems in any company of more than a few people is transmitting innovative ideas from the people on the front lines up the chain of command to the people with the authority to act on the information. To get an idea to someone who can act on it, you must typically navigate through several layers of people who don't have the authority to say *yes*, but who do have the authority to say *no*. What makes this even more challenging is the fact that you can't personally escort your idea all the way to its destination. In effect, you hand it off to someone, who in turn hands it off to someone else. This process is repeated until it reaches the leader who has the authority to give the go-ahead.

Anyone with a logical mind will be quick to point out that, if you have a hierarchical structure but then bypass some levels through direct communications, you're going to lose some of the benefits of the hierarchy. Actually, most will go further than that, intimating that, if you don't adhere strictly to the confines of the structure, you'll destroy the entire process and the result will be utter chaos. It would seem logical to say that if you break a system, in our case through bypassing certain levels, then the system will no longer work. But is this true?

Information could certainly bubble up from the front lines, through the levels of the hierarchy, to the leader with the power to act on it. However, would it truly break the system if there were also a "hotline," a direct path from the front lines to a higher authority? It wouldn't disrupt the normal flow of the hierarchy, for it would not be flowing through those lines of communication. Rather than getting all information from the preceding level of the org chart, the leader would instead also receive ideas directly from the people doing the work and who are in many ways the most qualified to speak about productivity and problems.

With today's technology, email makes instantaneous correspondence possible. It can be answered at your convenience. It's electronic, meaning that the information can be stored, analyzed, processed, and retrieved in almost limitless ways. And that's just the first and most obvious example. Is it effective and practical for the CEO of your company to get five thousand emails a week from the customer service reps? Obviously not. Some degree of management is clearly necessary. However, we have tremendous new information and communications tools available to us today. Sticking to old and outmoded structures just because it's the way things have always been done is pointless and inefficient. And potentially fatal if your competition joins the twenty-first century before you do.

You have hundreds of variations and options available to you today, and the ability to easily do what battlefield commanders of a few centuries ago would have given their favorite sword for. You can instantaneously get information from the frontline troops to the commanders. You're not taking advantage of that. You should be. As it currently stands, it's almost impossible for your most valuable resources to give you the time-critical information that you so desperately need to beat your competition.

RESIST COMPLEXITY THAT BRINGS NO TANGIBLE BENEFIT.

Another trap that people fall into when organizing things is actually exacerbated by technology rather than aided by it. Once upon a time, you had to spend a lot of time and money dealing with a print shop to get professional-looking forms, so they weren't created easily, often, or cheaply. Today, anyone who can waggle a mouse is capable of turning out high-quality invoices, forms, memos, flyers, brochures, procedures, and anything else that won't jam the printer.

This problem isn't limited to forms, computers, and other physical information systems. The urge to overcomplicate matters can show up anywhere. Another frequent example of this is bloated company guidelines and procedures.

You must resist any and all complexities that hinder you from getting your job done. Your work is what keeps your company strong and profitable. Paperwork is not. You can use any of a few tactics to help sidestep or eliminate these clusters of confusion. As in most things, the approach will vary depending upon how much power you wield.

Let's start with the leaders. Democracy, committees, listening to input from all parties, being objective and fair . . . all of these things are valuable. However, there comes a time when someone must simply have the courage to put a foot down and make a decision. If you preside over any procedures or technologies, build alliances with people who are experts in these areas. And then, unbeknownst to them, build another couple of alliances of the same nature with other people.

If you depend on one set of recommendations, particularly when you don't have any personal knowledge of the procedures or systems, you're allowing yourself to be driven by other people's agendas. In technology, that almost always equates to a lot of overcomplicated systems being created, because the people who create these systems enjoy it. Therefore, they may flat-out lie to you about what can and can't be done, all to promote their own agenda. If you have several sources of information, you'll be able to ferret out the truth and make an informed decision.

Listen to the people who have to deal with complex systems. They'll complain the loudest, and for good reason. They'll complain because they're the ones who are burdened with overhead when they should be getting work done. Between what you learn from your alliances and the needs for simplicity that you see from your people, make some decisions. Simplify as much as possible. Ignore the wails and protests of all the people who stand to lose if you cut their pet projects, and just do it. You're a leader. So *lead*.

When the smoke clears and your operations are much more streamlined and efficient, it will all have been worthwhile. And your people will love you for it. Nobody likes pushing paper for no real practical reason, and there's a lot of paper pushing in the corporate world. The more you can eliminate, the more time there will be to make trouble for the competition by outproducing them.

If you're not a leader, it will be harder if not impossible for you to make these changes. You have two options, and you should not hesitate to employ each when appropriate. First, if you can get the ear of a leader who is sympathetic to your cause, then you can help change and simplify the system as if by remote control. This is, of course, the preferred way when available as it makes lasting changes that benefit all.

If you don't have access to someone with enough horsepower to get the job done, then you have to ask yourself what's more important: getting your job done, or following the rules. In most cases, it's obvious that procedural work is a waste of time, and it's your production people who will have the best grasp of that. When deadlines are pressing and something has to go, take a look at what these people do. They simply ignore the tedious paperwork. Furthermore, if some information does need to be tracked to get the job done, they'll spend ten minutes at the computer and come up with something simple, elegant, and practical. Then they'll use it. Keep things simple, and focus on getting the job done.

ELIMINATE UNNECESSARY LAYERS.

Take nothing for granted. Many times, the systems we use were put in place long ago, and they remain in use unaltered because nobody ever thought to change them. Part of that is the old, "if it works, don't fix it" mentality, and there's a time and a place for that kind of thinking.

However, the reality is that many of our outdated systems are in place not because we've determined that they're still the best way to do things, but merely by default. No one ever considered reevaluating them.

Even fifty years ago, the business environment was radically different. For starters, there was no Internet. And there weren't even computers, at least not the personal computers that mere mortals use today. No email. No fax machines. If you wanted copies of something, you used a mimeograph machine. What it produced wasn't pretty, and it smelled bad at that. Business correspondences were done on manual typewriters, those ancient machines with which one had to do it right the first time. No backspace key. You used correction ribbon, and it wasn't pretty, either. Cell phones didn't exist. No one had heard of voice mail, and an answering machine was a human being who wrote things down on paper with a pen or pencil. Nor did VCRs or many of the other presentation methods we now take for granted exist. It was a primitive time by modern standards. As such, some of the organizational constraints we grapple with today actually made sense back then.

Does this mean that we must forever and completely abandon the hierarchical structures on org charts? No. Progress is a process of embracing new tools and procedures and eliminating old ones only when they serve no further purpose. The layered approach of the hierarchy is organizationally sound. However, many companies fall into the trap of adding abstraction just for the sake of it. It is, after all, what the high-level leaders were trained to do in school.

Once there were physical limits on the number of people that could be managed by one person. But, with our new computerized technology, that's not as true as it used to be. Sometimes it makes sense to divide your people into groups of ten, each with a leader, and then bundle them into hundreds, each with a leader, and so on. However, resist the temptation to follow default modes of thinking. Stop. Think. Analyze. Challenge. For every vertical layer you add, you create more communications difficulties between your people. By creating more tribes, you also promote an ever-increasing environment for tribal turf wars.

Don't be afraid to flatten your structures when you're confident that a single leader can manage a larger team. When you do have to add layers, try to come up with new and effective ways for communications to still flow easily, not just from leader to leader, but from any person to any other. An eight-cylinder engine is more powerful than a four-cylinder simply because of the greater number of pistons working together. If you broke up the engine block and scattered the eight cylinders across the country, you'd no longer have the raw power of V-8. You'd have eight one-cylinder engines that would be of limited or no use to you.

Layers divide, and your goal is to unite. Whenever possible, use the tools that you have to keep your people together. When you're a large enough corporations that departments are needed, assume nothing and reach for creative solutions. The less that artificial boundaries divide your people, the more you move toward a single, united empire.

USE AND PUBLICIZE A COMMON LANGUAGE.

It's common to organize companies according to division of labor, with each group categorized by its specialty or function. This makes sense, but an unanticipated side effect of this is that, as time goes on, each division starts to develop their own dialect, and sometimes even their own completely distinct language. For the people working within such a group, all the references will be well understood, and having a specialized language will improve and often speed up communications within the department. It becomes, in effect, the local dialect of the tribe.

The trouble starts when you reach the borders and find that none of the other tribes speak or even understand your language. An empire is a federation of many tribes that have chosen to merge their individual groups into the collective whole. There's nothing wrong with a little tribal consciousness here and there, particularly when the individual esprit de corps benefits the empire overall. However, when any tribal issue causes a problem for the nation, it must be addressed rapidly.

What are the steps, then, to building a common language in your company? First, talk to the tribal leaders and workers alike and get a list of terms that are unique to their tribe, along with their definitions. Along with this, ask for another word or phrase for it that already exists in the common spoken language of the people, such as English in the United States and in the United Kingdom. If there is no better way to express the term or phrase, simply state "None." It's a good idea to get as many people in each tribe as possible to help with this, and then have one person consolidate it into the tribal dialect. That way, even if one person doesn't know an effective way to express something in the common language, another person may.

Next, get a group to assemble these tribal languages into one document. If the concept being expressed tribally already has a word in the common language, use that and indicate that it is synonymous with the tribal word or phrase. After the compilation process is complete, you will have a document that contains common language definitions for every tribal thought. The document you've just built is meant to be a supplement to the common spoken language, as including it all would be too cumbersome. Instead, you now have a place to look when you need to understand how to communicate effectively with someone in another tribe.

You can make this a hardcopy paper document if it's small enough, and post it on bulletin boards around the company. It would also be easy to also provide this list as a Web page on your company's internal network, providing an easy way for someone to look up a tribal thought and how to express it in the common language. Of course, you can make this information available to your people in many other ways. The only important thing is to make it available, and to update it at least quarterly as a matter of procedure. In reality, it's best to add a new phrase immediately, so you should also have a plan that will enable people to easily get new jargon added to the common language.

Some will say that, instead of going to all this trouble, you should just employ translators, which is the way things are typically done in companies. The problem with this solution is you now have a bottleneck in your communications. Furthermore, you're dependent upon translators who very likely have an agenda or bias of their own. People will resist codifying a common language for two reasons. First, it removes a source of political power from them. That's rather the point. Secondly, it's a lot of work to implement. But get over it. It's for the good of the empire. Next year, when their bonus is bigger because improved communications made their company more effective in the marketplace, those who resisted the idea of a common language will be the first to sing its praises. People are funny that way.

BUILD CLEAR AND SIMPLE LINES OF COMMUNICATION.

It's entirely too difficult to get information from one person to another in most companies. The first and most obvious roadblock is bureaucracy, whether intentional or otherwise. And, yes, for any of you new to the game, people do block and mangle information intentionally if it suits their political desires. You've probably experienced more than once the mandate that to get a message to another person you had to "go through" a given individual or group. These people are gatekeepers, and they set themselves up in this position because it gives them power. If you try other means of communication, they will resist or protest, because bypassing them removes their control of the situation.

Yet another frequent obstacle to communications are procedures that show up in the guise of forms to complete, requests that must be approved, and many other types of paper pushing, whether electronic or physical. Once again, these procedures often show up because someone had nothing better to do than create them. Of course, they figured out either before or after that, if you control the paperwork, you have power, which means it will be a long and bloody struggle to eliminate it.

As you'll find in most turf wars and petty power struggles, the difficulties usually come from a single individual or a small handful of people. The rest of the rank-and-file workers just want to do a good job. Therefore, one of the best methods for obtaining clear communication is to build alliances with individuals in every group you can come in contact with.

Another benefit of building a network of alliances is keeping your ear to the ground so that you know of new developments in the company before they have a chance to affect you. If you have a flair for the dramatic, you can think of it as an underground network of spies, but, no matter what you call it, there's no substitute for the value of a real person working in a different department who's friendly to your cause. You need people who are willing to tell you the story of what's really going on, not the story that's broadcast to the masses after the politically adept have manipulated the message.

By building an information network, perhaps even meeting socially beyond the earshot of interfering busybodies, you not only set up a structure in which critical details can be passed immediately to the people who need them most to protect the interests of the empire, but you also have a little fun in the process. Socializing is good for morale, and these alliances will also come in handy any time you have an initiative that you need to move through unofficial channels. The difference between such an underground group of people and traitorous revolutionaries bent on the overthrow of the existing order is that your group is actually working for the good of the empire. And sometimes that means that you must resort to unconventional methods. If the normal lines of communication aren't clear, create your own, and keep it simple.

Beyond lunches or after-hours gatherings, we haven't discussed any of the physical methods of communicating. That's because in this day and age, it's the easiest part and will come naturally to you. We have telephones at our desks and at our homes, and cell phones everywhere else. We have company and personal email accounts, and usually a couple of disposable ones from free services as well. Web sites can be created both internally and externally. Information can be stored in word processor documents, spreadsheets, and databases, and transferred instantly to anywhere in the world. Scanners, digital cameras, fax machines, ground and air overnight services, and even standard postal mail offer numerous possibilities for communications, and this is not even a comprehensive list. If you can't find a way to physically communicate with someone else, you're simply not trying very hard.

One last word of caution: because we're occasionally breaking the rules in the name of better productivity and profitability, there will be those who oppose us. Always conduct yourself with the knowledge that business is war. Assume that emails can be intercepted. Printed documents can be read. People will eavesdrop. In short, if your correspondences need to be confidential, and sometimes they will, don't assume that any method is completely secure other than a two-person conversation standing in the middle of the desert. Even then, frisk them for wires first. Paranoid? Perhaps. But until you've been in the thick of tribal warfare, you'll never fully appreciate how devious people can be. Communicate frequently and effectively, but also sensibly.

MAKE EACH UNIT AWARE OF WHAT ALL OTHERS ARE DOING.

At a high level, many companies are managed with intentional walls of isolation between the departments. Oftentimes, it's not so much that they want to block the flow of information as it is merely a matter of efficiency. They simply don't see the need for Accounting to know what's going on in Manufacturing. It seems to be a waste of time and effort.

On a normal day, it's true that Accounting probably couldn't care less what's going on in Manufacturing, or any other department for that matter. The accounting staff has their hands full just crunching the numbers, and that's enough for a day's work. Furthermore, being two tribes of very different culture, most of the people in Accounting wouldn't appreciate what's going on in Manufacturing even if they knew. They have about as much interest in a drill press as the people on the shop floor have in debits and credits. Why, then, should one department know what another seemingly unrelated one is doing?

Let's look at another example. Manufacturing is in the business of physical production, and, for the company in question, they make a lot of metal fasteners, brackets, screws, and other such parts. In their quest to improve the efficiency of one of their brackets, they experiment with a new type of metal that provides greater strength with less weight. A series of tests and studies are performed, and it's determined that this new metal is a superior solution. Furthermore, the metal is 5% cheaper than what they've been using. Nobody else in the company other than high-level executives knows about this, and, frankly, nobody cares. Manufacturing isn't what they do, so it doesn't matter to them.

As is common in the Accounting department, one of the workers spends a fair amount of personal time investing in the stock market. As most good investors do, he also spends a lot of time reading and researching anything that might affect his investments. In fact, he just this week made a significant investment in the company that produces this metal.

What's not obvious to the rest of the world is clear to those who dig deep. Due to the direction that some related global events are taking, this stock is poised to go through the roof, along with the price of the metal. The fact that his company is about to be dependent on this metal and take huge losses when the price goes up is unknown to him. How could he possibly know? He works in Accounting, not Manufacturing.

If the company did a better job of keeping different departments informed on the daily goings-on throughout the empire, our accountant would of course immediately seen the danger. Alerting the appropriate people to his research, he would have saved the business millions of dollars in losses.

This is why it is imperative that you find a way to keep every single individual in every single department of your company up to date on what's going on everywhere within your walls. Not only does it bring tremendous power to bear on the problems and challenges that your company faces, but keeping everyone up to date also makes huge strides toward building unity. No longer do your people accept tunnel vision, thinking only of their small piece of the puzzle. By keeping them informed about the details of the business, they're suddenly passionate about every success that happens, across the company. Instead of forced ignorance with its related lack of response, the next time that someone in Accounting makes a brilliant move, the entire company cheers him. It's no longer something that nobody cares about because it didn't happen in their work area. Now it's personal. "Hey, look at that. One of our accountants just saved us $2.3 million because of his personal investment research. That's gonna look great at annual bonus time!"

Note that it's not "some accountant" but "one of *our* accountants." When you keep people in the loop, you give them a chance to make it personal, to take pride in the accomplishments of others, to cheer on people in distant groups, and to wake up every day and remember that they're part of a strong and exciting empire.

Again, there's no need to repeat the extensive list of technologies that are available to help you achieve the goal of keeping your people informed. The tools are there, they're cheap, they're easy to use, and most of your people are already highly skilled in their use. All you have to do is decide to use them.

MAINTAIN AN EXPLICIT AND OBVIOUS CHAIN OF RESPONSIBILITY.

After all this talk about circumventing hierarchies and maintaining underground networks, you might find it odd that one of the Stones of this Pillar involves an explicit command structure. In fact, much as we're doing with other bits of conventional wisdom, to understand the value of this you need to turn it upside down. Upon closer inspection, you'll notice that we're not talking about a chain of command, but rather a chain of responsibility. The two are not synonymous, as both a dictionary and the veteran corporate worker can attest.

In any company, there's never a shortage of command, because it seems like everyone in the building wants to be in charge. Command is seen in just that capacity, the ability and authority to give orders. In other words, it's the dream of small children everywhere: explicit permission to boss other people around. Look just beneath the surface of most of us and you'll find someone who's still sitting on the swing in the school playground.

The same cannot be said about responsibility. It's as though responsibility were a greased pig. Nobody wants to hold on to it very tightly. As we've come to expect when dealing with people, the motivations are numerous, and very few of them have the good of the empire at heart.

As an example of what this can do to a company, a friend of mine owned a software development company who often did programming work for hire in its specialty areas. Because he started out his career as a programmer and this technology was a pet project of his, he was personally handling this particular job. The company was hired to implement some bleeding-edge new Internet gadgetry, and time was critical. Millions of dollars hung in the balance.

His point of contact requested a preliminary demo of the system, expecting it to take many months. The customer's internal IT department was notorious for dragging its feet and indulging in tribal warfare. My client couldn't see dragging out the billing for six months or more while he went through the sequence of demos, revisions, and so forth. He knew that he could finish the majority of the entire production system in just a few weeks, and he wanted to knock their socks off. So he did.

His point of contact was naturally delighted, and the system worked beautifully. A modest handful of tasks remained, and it was decided at that point that the project would be transferred to supervision of the in-house IT department, meaning my client would now report to them instead of the business unit where his original point of contact resided. Of course, at this point the fun began, for the IT department had always wanted this project and resented it being outsourced. It was, after all, their tribe's turf.

I watched in the weeks that followed as more than half a dozen people in the IT department issued a continual stream of complaints that my client's system didn't work, that there were logistical problems, and also allegations that he wasn't timely with his deliverables. Of course, every high-level executive in the empire was copied on these correspondences, because the game was to take control of the project. When my client tried to respond and solve specific problems, no matter whom he communicated with, the story was always the same. Sometimes, the person he spoke with would simply pass the buck, leaving the issue unresolved. On other occasions, the correspondence was ignored altogether. The end result was that no one would take responsibility for being in charge, so there was no way that he could complete the work. After many months, the new system was still nowhere near being usable.

Plenty of people were in command of this operation. However, it had no clearly defined lines of responsibility and accountability. Although that worked out nicely for the IT department (which won another tribal skirmish by acquiring the project), there are some things they don't know. Losing millions of dollars tends to be hard on any empire. I'll let you come to your own conclusions about how this affects job security.

GIVE LEADERS AT EVERY LEVEL POWER AND AUTONOMY.

Managers from the old business model probably find this concept one of the hardest to grasp. One of the reasons that people work hard to rise through the ranks to a position of power is that they enjoy having the authority. They like being the one whom people have to ask when a task needs to be accomplished, and they relish the fact that they—and they alone—make the crucial decisions. All of this is great for the ego, but it doesn't help the empire.

But this dilemma does have a solution. Actually, like most problems, it has several solutions, depending on whether you're a leader or a worker. If you're a leader, you need to take a deep breath and start delegating the power you have to the people you're trusting to get the job done. They have to have the autonomy to get the job done in their own way. Don't tell them how to do it: just tell them what must be done. Express confidence in their ability to be brilliant, and, to back that up, give them the power to run their own show. Tell them to come to you if they need support and to keep you informed on progress. And then leave them alone and let them do their job for you. If you're unwilling to give them the reins, then you hired the wrong people for the job. Either replace them or empower and support them. There can be no middle ground.

If you're a worker, you're already familiar with receiving orders from on high that make no sense on the front lines. You have only two choices. First, you can sit there, follow stupid orders, and complain about how bad management is . . . and watch your empire slowly crumble as a result. If you take this path, make sure that you keep your résumé up to date. You'll be needing it.

Your second choice involves some risk, however: if you're not content to let bad decisions destroy a good company, then you're going to have to take some chances. If you get orders that are clearly not going to solve the problem (or will obviously make it worse), just ignore them. More specifically, develop a severe case of selective comprehension. You're a professional on the front. It's what you do. Therefore, you know how to solve the problem, even when you don't have the time or resources you need and have to resort to a little battlefield improvisation. This is where you shine.

So, determine how to solve the problem. And be sure you're right. Then, read the orders you've been given. Because political people don't want to leave themselves open to accountability, your directions will often be on the vague side anyway. Go through each and every line and find ways to misunderstand, reinterpret, or just flat-out play dumb so that what you've actually done will appear to be nothing more than a misguided action by a poor, dumb simpleton out there on the front lines who wasn't smart enough to understand the orders.

And check your ego at the door. We're trying to save an empire here. This is your defense against charges of gross insubordination. You weren't insubordinate. You just didn't understand. You're very, very sorry, and you promise that it won't happen again. Remember, it's always easier to ask for forgiveness than permission. After they've grudgingly accepted your atonement for your sins, you then mention that, by the way, your efforts just happened to solve the problem. By sheer dumb luck, of course. Would they like for you to reverse what you've done and return the problem? It would be no problem. Really. You'd be happy to comply.

Yes, there's personal risk. But if you don't stick your neck out to save your business when it needs you, then one day there may be no company. That's even riskier, and it affects more than just you. It would hurt everyone in your company. Even if it's a cliché from an old Musketeer tale, like most clichés it contains a truth: everyone in the empire must at times stand together to defend one of its people. And there are times when one person must risk it all, to defend everyone in the empire. From such actions are legends born.

DESIGN RULES THAT CAN BE BROKEN.

No matter how well you plan, how thoroughly you prepare, and how meticulously you organize, the enemy gets a vote. The minute you step into the real world to implement your ideas, the situation becomes dynamic. Things change unexpectedly. Stuff happens. If your people are tied to rigid, inflexible rules that were determined before the battle began, then, when the shooting starts, you're asking them to fight with one hand behind their back. Or to not fight at all.

The key to any successful long-term plan is *options*. Consider the daily reality of the workers who man your customer service phone centers. These people are usually equipped with a telephone headset and a computer screen. In the modern age, it's not the people, but the computer systems that make the decisions. When a customer calls in with a particular problem, the service rep doesn't make a personal evaluation based on experience and then decide how best to take care of the customer. Instead, the appropriate form is brought up on the computer, data is entered, checklists are reviewed, and the computer informs the rep what can and cannot be done. Of course, that's inflexible enough in and of itself.

Because companies have invested so much time and effort into building these systems (all with efficiency in mind), the notion of a customer service reps arriving at their own conclusions on how to handle a customer's dilemma is completely intolerable. Therefore, strict rules are put in place, and, when a customer calls, reps will follow the procedures on the computer, without exception.

Then, one day, somebody trips over a wire in the server room, and the entire computer system goes offline, right in the middle of peak calling time. Initial estimates indicate that the system will be down for the rest of the day. Customers continue to call in. Now what?

Let's say that you work in a call center as technical support for a particular software package. Furthermore, let's say that, out of the twelve reps working in your area, three of them actually know the software very well. Your computer system suddenly goes down, but of course the phones keep ringing. As an alternative, you could quickly gather together, and, realizing that many of the problems could be solved from your combined personal knowledge and prior experience, you enact a backup plan.

The three experienced reps take off their headsets and don't take calls, each one standing and helping three of the other nine reps, who continue to field calls. They first ask the obligatory simple questions that everyone must endure, such as "Are you sure your computer is plugged in and turned on?" If the problem is a legitimate one, each rep coordinates with the experienced rep standing in their group, and they work through as many problems as they can. Some customers are still told to call back later. Most customers have to wait a little longer to get help. However, 85% of all the calls are successfully fielded for the rest of the day, and, despite the failure of a critical system, the customers are taken care of and hang up happy.

The rule was that you used the computer system. Period. These reps staged a mutiny and broke the rules. Should they be rewarded or punished? For any sane and productive human being, the answer should be quite obvious.

Clearly, the most important rule is the one that has the least restrictions, which falls back on previous discussions that—whenever possible—you should tell someone what to do, not how to do it. The thing to keep in mind when setting up any kind of structure or rules is to realize that, no matter how well you plan things out, it's almost certain that the rules will need to be broken at times. Your planning shouldn't try to solve all possible problems. You can't do it without a crystal ball. What you should do is build an environment in which you have organization, order, and solid support for your people to do their jobs, and at the same time a loose-enough fabric to allow your people to think on their feet when needed. Ask yourself this single question: if your people had to improvise, what system could you design to give them the maximum support when they most need it? When your rules are designed to be broken, then, in the worst-case scenarios, your people will show you their very best.

NEVER CREATE A FOOLPROOF SYSTEM.

The example of a customer service call center points out another practice that's becoming increasingly common in the corporate world. With the power of modern computers, technology, and information systems, people have become convinced that they can automate processes to the point that highly skilled individuals are no longer needed. A very large segment of the business world today truly believes that they can build a system so comprehensive and complete that even an idiot could do the job.

In fact, this is part of many business plans. Skilled personnel cost money after all. If you can automate your work to the point that the system walks you through every step of the way, then all you really need are minimum-wage workers who will follow instructions. That's about as easy and profitable as it gets, right?

Obviously, a lot of companies think so, for this is quickly becoming the norm in many aspects of corporate life. There's only one problem with this idea. If you automate to the point that even an idiot can do the work, then *you will have idiots working for you.*

If that doesn't run a chill down your spine when you think about the long-term implications for your company, then we may have a position for you in one of our automated call centers. Of course, this applies not just to customer service, but to any and every operation in your company that can be automated or defined by procedure to the point that it's nothing more than a job of connecting the dots. Also, it's worth stating that not everyone who works in an overly automated job is an idiot. Some are quite capable. The point is that such a system allows—and in fact encourages—hiring from the bottom of the barrel.

Can you quantify how much business you lose every year because your customers dealt with idiots, got disgusted with you, and went to the competition? No. Customers do not take the time to call you up to say, "By the way, I've decided that I'm no longer going to spend my money with you, and here's why." And, even if they did, you'd never know because there's no computer screen in your automated system to capture that information. The customers just silently fade away. You'll never know how many, and you'll never know why. You'll just spend your time trying to assign the blame somewhere else for your company's continually diminishing performance.

There is no substitute for a capable, knowledgeable, motivated, and inspired human being when it comes time to get the job done. If you want to build an invincible empire, designing your systems to use the least-capable people you can find doesn't even make sense on paper.

Real people can find real solutions. Automate *tasks*, not *thinking*. Use your software and automation products to do the mindless work. They're tools, nothing more. Remember, a hammer is much better at driving a nail than it is at determining where the nail should be placed.

Build robots to take out the trash. Leave thinking, creativity, and problem solving to the ones who do it best: your people.

Organization should be structural support for your people so they can be brilliant. It should not be a stifling or restricting prison that traps them into the same poor performance, day after day. Your people want to succeed. They want to outperform the competition, and they crave the thrill of victory. No matter what part they play in your operation, from waste disposal to the accounting and legal departments, they are your experts. They're the ones who do the real work in the real world. It's critically important that you reevaluate your structures, procedures, and organizational procedures, eliminating anything that ties their hands and makes their job more difficult, or keeps them from getting critical information to the people who can act on it.

Don't be afraid to break new ground. We have tools and technologies at our disposal today that were the stuff of science fiction even a mere fifty years ago. You're not using it in a productive manner. Forget about how things have always been done in the past. Blaze a trail for the future. Find new ways to organize for the new era in which we live. For your people to join together, work as one, and achieve greatness for the empire, you must remove the artificial walls that separate and limit them. Using flexible, simple structures that leave room for your people to fill in the blanks, they will blind the competition with the light of their combined achievements.

ORGANIZATION

B uild a structure that allows your people to be ingenious.

◎ Make it easy for good ideas to reach decision makers.

◎ Resist complexity that brings no tangible benefit.

◎ Eliminate unnecessary layers.

◎ Use and publicize a common language.

◎ Build clear and simple lines of communication.

◎ Make each unit aware of what all others are doing.

◎ Maintain an explicit and obvious chain of responsibility.

◎ Give leaders at every level power and autonomy.

◎ Design rules that can be broken.

◎ Never create a foolproof system.

IV Mobility

Improvise. Adapt. Overcome.

Throughout the course of human history, the glory of the charge has always belonged to the cavalry. Fast, maneuverable, and powerful, these forces are the vanguard of military might. Although not always mounted, the motto of this elite has always been to adapt to change and think creatively to overcome adversity. Whether you're attacking or defending, the ability to be flexible in your application of power is a vital one. Tomorrow is always uncertain.

In the business world, as in battle, the only constant is change. Unfortunately, change strikes fear in the hearts of most people. What they fail to understand is that change makes new successes possible. Because of their fear, they cling to entrenched habits instead of becoming more adaptable, never realizing that mobility is freedom, and that freedom is power.

No matter what part you play, expanding the empire requires constant change. Therefore, because it's an inescapable fact of everyday life, the only proper way to approach it is to cast your fears to the winds and embrace the excitement of it all. If you do, it will be the ride of your life.

UNDERSTAND THAT ATTITUDE IS THE HEART OF MOBILITY.

No matter how well you plan or how stable your daily routine, you're going to have to deal with change. You can't avoid it. If you ignore it, it won't go away. Instead, it will pounce on you when you least expect it. And, of course, because, you weren't expecting it, you're not going to fare very well in the exchange.

Your ability to shine when surrounded by chaos is rarely a matter of preparation. Rather, the single most important aspect of improving your adaptability is attitude. Look around you. The people who spend all their time and energy grumbling and resisting every change in procedure that occurs are almost never productive. Furthermore, their bad attitude does nothing to help them cope with the very change that they so dislike.

Now look on the other end of the spectrum. People who are quick on their feet and accept the fact that nothing is forever tend to greet each new change as an interesting and exciting challenge. It's a test of their abilities and a chance to hone their skills. They pour their time, energy, and creativity into finding novel new ways to be productive and prosperous in light of the new events. Not surprisingly, these are the people who are the most successful in any organization, as well as in life. The most fundamental difference between these two types of people is nothing more elaborate than attitude. And attitude, unlike change, is something you *can* control.

You must not only embrace change, adapting to each new adventure with excitement and anticipation, you must also reinforce this mindset in your people. Once again, it doesn't matter if you're a leader or a worker. Although the leader's position and approach is clear, even the worker can make tremendous improvements in the group when it comes to increasing mobility. One enthusiastic voice leading the way, showing that it can be done and keeping spirits up, is all it takes. Be that person, and watch the ripple of excitement pass through your peers. Lead from the middle, and lead by example. Before you know it, even the stodgiest among you will be standing side by side with the others, if for no other reason than their realization that there's strength and safety in numbers.

Furthermore, take pride in your ability to dance around the edge of danger and always prevail. When you seek change rather than fear it, you become the surprise of the lightning charge, the irresistible force of the heavy cavalry, and you will be untouchable. Those who embrace change control the day. The ability of your group to live in this manner is something to be proud of. It's up to you to make sure that your coworkers know this. Lift their spirits and sing their praises with each new success, and see how much faster they maneuver on the next adventure.

BE QUICK ON YOUR FEET OR BE A TARGET.

Another aspect of mobility also accompanies the ability to change and mold your plans to any new events. As any zebra in Africa can tell you, the lions don't attack the strong, fast, and maneuverable. They prey on the weak and the slow. This is why you often see zebras at the local gym on their off hours. Look around your office. Does anyone you know look like they would make a nice midmorning snack if they were a zebra? Perhaps even you? The simple fact of the matter is that, if you don't learn to move quickly, you're going to be an easy target every time there's a shakeup in your company. Next time you're at the gym, ask the zebras what that feels like.

A lot of people get far too focused on their long-term plans. They have a structure in mind, and they work hard to make sure that their work, their career, and their day-to-day life in the company all fit within that neat and tidy plan. They do a lot of nest feathering, building any little perk into their jobs that they can find and just in general trying to make their position as comfortable as possible. There's nothing exactly wrong with that, but the problems begin when change comes. Instead of creating a job description or set of department procedures that can be easily altered to each new reality, they have instead built an entrenched position that's comfortable and pleasant but difficult to alter. When the tornado comes, it's far better to have a fast pair of sneakers than a comfortable pair.

It's not only important to be quick on your feet; you must also have to be able to turn on a dime when necessary. If your company develops Hula Hoops when the fad is hot, you may be making a great living . . . for a time. However, one day, the fad will end, and, when it does, anyone who hasn't retooled their businesses will be left sitting out in the cold with no jobs and no future. On the bright side, at least they'll have a Hula Hoop to play with.

The people who can think on their feet, however, will have realized that change is upon them, and they will have noticed that all of the equipment necessary for making Hula Hoops can also be used to make bicycle inner tubes. While the rest of the industry is panicking and suffering devastating setbacks in revenue, yours will continue to prosper because in the heat of the crisis you realized that, if you simply pour a more flexible type of material into your mold, you could make a quick transition into a new industry. Years later, when Hula Hoops are mentioned only in the history books, your company will have grown into a prosperous manufacturer of inner tubes.

SEE TROUBLE COMING AND BE GONE BEFORE IT ARRIVES.

The people who are now making a good living selling inner tubes can thank not only their quick feet and their ability to turn on a dime, but also their insight and vision. If you wait until hard times are already upon you, it's going to be too late to do anything about it. Therefore, you must develop the abilities and instincts to see trouble coming long before it arrives, and be somewhere else when it does land. The difference between an inner tubes tycoon and a Hula Hoop disaster is simply the ability to look ahead. As in the martial arts, the best way to block a punch is to just not be there.

The external threats—namely your competitors—are obvious to those who work at the highest levels of your company. Additional external threats include such subtle things as the economy, general market conditions, supply and demand, the cost of labor and materials, and other such things that appear as general rather than specific threats.

Not only should you be concerned with your surroundings in terms of the outside world and the overall business environment, you must also be aware of what's going on within your own company. Here, too, the dangers are ever present and not always obvious. Workers must contend with both peers and bad leaders who are more concerned with personal gain and self-interest than they are in simply getting the job done. Politics come into play at every level of the organization, at the expense of both the workers and overall productivity.

Not only do productive people face danger from the antics of the ambitious as they jockey for position, some very real and legitimate constraints are placed upon every department that can pose both difficulties and dangers. For example, finite budgets will dictate what resources are available to both leaders and workers. Bad things often happen when money runs short. It's far better to see this sort of thing coming and have your résumé on the streets than it is to find out at the last moment that your entire department has been eliminated due to cash flow problems.

It's also important to have a sense of which direction the company is heading and how that will affect your department. Do the new markets being pursued represent an opportunity for you as an individual? Is the overall health and financial stability of your business such that layoffs are imminent? Do the changes mean that you will soon face a situation in which you desperately need more people than you currently have just to get the job done? Does this mean having to work countless hours of overtime? These and many other things could have an extreme effect on both your life and the well-being of the empire.

So you must always keep a crystal ball handy, as it's critical to have a sense of which way the wind is blowing, both fiscally and politically. You must always keep an eye to the horizon and make it part of your everyday posture to see every potential change that could come your way.

Part of the reason for looking ahead and being aware of which way the wind is blowing is to know where the smoke will end up when the next fire breaks out. In other words, you need to make sure that you are always upwind or at least have an escape route planned. Your goal, overall, is to do everything you can to aid in the expansion of the empire. Sometimes, however, that's going to require that you rapidly exit a bad situation to continue meaningful and productive employment. You're useful to the empire only if you live to fight another day.

Your first and most fundamental responsibility is to make a living and provide for yourself and the people you care about. Having joined a company to do just that, you also adopt the responsibility of looking out for the company. You're not much good to either family or company if you allow yourself to become a casualty. Keep an eye out for trouble, make a habit of constantly playing "what if" in the back of your mind, and speculate on the potential for trouble in every new development that you see. And always have a plan to escape that danger should it actually materialize.

BE IN AND OUT BEFORE THE ENEMY KNOWS WHAT HIT THEM.

The business world is full of brilliant strategists, no matter what level of the company they inhabit. Unfortunately, it is often this very talent for planning that is the downfall of otherwise excellent initiatives. When plotting and preparing for a better future, it's a real temptation to let the vision get out of hand, creating battle plans that are so large and complex that they take a long, long time to follow to completion. The problem is that your company, your competitors, and the marketplace are always changing. What may have been a wonderful plan last month can easily turn out to be a disastrous move this month due to an unexpected change in conditions.

Does this mean that we should never think in terms of long-range plans? Of course not. However, if your plan is so complex and interconnected that it must be executed in its entirety to be effective, then you've created a tremendous vulnerability for yourself. Things change, and they often change quickly. Grand and monolithic schemes look impressive and powerful on paper, but they rarely survive the *blitzkrieg* that is modern business.

It's easy to look back and shake your head at the tactics initially employed by the British and the colonists during the American Revolution. Following the tradition of how wars had been fought in Europe, huge armies marched to the battlefield, politely lined up in opposing rows, and then opened fire. If ever there were a bad day to have a front-row seat, this was it. From a purely tactical point of view, it boggles the mind that generals would voluntarily line their troops up in pretty formations and present the most orderly of targets for the enemy to shoot at.

The Native Americans employed a far more practical approach to warfare. They operated in smaller, mobile units. Springing up from out of nowhere, they then attacked, making use of whatever was available as cover from the enemy's fire. Employing huge formations and presenting such vulnerable targets were the last things on their minds. Furthermore, it's a long and obvious procession to move and maneuver a huge army. Small, mobile forces can react quickly and be somewhere else in the blink of an eye. The same rules apply to every business or professional endeavor.

The problem with large, grand schemes that must run to completion is that nobody is going to stand there quietly and allow you to put them into place without opposition. The universal variable in business is people, and people always have ambitions and agendas of their own. The moment you begin to act on your plans, your competitors will analyze what you're doing, calculate the effect it will have on their own initiatives, and begin plotting counterattack and resistance measures. If your scheme takes months to complete, you're exposing your flank in such a long and stretched-out formation that their biggest problem will be deciding which of the dozens of perfect targets you've given them that they should attack first. Those are nice problems to have, if you're the enemy that is.

Naturally, when embarking on plans to improve the empire, you'll want to employ some long-term and strategic thinking. Grand schemes are not only good, they're absolutely required if you want to do anything other than sit still in the marketplace and let the competition chip away at your defenses. However, whether it's a market-driven initiative to move your entire company in a given direction or it's the smaller, day-to-day concerns of your department toiling on the front lines of your company, you must realize that you can't change the world overnight. As such, long-term thinking must further be subdivided into smaller incremental steps if your ideas are to survive.

To keep competing ideas from derailing you before you have a chance to finish what you started, you must plan your initiatives so that you can execute them quickly.

The principals are the same regardless of whether you're the CEO trying to take over a competing company or the guy on the loading docks trying to push through a new plan for organizing inventory that you know will make things better for your coworkers and the company. Think big. Move small. Employ lightning strikes, and never present a target for those who oppose you.

STAY ORGANIZED BUT KEEP THE STRUCTURES FLEXIBLE.

General Patton once observed that fixed fortifications were monuments to the stupidity of man, reasoning that if mountains and oceans could be overcome, so could any obstacle created by humanity. This is just as true in business as it is on the fields of battle.

It's an extremely common sight to see people at every level of an organization implementing procedures and making static plans designed to last until the world stops spinning. If nothing ever changed in your company, this wouldn't be a bad idea at all, would it? However, by building fixed and immovable organizations and procedures, you'll find that you've effectively tied an anchor to your foot if you ever have to react to a new situation. This applies to physical as well as organizational structures.

When I was a young man just out of high school and needed a job, I worked for a time in a factory that did high-volume manufacture of prescription eyeglasses. This was a typical assembly line. The process of taking a prescription and turning it into a pair of glasses was a sequential one, starting with the raw blanks for the lenses, walking them through various groups where they would be cut, ground, and polished, and then continuing the journey into the area where they were cut for the frames, treated for shatter resistance, and finally assembled.

Because the factory produced tens of thousands of glasses per day, load management was a significant consideration for optimal workflow. Naturally, the majority of the people hired was trained in one specific operation and did that all day. Some of us, however, for a variety of reasons had the opportunity to learn different jobs. I ended up learning virtually every step in the entire process, and because of my nature I always wanted to be the best producer in the group, just for the sport of it.

As a result, I was part of a small group of people who could float. Although I always had a given job and position where I spent the bulk of my time, occasionally people in another group would call in sick or work would get backed up in another area for some reason. At such times, the handful of us who could work other operations were shifted over to the problem area, reinforcing the group there until the crisis passed and the flow was smooth again.

Because only a few of us had more or less acquired the diversity of skills on our own—whether through boredom and appropriate maneuvering—even this shift in labor wasn't enough to keep the factory from having a bad production day, but it did help. Nonetheless, when your volume is in the tens of thousands, even one bad day can be an extremely costly problem.

Now imagine the result if the entire workforce had been trained, over the course of time, to perform all operations instead of just one. Instead of a static structure that required each person to know one and only one job, and therefore be forced to sit there and drink coffee for several hours because production was backed up, the entire composition of the workforce could dynamically flex. Large effort could be poured into areas where it was required, overstaffed areas could be diminished by routing people to needed areas, and the load balancing of production could be shifted in real time to always maintain the maximum possible output of the factory.

No matter what you're organizing or building, if you think in terms of flexibility instead of building large, permanent procedures, you'll have the mobility to react and adapt to every situation you encounter in the course of your work. Consequently, you'll always prevail.

BUILD A COLLECTION OF SMALL, FAST UNITS.

You can have something large built for power, or you can have something small built for speed. You can rarely have both. Therefore, if you can choose only one, small and fast is the way to go.

Think of it this way. If, back in the days of horseback warfare, you had elephants, well, that would be an impressive and mighty steed indeed. Elephants are large, powerful creatures. You could hitch a rope to them and pull down trees, and do many other such things that horses just don't have the, well, horsepower to accomplish. However, once the battle is joined, the enemy will know exactly where your elephants are. And, five minutes from now, their position isn't going to be that much different. Elephants are not known for burning rubber. Consequently, your enemies, mounted on small and fast war ponies, continually sweep in for an attack, run circles around your elephants, shower everyone with arrows and spears, and then quickly ride back out again before the elephants can catch them. Speed and mobility are an obvious tactical advantage.

But what if you had an army mounted on horses and needed to pull down some trees or gates? Your steed doesn't have the physical strength of an elephant, so you're out of luck. Well, you would be if you had only one horse. However, by harnessing the efforts of several horses, you'll find that the gate comes crashing right down, at which point you can go back to running circles around the elephants.

The small, fast, and mobile can offer the best of both worlds. The large, powerful, and lumbering cannot. Are you beginning to see the business applications of such a concept? If you read your corporate history, you'll likely find a great many examples of small, nimble companies that outmaneuvered the giant, monolithic corporations that dominated their industry, resulting in a new balance of power and redistribution of market share. As does every other concept we'll touch on, the lessons that apply at the company level work all the way down the line, and everyday workers can use them in their individual jobs.

We discussed earlier the advantages of being in and out before the enemy knew what hit them. Small, mobile units will pull this off much more easily than an army of five hundred thousand soldiers. Even if they do have elephants. Big companies, by their very nature, move slow and don't maneuver well. If the enemy is a competing company, you can certainly use that to your advantage. Even if the competition you're facing is the tribal warfare within your own company that you're trying to bring to an end, the same principals apply. Just as you don't want to build huge, complex, grand schemes that have no way of responding to change, so too do you want to organize your people and your efforts into small, mobile groups.

If you need the power of a hundred people to get your project completed, don't build a single group of one hundred people. Specialize, and then cross train. It is far better to have ten groups of ten, each of whom can perform multiple tasks. When you give them a task to accomplish and turn them loose to be creative and brilliant in their execution, the small groups will have much better communication, far less bureaucracy, and a higher level of esprit de corps. They will get in, get out, and get the job done before anyone even knows they were there.

When there's a task too large for ten people, unite two or three groups and have them attack the problem from several sides at the same time. Although a job must be done in a sequential order at times, very often you'll find that several small groups can do concurrent work, thereby maximizing the use of your calendar time.

If your department, or your entire empire, is a collection of small, effective, versatile, and mobile groups, it will adapt to any problem thrown at them. And its people will surround your competition and pick them to pieces with impunity, just as our horsemen were able to overcome the elephants. Even when you need one hundred thousand people on the field, don't line them up as one group as they did in the old days of European warfare. Instead, subdivide them into a collection of smaller groups and attack the enemy from all sides. You still have one hundred thousand people on the field. They just don't make as good a target.

USE DIFFERENT APPROACHES FOR DIFFERENT SEASONS.

Fireplaces and winter coats don't get a lot of use in the summer. In a similar fashion, bikinis and air conditioners are inconvenient at best when the temperatures drop below zero. If this sounds like an obvious exercise in common sense, that's exactly what it is. Nonetheless, as you've no doubt experienced, common sense is often in short supply in the business world.

Of course, like all the Stones, this one speaks to a concept rather than a literal time of year. However, in this particular case, let's first take a look at this from a literal perspective, just because it's convenient to do so. Most countries have different times of the year when major holidays and festivals create increased commerce for retail merchants. In America, the winter months prior to the Christmas season are the busiest shopping days of the year. In fact, many companies make the majority of their money in just those few months, with only a trickle of business throughout the remaining months of the year.

If you work in such a business, any initiatives that you wish to embark upon should have the time of year as its highest consideration. An example of this is hiring. Part-time people are rarely as dedicated and dependable in terms of looking out for the company's bottom line as are full-time employees. The simple fact is that, whereas people who work part-time are just as capable and ethical as anyone else, they're very aware of the fact that they won't be around to receive long-term benefits. For this reason, they have less incentive to cut costs, increase sales, or boost productivity than do the people who know they'll be there another ten years.

From this perspective, then, it would make sense to have full-time, permanent employees. But what about the huge spike in the workload when the holiday shopping season arrives? Should you build up a larger staff by hiring more permanent people? If you do, when the season is over, you'll be massively overstaffed, and simple profit and loss numbers will demand that you fire a large number of them. Do this often enough and you'll generate bad publicity and garner a bad image such that no one will want to work for you, and, even further, many may avoid your products simply for philosophical and ethical reasons.

Of course, in this case, it makes sense to hire part-time, temporary people during the holiday season. Because they understand that it's a job for the season alone, they have no hard feelings when the gig is up, and you have the flexibility to manage your labor costs sensibly. However, what if you determined that hiring would be simpler if you just did this all year long? Of course, you'd never have any permanent people, and, beyond the obvious fact that no one would be dedicated to the betterment of your company, you'd also have no accrued job skills and expertise. Simply put, the hiring practices of one season do not make sense for all seasons, and each requires an individual approach that is tailored to dynamics of the given situation.

What are the seasons in your company? Do you have cycles based on the time of year? Is there an ebb and flow based on the economy? Do your finances change based on the acquisition of major contracts? Think it through all the way down to a very small scale. If you work for someone who is encountering personal difficulties at home, their mood is going to be much different than it is when things are going well. How you interact with this person should vary according to the state they're in. What works when they're in a good mood will fail miserably when they're cranky or depressed.

No matter what your seasons—be they physical, economical, logical, or emotional—you need to be aware of them and tailor your approach accordingly. Life is not a one-size-fits-all proposition, and business is even less so. Even when you're employing long-term thinking and have long-term plans, you must always maintain flexibility and perceptiveness and adopt a different approach if the season suddenly changes on you. Although surfers are known to throw parties when a hurricane approaches, the sensible among us will typically bring the boats in and eat dinner in the basement. It's all about taking the appropriate action for the moment. And of course, keeping a spare towel never hurts.

ALWAYS KEEP AN EYE ON YOUR SUPPLIES.

No matter how mobile you keep your endeavors, horses don't go far without water, and tanks are reasonably useless without gas. In a similar manner, people don't get paid without budgets, and your Hula Hoop factory is going to come to a grinding halt if you run out of plastic. One of the easiest ways to lose the battle, and perhaps even the war, is to neglect your supply lines. This is exactly what happened to the German army when they tried to cross the broad expanse of the Russian steppes.

In the earlier years of human history, many civilizations survived through the practice of being nomadic tribes. Their housing was portable, typically tents of one sort or another that could easily be taken down, transported, and set up elsewhere. They lived like this for a simple reason: they were able to move with the supplies. Additionally, this flexibility allowed them to adapt to the seasons, relocating to warmer or cooler locales according to the season.

The practice of moving with the supplies is one that can also be applied to the corporate world. Clearly, because most people are hired and go to work in a certain department doing a specific job, this is not to suggest that the solution to supply problems is to continually change departments. In a practical sense, that's just not going to happen in most companies. So, what does it mean to move with the supplies?

The three most prevalent and important types of supplies for most companies are money, people, and power. When thinking in terms of the nomadic tribes of a hunter-gatherer culture, moving with the supplies meant actual physical relocation. Because we've already established that this is not a practical approach in the business world, how do we stay in touch with our supplies? Simply put, if we can't move to the supplies, we just bring the supplies to us. Armies have been doing that for ages.

Power, money, people . . . all of these supplies can be made available to you by a process that's as simple as the barter method and as old as the trade alliances among kingdoms. When you don't have the supplies you need, and can't obtain them through official channels, use unofficial channels: trade with your allies. Bear in mind that mutual consideration is a critical factor in such successful negations and relationships. Much of that can be maintained by constant vigilance on your part.

Always keep an eye on your future needs and the current level of your supplies. Project future requirements, plan ahead, and always try to keep a little in reserve when you can to avoid self-generated crises.

Just as you keep an eye on your stores, you should take another note from the nomadic tribes of old. Never stop foraging. You should have people in your group who continually look around, make connections, and keep their ear to the ground for the possibility of new alliances and new supply lines.

It also works the other way. Don't wait for others to seek you out for help. To build a strong network of allies, your scouts should actively monitor other tribes, make connections with them, and keep up with their general state of health and well-being. When you see that they're about to fall on hard times, initiate the help yourself before they come to you. The first step in forming powerful and long-lasting friendships is, well, taking that first step. People may assume, for a variety of invalid reasons, that you're not approachable. By taking the initiative and offering help without having been asked for it first, you have an opportunity to create an excellent first impression, thus laying the groundwork for not only a great trade alliance but for a solid partnership in all your endeavors going forward.

Everyone needs supplies, including you. Manage yours well, continually look for new opportunities, and build alliances wherever possible. When you finally do find yourself in a protracted skirmish to accomplish your objectives, you'll be well provided for and can endure the amount of time it will take to succeed.

CONTINUALLY LOOK FOR NEW PURSUITS.

The company with only one product is vulnerable, and the person with only one skill is easily replaced. Besides that, most humans have difficulty with monotony. No matter what the task and how much you enjoy it, if it's all you ever do and you have no variation in life, you will eventually burn out. Because of this, both as a company and an individual, you should always be on the lookout for new pursuits.

Additionally, diversity increases the power of the empire and also aids your quest for mobility. Any time you have a problem to solve, you're going to fall back on your personal toolkit to solve it. If you have only one talent or skill in the bag, your options are limited. The one trick you have up your sleeve may or may not be adequate to meet the need. However, if you're continually looking for new things that interest you and new capabilities that you can add to your repertoire, you're going to have a much greater chance for success no matter what challenges you face.

So how do you expand your talents? Like many other things we've looked into thus far, the answer starts with a very simple step. Most people never expand their capabilities because they never think about doing so. It doesn't happen by magic in your sleep. If you want to expand your usefulness to the company and create better opportunities for your own career, the first thing you should do is treat yourself to a nice relaxing chair, your favorite music, a little quiet time, and active contemplation.

The easiest way to approach this is to start with the things in life that you enjoy. If you have a love of the visual arts, you may have at one time considered being an artist, only to discard it because of the lack of financial stability. And yet, talents in the visual arts can be applied in an extremely wide variety of ways, particularly in the electronic age. Whether it's helping with advertising flyers, creating logos, or even enhancing the company letterhead, it all amounts to talents that the company can use that coincide with things you enjoy personally.

How many passions and talents do you keep inside that may have cousins in other industries? Spend some time in your favorite chair considering these things. Then, go to your local bookstore and browse the shelves. It's a great way to brainstorm if you allow yourself to indulge in a little free association. Let a thought that occurs to you glancing at one book lead you to a completely different section of the store, and bounce around from topic to topic considering the many ways in which the emotions and desires you feel inside can be expressed in alternate ways.

When you've come up with a few new ideas, some of them will speak to you more strongly than others. Grab a book, subscribe to a couple of magazines, visit some Web sites, or join a local special-interest group. As you explore, you'll find that, after a little initial investigation, some ideas leave you cold. But others will light that fire in you, keeping you up at night thinking about how much fun it could be to pursue them. These are the winners. Look for ways that you can bring these talents to work, and pursue them.

The next time there's a problem, crisis, or opportunity at the office, chances are you may be able to contribute some of your newly discovered interests that you've been pursuing in your spare time. Those you work for will consider this an extreme bonus, as you didn't have these talents when they hired you.

Change is the only constant in the universe. When the occasional crisis or unexpected development arises in your company, many may panic or handle the situation badly. Fear sets in due to many people's deep-seated fear of the unknown. You, however, simply react to the problem with an unexpected solution, saving the day. The more talents you have at your disposal, the greater your mobility.

NEVER LEAVE ONE OF YOUR PEOPLE BEHIND.

This last point is not so much about how to be mobile, but rather the lifestyle and atmosphere a highly mobile group must adopt to thrive as a community. Year after year, your company and your department will encounter change and the unexpected. Some events will be minor, and some will shake the very foundation of your enterprise. You, and most people like you, will improvise, adapt to the new situation, and overcome any difficulties that confront you.

However, it's an important thing to remember that not everyone is like you. Many people, for a variety of reasons, will flounder and be overcome when the world that they thought they could depend on suddenly changes right in front of their eyes. Some people adopt a very callous attitude in the workplace, looking after their own well-being and actively criticizing those who don't do the same rather than offering a hand. This is *not* how you unite the tribes.

Dealing with change is difficult even for those who apply themselves to the task. Creating an environment of mobility and building an atmosphere of an elite unit who can handle anything that gets thrown their way require overcoming many fears and self-perceived limitations. When things start moving fast, some of the people among you are not going to be able to keep up. If you abandon them to their fate, you can count on your entire group eventually giving up the idea of pursuing mobility. Being quick on your feet and developing a fast, maneuverable approach to doing battle brings certain risks. The minute that people see that they're working without a net, they'll give up in fear and go back to the perceived comfort of a static atmosphere. Who can blame them?

When changes come and even one of your people is in danger of any kind, it is imperative that the entire group come to that person's aid, and do so not grudgingly but with an enthusiastic sense of camaraderie. This will demonstrate to all that mobility is about more than being responsive and quick on your feet. A truly elite unit has its strength not in overwhelming numbers, but in the talents, tactics, and abilities of its members. It cannot afford to lose even one of them.

Furthermore, sometimes in the heat of the fight, you'll realize that quick and sometimes risky decisions must be made, for to stop and consider it in committee would mean to lose the opportunity. If people are punished by being abandoned when they slip and fall, then no one will ever take any chances. Showing support for those who fall off a horse demonstrates to each individual that they're not out there riding alone and vulnerable, but are instead just one soldier in a highly responsive force. Doing so will make your people fearless, and the fearless are the most mobile people on the planet.

Your treatment of those who, at least in the beginning, can't keep up also sends a very loud message to the rest of the empire, even if this person is perceived as the least valuable person in the building. Your company needs flexibility, mobility, and fearless riders who are willing to stop or turn on a dime even when they're traveling well beyond the posted speed limit. You need creativity and people willing to take chances and risk it all for the good of the group. When you make a conscious and dedicated decision to never leave one of your people behind, you build an internal loyalty among your own group, and you inspire all other tribes in the empire as well.

Remember, although we may be speaking of mobility at the moment, never forget the underlying theme: the path to personal and corporate success and stability is to unite *all* of the tribes into a single, powerful empire that can provide for all of its people. And the best way to lead is by example. When you demonstrate not only an agile unit but an extreme and intense loyalty to each other, you paint a picture to the entire company of what all could experience by joining forces and looking out for each other.

Change happens. Deal with it. Adapt an attitude of speed and mobility that embraces change and profits from it. And, above all, make a solemn vow to each other that you will never, *ever* let one of your people fall by the wayside. Together, you are the lightning charge of the elite.

MOBILITY

Improvise. Adapt. Overcome.

◎ Understand that attitude is the heart of mobility.
◎ Be quick on your feet or be a target.
◎ See trouble coming and be gone before it arrives.
◎ Be in and out before the enemy knows what hit them.
◎ Stay organized but keep the structures flexible.
◎ Build a collection of small, fast units.
◎ Use different approaches for different seasons.
◎ Always keep an eye on your supplies.
◎ Continually look for new pursuits.
◎ Never leave one of your people behind.

V | Competitiveness

Promote excellence through
a culture of conquest.

One of the biggest killers of productivity in any company is complacency. Sometimes it's due to personal laziness. Other times it's the result of stifling bureaucracy. Most of all, though, the greatest danger to the long-term health of the empire is clinging to the status quo, that feeling that if things are okay today, then it will always be so. This inevitably results in an organization of people who sit on their hands and do nothing to prepare for the challenges of the coming day. The result is always the same: decline, and ultimately, failure.

In a race, the horse that slows to a stop will soon be passed. If you have a very keen ear, you might also hear the other horses laugh as they gallop past. Does this seem self-evident? You'd be surprised how often the very, very obvious can escape people in the corporate world. It's quite simple. If you're not preparing for tomorrow's victory, you will without a doubt experience tomorrow's defeat. The only way to perpetuate an empire is for all its citizens to dedicate themselves to making it stronger every day. Only by making your company more powerful with each passing month will you be able to ensure any kind of stability for your own future. If you decide that today is a good day to stop sharpening your sword, you'll soon discover that your competition didn't share these sentiments.

To enjoy personal prosperity and security, you must build an invincible empire and see it as an unstoppable force. Additionally, you must develop an attitude of conquest and see every competitor in the field—whether or not they seem to be a threat—as a distinct danger to your health and well-being. With this perspective, there can be only one choice: you must either conquer the competition or be conquered yourself. Although there are many short-term ways to bring this about, we're not interested in quick-fix results. If you want to be bringing home a paycheck many years from now, you're going to have to turn your thoughts to the kind of strength that lasts. That longevity comes from providing superior products and services and outflanking your adversaries at every turn. Only through excellence can you prevail in the competitive world of business.

FOCUS ON A COMMON ENEMY

Too many companies are divided by internal strife and petty turf wars that don't serve the common good. Individuals concentrate on their personal career paths to the exclusion of all else. Departments develop a tribal consciousness and view all other departments as opposing tribes, devoting their time to overcoming them. Your competitors in the marketplace love this because you're fighting the wrong enemy. It will cost you the war.

Any student of human history will have noted that one of the most common ploys used by conquerors in uniting their land is that of defining a common enemy. Because of this newly discovered menace, people immediately turn their focus from petty internal squabbling and bickering to the dangers of an external enemy. Suddenly, instead of a collection of continually arguing tribes thinking only of themselves, they instinctively band together to fight something that threatens them all. In place of divisiveness, unity and a sense of common purpose prevail.

When the threat from your competitors is real and obvious to all, it isn't difficult to highlight the dangers. However, even though your competition represents the most legitimate and immediate threat to the health and well-being of your company, this doesn't mean that your people are going to realize it. More often than not, they need someone to point it out before they will come to realize the critical nature of the situation. The bigger and scarier you can make this opposing force sound, the better. People who are fighting for their lives work much harder than people who feel they have little to lose.

First, let your instincts point you to the obvious results that would occur if your company were to take no action whatsoever and your competitors were to continue on a normal and sensible approach to expanding their own empire. The consequences for the workers and leaders in your company are easy to see and include such things as longer hours, pay cuts, and even massive firings as your company scrambles to cope with the revenues lost to the competition. When people realize that their apathy toward their common enemies will cause them to suffer personally, they'll suddenly be very passionate about the issue.

From there simply connect the dots. Your starting point is the general perception of the state of affairs shared by the people, and your ending point is the catastrophe that you know will result if your people simply choose to sit on their collective hands and accept the status quo. All that's necessary to make it real to the people you address is to fill in a few more dots between your starting and ending point, painting an obvious and likely series of events that can lead from your current bucolic setting to an end of widespread layoffs and financial hardship. Make sure that each step you show between the present and the future is realistic and appears as the next logical step based on the one preceding it.

The result is a line of reasoning showing the common enemy that threatens the entire company and the evils that can befall it accordingly. When you've done this, you'll have a line of reasoning that you can present to anyone from the board of directors to the cleaning crew and that will have a resounding effect on them personally. That's how you get their attention.

Your goal is to ensure that—at every level of the organization—your peers, the people working for you, and the people to whom you report all band together rather than fight amongst themselves. In your water cooler conversations, in high-level boardroom meetings, and in the day-to-day interactions that you have with people in the hallways, spread the word. You must continually emphasize that every one of your competitors in the marketplace fantasizes about putting you out of business. Of course, if this happens, you'll all lose your jobs. Connect the dots for them, and lead them down the path until they see the danger. And then make it real to them.

When everyone in the company sees the competition as their common and most dangerous enemy, understands the threat that they pose, and is both willing and enthusiastic to fight them, your productivity will skyrocket. The results will be greater efficiency and tremendous morale. This in turn will generate an overpowering and unified force that your people can pour into the growth and protection of the empire. Your adversaries in the marketplace will find themselves reeling from the strength of your efforts.

HARNESS INTERNAL POWER STRUGGLES.

People are competitive by nature. It's part of our animal instincts, and many people love a good fight just for the sake of the conflict. So, even when there's a clear and present danger, a common enemy that all acknowledge, you'll always have internal power struggles. This is obviously a destructive and wasteful way to live your life, but you'll have a better chance of convincing the sun to sleep late tomorrow morning than you will of altering this fundamental aspect of human nature. If you don't learn to recognize this when it's happening and find a way to redirect the resulting chaotic energy, it will tear the empire apart.

Some people compete and struggle because they want the perceived reward, namely power. Many, however, are more interested in the competition itself than in what they're actually fighting for. They simply enjoy the thrill of battle. Of course, they may be entirely unaware of this.

Actually, people of this sort are often the easiest to deal with. They like to fight, and you both have a common enemy in your competitors. Get them involved in *that* conflict, and show them how their creativity, productivity, and drive for excellence can be used to destroy the competition. Convey this effectively, and they'll be so busy helping the empire defeat its adversaries in the marketplace that they'll forget all about their petty internal quarrels. Furthermore, when they see rewards for their part in making the company stronger, they'll become even more enthusiastic and dedicated to the task.

This can easily be used to motivate those who are driven to struggle because they want to achieve a goal. Those who are ambitious and wish to climb the corporate ladder can be shown that working together as opposed to working against each other is the best path to success for their personal careers. To do this, you need to get them thinking in terms of victories against the competition. Fuel their lust for conquest.

Furthermore, encourage them to document their adventures. Each and every time that they succeed in their efforts such that the empire prevails, they've added one more notch in their gun belt and given their superiors yet another reason to promote and to reward them. In other words, show them how their own personal needs can also be met by fighting the external enemy instead of struggling with their coworkers.

Internal political struggles are an incredible source of power. Learn to recognize them when you see them, and start practicing your dialog to distract them from their smaller fights so as to divert their attention to the larger struggle that the company as a whole is engaged in. For the particularly ambitious, the quickest way to get their attention is to point out that the greater the battle, the greater the chance for fame and prestige. Whether it's the petty satisfaction of overcoming a coworker in some pointless argument or it's the spotlight that results from leading your group into battle and demolishing all competitors in the marketplace, all who yearn for conflict crave glory. Use that, steer it in a productive direction, and you'll have a highly enthusiastic group of people who are more than happy to work together for the good of the empire.

BE BOLD WITH THE ENEMY BUT HUMBLE WITH EACH OTHER.

Without a doubt, you want to foster a spirit of superiority in your workgroup and in your company. You want a building full of fierce competitors. Your goal is to fire up each individual, regardless of what part they play. Make them aware of the battle, show them the common enemy, and make the situation real and personal enough to them that they care passionately about joining that conflict and prevailing.

The empire needs a culture of winners. Each of you, worker and leader alike, should do your utmost to encourage this, empowering every individual with a sense of boldness that borders on the brash. Of course, not every person is aggressive by nature, and you should not attempt to turn a gentle soul into someone they're not. The nonaggressive personalities will serve brilliantly in other aspects of the empire, as we'll see later when we discuss supporting positions. Nonetheless, for the competitive, you can easily direct their energies and their passions towards the greater good. As your workgroup, department, or entire company begins to acquire this attitude, the momentum itself will strengthen every person involved. Before you know it, your business will be bursting at the seams with enthusiasm, vigor, power, and a desire to be the very best, conquering all who stand in your way.

Unchecked, however, all this confidence and enthusiasm can have a downside. Arrogance divides, and that's just what you'll have if you allow this competitive spirit to spread recklessly without some degree of control. Professional athletes often psych themselves up before a game by chanting that they're the best, that all other mortals are inferior, and that no one on the planet can touch them. This attitude is fine as long as it's applied in controlled situations and directed toward your opponents. However, when people start believing their own press statements, it's easy for this kind of thing to get out of hand. Before you know it, they'll be walking down the halls of your company feeling the same way toward their coworkers. It doesn't take much imagination to see what kind of an effect this could have on morale. A cocky, arrogant attitude expressed internally will do nothing but alienate coworkers and create divisions within the empire. For obvious reasons, this must be avoided.

You must be fierce with your enemies and yet at the same time treat each other with kindness, respect, and humility. It's the only way to unite rather than divide your empire. Toward this end, you should do everything within your power to foster a sense of family among all people, regardless of position. Teach others—and demonstrate by example— that the greatest and most gratifying praise is that which comes from someone else, not yourself.

Along those lines, look for every chance that you can find to compliment the efforts of both the individual and the group. The more you can build esprit de corps, the more you'll minimize egotism and bickering. Build pride in being a member of the group, and build a group pride in being a member of the empire. Do this by demonstrating the benefits of inclusive thinking. This shouldn't be difficult to do because, for any endeavor, the power of a group will almost always exceed the power of the individual. Because people love to be on the winning team, they'll enjoy this increased horsepower. If you make it clear to people that mutual praise strengthens their power and that arrogance diminishes it, you'll be able to show in logical and practical terms why the individual benefits personally by displaying nothing but a positive and supportive attitude toward all others in the group.

PROMOTE POSITIVE COMPETITION.

So far, we've been concentrating on directing our competitive efforts toward the enemy. That's not to say that internal competition has no value. In fact, contests and games can offer great boosts to productivity. As we've already noted, the most important thing to keep in mind when trying to increase a competitive nature is to make sure that your competitions unite rather than divide.

A game that illustrates this concept is a dice came often played at parties. It's a street game, and so goes by many names. One of them is *Farkle*. This game is played with six dice, with certain dice combinations being assigned points. Each person rolls all the dice, and then pulls out any combinations of points from that roll that they wish to keep. With the remaining dice, they roll again. As long as each roll produces points that they can take, they keep rolling. When all dice have been rolled into points, they pick up all six and continue, with the points still accumulating.

When they've pushed their luck as far as they think they can get away with, they stop rolling and take the points that they have accumulated thus far. They must choose to stop and take their points for them to count. If they instead roll the dice and no points are present, they lose all points that they have accumulated for this turn and must pass the dice to the next player.

As you might imagine, this game, with each person rolling the dice, builds up quite a bit of personal momentum. As the point tally for the current turn increases, both the excitement and the anxiety rise. It's a form of gambling, of tempting fate, pulling back only at the last moment when you've built up all the points you think you can get before a farkle turns up.

In most games, everyone crowded around the table would be hoping that the person rolling failed, because they want to win themselves. The entire group would, individually, be focusing on the person rolling and quietly or loudly wishing the current player to farkle and lose their points.

However, in *Farkle*, the entire group sincerely cheers on the person rolling, even though you're all competitors. Everyone loves a winner, and, in this particular game, you encourage each person's success the same as you'd cheer a horse that you'd bet a week's wages on. With each successful roll, the excitement builds, everyone hoping that a new record will be set. When the person rolling the dice completes a successful turn that earned them points, everyone is excited and happy. Sound different than your average cutthroat game? It is. It's also big fun.

Rather than destroy the competitive spirit, in *Farkle*, the greater each individual success, the greater the excitement experienced by all. Therefore, each person, fueled by the group spirit and camaraderie, is as motivated as possible to do their very best. This combined enthusiasm can be incredibly contagious, building to an almost fever pitch and bringing the very best out in everyone. Of course, that's rather the point.

At the end of the game, there will obviously be just one winner. However, unlike many games that have winners and losers with only the winners feeling good, in this game everyone enjoys an uplifting experience of being cheered on by others throughout the game. Of course, *Farkle* is just one example.

Regardless of what your competitions are, it is imperative that you manage the atmosphere and keep all such activities positive and unifying. Remember, one champion and a room full of losers will never be as powerful as a roomful of people who feel like champions whether they won or lost. Change the way people play, and you'll change the way that they work.

SHARPEN SKILLS THROUGH FREQUENT GAMES.

In addition to the group-building and morale-lifting aspects that we've just looked into, competition can also be a great incentive to improve at what you do for a living.

As I mentioned previously, I spent a number of years doing factory work, and, as anyone who has put in eight hours on an assembly line can tell you, it can be a long and tedious day. The very nature of mass production ensures that you will do the exact same task, over and over again until your mind goes numb. At such times, most people aren't thinking about the good of the empire. All they're thinking about is quitting time. When they leave for home, you can bet that they're not going to spend the rest of their evening considering ways to make the company more productive. Factory work, like so many other jobs in the business world, is often little more than a test of mental endurance.

I was struck by this sensation early on in my first job of this sort, and for a while it bothered me a great deal. I don't particularly care for mind-numbing experiences, and I have a very low threshold for boredom. Before long, I realized that I'd either have to come up with some way to survive the monotony or get another job. I chose the former. I hate admitting defeat, even if the adversary is the job itself.

No matter what you do for a living and how large or small your workgroup, a keen eye will quickly pick out several fundamental personality types in any environment. I knew what I was looking for. I needed to find someone, anyone good natured, who had a little pride and liked to compete. Of the several people doing my particular operation, one of the guys clearly stood out as a kindred spirit. Consequently, in a light-hearted manner, I told him that I thought he was really good at what he did, and, of course, that I could also leave him in the dust any time I chose.

The result was exactly what I was hoping for. He raised his eyebrows slightly, smiled, and told me that I couldn't beat him in my wildest dreams. And so, we were off. Of course, not every day was a game. People get sick, personal problems follow you to the job, and sometimes you're just so tired from the rigors of everyday life that all you can do is merely maintain the status quo. However, for the overwhelming majority of the days that I spent there, my newfound friend and I raced and competed with every job skill that we could clearly define.

Of course, I'll tell you that I always won. However, he might have a slightly different story, and, in truth, neither would be completely accurate. No matter who produced the most at the end of the shift, we were pushing ourselves to the absolute peak of our abilities because it was fun to do so. It took the tedium out of the work, introduced camaraderie between us, made the days shorter, and gave us a lot of excuses to laugh. Our productivity, not surprisingly, skyrocketed. And so, there wasn't just one winner each night. There were three. He won, I won, and the empire won.

As this example illustrates, you can lead very effectively from the middle. My partner in crime and I had no position or official power, no authority to pass out bonuses or money, and in short were nothing but a couple of working-class, minimum-wage stiffs. And yet, just because we decided to have some fun and shake off the tedium of assembly-line work, we raised the spirits and productivity of many other groups. You don't have to be a leader to lead.

Build an atmosphere of champions where you work, and use the power of games and competition to hone your skills to a fine edge. As you build these games, however, give much more attention to the spirit in which they're played than to any other aspect. When pursued properly, as they were in our examples here, the electricity and excitement that it generates among your people will allow you to outshine all other empires.

GLORIFY ALL WHO COMPETE, NOT JUST THE CHAMPIONS.

Frequently, people join together in company competitions and, motivated by the thrill of the contest, go on to achieve greater individual productivity than ever before. Far too often, however, all of their hard work and personal achievements are completely ignored at the end of the games because the only people who are recognized are the few champions who won their particular prizes. As you might imagine, this has quite a demoralizing effect on everyone else. People who have worked their tail off to deliver the best results of their career will be insulted that their efforts are trivialized at best or completely ignored at worst. Furthermore, they will resent the winners for being the only ones praised for their accomplishments. This in turn diminishes the good feelings that normally come from winning, so even the champions are robbed of the uplifting experience that was supposed to be the entire point of the game.

Anyone who approaches internal contests with a goal of gaining specific and measurable increases in productivity for the duration of the event is thinking far too small to be of any help in building an empire. The greatest benefit from any competition is *enthusiasm*.

Therefore, esprit de corps, not a temporary rise in productivity, is the point of this endeavor. Your goal should be lifting the spirits of everyone who participates so that, for here on out, they'll be happier in their work and enjoy each other's company that much more. Happy people are the most productive people. Consequently, we're organizing games to improve unity and to experience a common bond. In a word, we're building *passion*. Not just for today, but for all days to come. All other things being equal, the force that is the most fired up and motivated will win the battle every time. In fact, even when things are not equal and that group is the underdog, it'll still win most of the battles. You simply cannot put a price on enthusiasm, for it is the force that moves mountains.

Regardless of how long your competitions run, you must each day give thought to how you can make every competitor feel like a winner. When you succeed in this effort, you will have transformed your department from a collection of people who come in and do their jobs to a group of winners, people who see themselves as success stories. As everyone knows, people who feel like they're successful become just that. It's a self-fulfilling prophecy. Because of this, you need to evaluate the performance, and the state of mind, of every contestant on a daily basis. If your games are on a large scale, this will of course be delegated to those who lead the various individual groups.

The same applies at the awards ceremony: leave no one out. Give glory to your champions, and make them feel like the winners that they are. However, make sure that, in the course of the evening, the spotlight shines briefly on every single person in the room. Do keep in mind that your praise must be absolutely sincere, or everyone will simply roll their eyes and mutter about having to endure a bunch of phony corporate hogwash. You will have gained nothing. In practice, it's actually not that hard to find sincere and realistic things to praise about every single individual you work with. The only difficulty in the typical workplace is the fact that most people never make the effort. Fortunately, this is very easy to change.

When the room has emptied out and people are sweeping away the confetti, you want your awards presentation to have had one crucial lasting effect. The very next workday, if you've done your job right, every single person will walk into the office with their heads held high, feeling like a winner who is capable of doing their best work ever. If you continue to reinforce that as time goes on you will never lose these gains. All who competed, in turn, will be that much better at their jobs and will also enjoy the experience more. Everyone loves being a winner. When your contests have no losers, only a bunch of winners who just happened not to get the prize this time, you will have taken your people to yet another level, and they will be all the more effective in battle. Not only will the empire be stronger, but everyone's lives will have been enriched in the process.

RAISE SUPPORTING POSITIONS TO A PLACE OF HONOR.

Throughout these Pillars, I speak in terms of battles and enemies, struggles and triumphs. Against such a backdrop, some of you may feel out of place. Not everyone has the aggressive nature of a warrior. Many people of good heart and conscience shy away from conflict and prefer the harmony of cooperation to the adventure of conquest. Is there no place in an expanding empire for such people? Must everyone hold a frontline position, going nose to nose with the enemy?

It would be a very unrealistic view of the business world if such were the requirements, and it is precisely such realism that must ever be the bedrock in which our pillars are rooted if we wish to build a stable and lasting empire. In business and in combat, the warriors cannot possibly prevail on their own. The nature of battle is an extremely complex one, with many aspects that must come together to assure victory. To ignore or minimize the importance of even one of these is to risk being soundly defeated, whether you're swinging a sword or selling a product.

Around the time of World War II, a new phrase came into being: *the military-industrial complex*. It referred to the large collection of manufacturers and related industries that were necessary to build the weapons and equipment of war. It would have mattered little how brilliant Field Marshal Erwin Rommel, the Desert Fox of the German Army, was on the sandy battlefields if he had no tanks to command. He could have had the most capable and highly trained tank crews on the planet, but, without Panzers to drive, they would be little more than riflemen. Consequently, the industrial production capabilities of every nation in the conflict were just as crucial as the strategic skills of their leading generals. You can't have a shooting war without bullets.

The factories and people who produced the planes, guns, parachutes, and even socks and toothbrushes were therefore extremely important to the overall success or failure of the competing nations. Any question of this can be laid to rest by the dubious honor they received of being the targets of most of the aerial bombing raids that took place. No country is going to waste precious resources bombing the local cattle. Instead, they're going to attack those operations that can provide supplies to the frontline troops, explicitly acknowledging the critical importance of support operations. The cows, of course, couldn't be happier about this.

Fortunately for those of us doing battle with our competitors in the business world, we don't draw the kind of attention that would cause us to scurry to the nearest bomb shelter. Nonetheless, it's equally important in our domain that we understand, and honor, the importance of the supporting positions in our companies.

Without supporting people, your company cannot complete its transactions. You would have no appointments or sales. Your paperwork would get lost. Even if it didn't, it wouldn't matter, because there would have been no one to deposit the sales revenues into the company bank account. In short, without the backing of all these support organizations, your work means nothing.

As ever, you should also build a sense of pride and unity, continually reinforcing to them that, of all the support groups in the company, yours are the absolute pick of the crop. This isn't divisive because, at other times, the empire as a whole will celebrate the fact that, combined, its support system is superior to every competitor in the marketplace.

Both at the tribal level and in the empire at large, you need to hold up your support people as an example of value and excellence rather than holders of menial positions that could be filled by anyone off the streets. If you work in a support position, you should also do the same for all other groups in the company's infrastructure. When your supporting positions are widely recognized and treated as positions of honor, every single person will hold their head high and give heart, body, and soul to whatever task they perform, confident in the knowledge that they are making a very real contribution to the health and well-being of the empire.

GIVE YOUR PEOPLE HEROES TO CHEER.

It's easy to visualize how heroes are created in the context of company contests. Frequent games are in fact a good idea, but there will always be those periods in between, when you're all engaged in the everyday business of just getting the job done. What then? Where are your heroes then?

No matter what the position, and no matter what shape your company is in, people are constantly showing up and doing more than their fair share, performing above-average or sometimes even spectacular feats, and usually without notice. If you take the attitude that they're just doing the job they were hired to do, you're missing out on some very powerful motivating actions that you could take.

Just for the record, what if they *were* just simply doing their jobs? Maybe they were hired for high-profile and high-stress situations, leadership roles, or in some other way were given their job because they were expected to perform the miraculous on a daily basis. Who cares? How does it benefit you, or the company, to shrug your shoulders and just leave it at that?

Additionally, being a hero is a somewhat relative thing. The media may hail as a hero the soldier who stormed a machine-gun nest. On the other hand, to him, he was just a guy doing his job. Someone had to deal with the situation, and he happened to be there to get it done.

Very often, the people doing the work don't really need to be put on a pedestal and glorified for doing what they consider to be all in a day's work. Although everyone needs recognition for what they do, which is a topic we're continually considering from a variety of angles, in this particular case the need to glorify our champions isn't just for the benefit of the heroes themselves. More important than giving them credit and accolades for the good work they do is the effect that a good old-fashioned hero can have on everyone else.

The position of the hero is a relative one: they serve to show that, although our fears tell us that we must stop now or perish, many more steps can safely be taken. The critical difference between success and failure is very often one of hope, belief, and inspiration. If two groups possess the exact same capabilities, the one who loses hope will fail, and the one who can stay inspired will succeed. This is what our champions give to us.

We often think only of conspicuous leaders when looking for our inspirational figures. The hero is often not at the head of the pack, but in the middle or even the rear. No matter what your position, as a leader or worker, make it a part of your job to look for and seek out such people in your own organization. You won't always be able to reward them with a ticker tape parade. You can always, however, raise your voice and gather the people to lift their coffee cups in a toast to the one who goes that extra mile, achieves the difficult or impossible, holds out just a little longer when all were ready to quit, or performs any other task that can be used to raise the spirits of the group as a whole.

Remember, although those who take that extra step truly do deserve the praise, your people need the *example* even more. Some of your heroes will be reluctant ones. Make them see the good that others will receive by allowing you to make an example out of them. Your people work hard, and they will have moments of doubt. The only way to tilt forward into the wind and persevere is to keep the faith. Celebrate your heroes wherever you can find them, and do it often. It will help you all to reach for greater heights.

CELEBRATE VICTORIES WITH GREAT ENTHUSIASM.

Just as your people will always need inspirational figures to cheer to raise their own hopes, celebrating victories lightens the heart and lifts the spirits. Leaders will always urge you on to the next set of goals, the next plateau, the ever-higher mountaintop. No matter what you do, you will always be asked for more. Such is the nature of expanding an empire.

Even if you achieve success after success, if each accomplishment is immediately followed by the declaration of yet another goal, you're going to get tired and burnt out. You'll see nothing but an endless road of labor and never a rest area where you can take a break. You'll also see little point in succeeding because all that your accomplishments will produce will be another set of labors. Accordingly, your efforts will begin to diminish, and, instead of expanding to ever-greater conquests, you will begin a steady decline into depression and failure.

For as long as humanity has gathered in societies, major festivals have been held at certain times of the year. In the spring, there is much work to be done. It is the season of birth and growing. Ground must be prepared, crops must be planted, livestock attended to, and homes and structures built and repaired, all while the weather is good. The list of chores can seem endless, but all are necessary for the survival of the village. Slack off now, and you're going to be very cold and hungry later.

Additionally, spring comes after the long, hard winter. In the old days, winter wasn't something we watched on television from inside our comfy, heated apartments. It was a devastatingly challenging season that many people did not survive.

Consequently, when the winter passed and spring came along, people in villages everywhere prepared to party. Bright costumes helped to brighten attitudes. It was a time to drink, dance, and be glad you were still alive. You worked hard and endured for the entire gloomy season. You deserve a celebration and a chance to enjoy some of the good things in life that you worked so hard to maintain. Having had a chance to celebrate and enjoy life for a while, you were then rejuvenated and prepared both mentally and physically to step back into the hard work of the planting season.

These days, those of us making a living in the business world are not as concerned with the changing of the seasons, at least not in such critical, life-and-death ways. Nonetheless, the lessons learned from the major festivals of spring and fall should be applied to the daily lives of every company.

It's very common for us to be hard working and dedicated by nature. It's also equally prevalent thinking that hard work is the responsible thing to do, but that parties and festivities are frivolous and unimportant affairs. The hardcore from the old business model may even openly state that all that time you spend frolicking could be put to more productive use by working.

Once, maybe. Twice, perhaps. But I'll guarantee you that, in the long run, the company that parties until the cows come home every time they achieve success will kick your company's stoic rear end. You may be good, but you'll get tired and worn down after a while, and then you'll be little more than stationary target practice. Not only that, but, once they demolish your company, they're going to kick back and laugh loudly about it afterward. The world's greatest warriors also threw world-class parties.

The nice thing about this is that it works even if you're not in charge. Where is it written that only leaders can throw parties? If you're just another working-class stiff in a group of working-class stiffs, and you know you've all just done another landmark job, stand up and declare a party! You've all worked hard. Once again, you've beaten your competition into the ground. Who cares whose idea the party was? You all deserve it, and the group that plays together moves mountains together. Make celebrations an important part of your company's culture, and you'll be amazed by the spirit and achievements of your people.

ALWAYS LOOK TO THE NEXT CONQUEST.

We had to look at the various ways that we can cheer each other on and celebrate before we could get here, or it would simply be unthinkable. All work and no play not only makes Jack a dull boy, it also ensures that the quality of Jack's work will eventually be mediocre at best. All of the greatest things in life are born from a cycle of tension and release. Think about that the next time you watch a good movie. Even the ocean doesn't stay at high tide all day. Work hard, and then play hard.

However, the reason we play hard is so that we can once again work hard. The competition never sleeps. Each day, they get up and try to think of a way to put you out of business forever so that they can have your turf, your customers, your money, and your staff. If you allow yourself to become complacent, you will end up soft, lazy, and vulnerable. And your competition will eliminate you. Therefore, you must always keep moving forward, on to the next victory and the next accomplishment in the marketplace.

Some of these goals will be obvious. More sales. Expanded product lines. Greater market share. Reduced competition. These are all things that can be thought of in terms of the empire as a whole.

Although it's important to employ long-term thinking and envision grand schemes, it's even more critical for you to look for the next conquest on a much smaller scale. In all the various, small groups throughout your company, you have work and goals to accomplish. The same can be said for the individual. If each person, each small group, every larger department, and massive division, all the way to the top, continually looks to the next victory, your entire company will throb with life, excitement and productivity. Your ambitions, plans, hopes, and dreams must exist at every level of the business to keep you alive and growing.

Each day, driving in to work, you should take some time to think about the overall nature of the business world, for in that world your company, and therefore your paycheck, finds its home. Business, by its very nature, is an extremely competitive environment. Your industry is full of sharks swimming through the waters of the marketplace, devouring all who stand in their way. You must be willing to join in your company's competitive efforts so that you will prevail in this cutthroat environment, or you'll find yourself without a job. Therefore, your empire must be fierce, powerful, and completely effective in the battle for profitability.

Whether you're one of the warriors on the front line who lives for the fight or you're the solid, dependable support staff who makes the victory possible, embrace the spirit of competition and dedicate yourself to doing your absolute personal best in the part you play. This in turn guarantees victory for the company that provides for you. When the spirit of positive competition ripples through your company, you will continually urge each other on to greater heights, and you will unite in your efforts to compete in the outside world as an invincible empire.

COMPETITIVENESS

Promote excellence through a culture of conquest.

◎ Focus on a common enemy.

◎ Harness internal power struggles.

◎ Be bold with the enemy but humble with each other.

◎ Promote positive competition.

◎ Sharpen skills through frequent games.

◎ Glorify all who compete, not just the champions.

◎ Raise supporting positions to a place of honor.

◎ Give your people heroes to cheer.

◎ Celebrate victories with great enthusiasm.

◎ Always look to the next conquest.

VI · Persuasion

Never forget that you're dealing with people.

I t doesn't matter what industry you're in or what you do for a living. You have a set of responsibilities that contribute to the overall health and well-being of the empire. You also have a career to look after. Particularly if you do something you enjoy for a living, it's easy to get caught up in the work at hand. In fact, many people spend years at their jobs operating under the mistaken impression that, if they simply attend to the skills for which they were hired, everything will work out. But nothing could be further from the truth.

Competing tribes will derail your projects. Ambitious coworkers will compete for your promotion and resources. For a wide variety of reasons, no matter what it is that you're trying to accomplish, and regardless of whether it's for the company or your career, things will rarely go as planned. All of this is for a very simple and understandable reason: people are involved. So remember that, whenever three or more people are gathered, you will have to deal with politics.

Each person will be doing their very best to promote their personal agenda. And you have an agenda to promote as well. That's a fact that escapes a surprisingly large number of people, workers and leaders alike. Most seem to think that the only ones in the company who should be concerned with navigating the political waters are those who are trying to climb the company ladder.

Because of this incorrect assessment of the situation, some people cling—often in a very haughty manner—to the fatal assumption that they shouldn't have to play political games. They were hired to do a specific job, so, therefore, that's all that merits their attention. By refusing to acknowledge the realities of group dynamics, they relegate themselves to the status of a stationary target. Consequently, their projects fail and their careers stall. The productivity that they are truly dedicated to providing for the company never appears, all because it was hijacked by the most common villain in any social gathering, that being human nature.

It doesn't have to be this way though. No matter what your job, to succeed both for yourself and the company, you must master the art of presenting your agenda. The finer points of persuasion represent a basic skill set for those who work in sales and marketing, but for most everyone else it's a complete mystery. However, even if you do make your living among the persuasive, it never hurts to go back and review the basics because they never change. For the rest of us, however, it's critical to realize that every day is an exercise in sales. Realize this and use it to your advantage. It will make you, and the empire, that much more effective.

MAKE A FRIEND.

No matter what you're trying to accomplish, be it closing a million-dollar sale or just trying to convince the other members of your workgroup that your new idea is worth pursuing, the first step never changes. If you want someone to go along with your desires, you need to make them a friend. We all go out of our way to help people with whom we feel a personal connection. In contrast, the demanding or presumptuous individual who simply walks in and makes demands rarely gets either our sympathy or our support.

Particularly if you're speaking to someone with whom you have no prior relationship, you need to establish a relationship before doing anything else. However, even if it's someone you've worked with for twenty years, you still don't want to walk up and dive right into business. Things will go much more smoothly if you'll take the time first to warm them up a bit. In sales parlance, this is known as establishing rapport, and it's really not that hard to do.

The first step is finding something in common. Given that we're all humans, that identifies a very broad area right off the bat. Basic human needs and desires vary little from person to person or even culture to culture. We need to make a living. We want to enjoy the companionship of family and friends. We're also pretty enthusiastic about eating on a regular basis. These and many more such things can form the basis for some light, casual conversation. The reason that talking about the weather is such a cliché is due to the fact that it's a guaranteed point that everyone has in common. We're all affected by the atmospheric conditions in our area. Particularly if we happen to be standing outside without an umbrella when that atmosphere begins to descend upon us.

After striking up light banter about something you have in common, the next step is to find things you can agree on. It's easy to point people in a direction and let them go. You'll find that they will tend to follow the same path until something comes along to alter their course. For this reason, if you start out talking about things that prompt them to say "no" or become negative in any way, that's extra inertia you'll have to overcome when you want them to become positive and say "yes." Therefore, it makes sense to start out on topics that get them in a positive frame of mind. By touching on areas where they're likely to say "yes," reaffirming whatever it is that you're discussing, you've won the first battle. You want them to say "yes" to your particular desire, and you've already got them in a yes frame of mind.

Along those lines, you also want to avoid doing anything that would make them perceive you as a threat. Basic animal instincts will kick in immediately anytime we feel that our safety or well-being is in danger. Consequently, even if it's something as trivial as discussing a topic about which you're highly knowledgeable and they realize that their opinions are uninformed, you're in trouble. They're going to become defensive, even if they don't realize it, and, when it comes time to get them to agree with your ideas, they're instead going to resist you. They may not even understand why on a conscious level, but if you've flipped their switches and made them feel threatened, they'll crawl out a back window before they'll agree with you. Therefore, practice being as harmless and non-confrontational as possible in all such encounters. When you're done, you want to walk away with not only the approval of your desires, but also with new allies, not new adversaries.

LEAVE YOUR EMOTIONS AT THE DOOR.

Something else to bear in mind is that most conversations and meetings tend to go sour or get heated the moment emotions come into play. Just as in our previous example, when people's plans are challenged, they will become defensive, angry, sullen, and unreasonable. You've doubtless had your share of experience being on the other end of these feelings, and you know how it comes out in the end. The conversation almost always shifts from a discussion of the matter at hand to one of personal attacks and hurt feelings. There's not much chance of anything productive being accomplished at that point. This deterioration into emotional bickering is one of the most common and fundamental reasons for tribal warfare, and the weakness of your empire.

When things start becoming personal rather than professional, look for the first plausible excuse you can find to wrap up the conversation. Glance at your watch and frantically remember a fictitious appointment for which you're now late. Nothing good is going to be accomplished at this point, and there's a high potential for people to make mistakes and say things that will have a long-lasting and unfortunate effect, perhaps permanently damaging some relationships. Know when to walk away.

Up until now, we've been talking about everyone else's feelings. Although you don't always have complete control over another person's reactions, that limitation doesn't apply to your own. When you approach one or more people to promote your agenda, leave your emotions at the door. They'll only trip you up.

Consider this. How many times in your life have you been caught in a heated and volatile conversation? How clear was your thinking then? Was your logic impeccable, or were the lines blurry as the adrenaline worked its way through your system? If you'll think back, chances are you were also quite reactionary. When you feel like this, you're very easily manipulated, although you may not realize it.

When you are upset or are otherwise out of balance emotionally, it's very easy to see which way you'll respond. If someone wants to lead you down a certain path and you're angry, then they merely need to harness your hostile emotions by manipulating your very predictable reactions. By finding a line of reasoning that makes you progressively more upset, they'll continually poke you in the ribs and direct that anger towards the conclusions that they've plotted out. Before you know it, you may find yourself angrily making their point for them. This is just one of the many ways that people can manipulate the emotionally unbalanced, with all the skill and finesse of a highly trained martial artist.

Another problem with becoming upset is that doing so diminishes your respect and credibility. If you're in a meeting and someone wants to make you look bad, the first tactic they try may be to get you to lose your temper and react brashly. All they have to do at that point is maintain a calm, even disposition in the face of your emotional tirade. To all who are present, it will seem clear that your antagonist is a perfectly reasonable person who should be listened to and you're an uncontrollable hothead who doesn't know how to act in a professional environment. It won't matter that your plans and ideas are better. You will have lost the chance to sell people on them because you lost your credibility at the same time as your temper.

Additionally, you need to learn emotional discipline due to the nature of promoting your agenda in general. If you have ideas that you want to sell, you may be successful most of the time. However, you will have those moments when you lose. Furthermore, even when you're winning, the path to acceptance may require persevering through several rejections. If you lose your composure or become depressed each time someone tells you no, you'll give up far too early in the process. And, once again, if you allow people to see your negative emotions, you'll garner the reputation of a fragile and unstable personality who can't be counted on in day-to-day affairs because your reactions will always be in question.

Keep your cool. Maintain your balance. And, whenever you engage in the business of the day, leave your emotions behind. You can pick them up later, on your way to the victory celebration.

SPEAK THE OTHER PERSON'S LANGUAGE.

One of the most important steps toward successfully promoting your agenda is learning how to communicate effectively with others. You can have the most brilliant idea in the history of the company. You can have your plans perfectly laid out and every item justified with impeccable logic. And yet, if you can't speak the language of the people whose support you need, it all comes to naught, for they simply won't understand what it is that you're proposing. It's not enough to share the same spoken language. You have to share your vision in a manner that's meaningful to them. It's the only way that they can get excited about it.

If you're from Spain and you travel to Japan, you might have some problems communicating if you try to speak to the people on the streets in Spanish. Although you might find the occasional person who knows more than one language, in general the most you're going to get are blank stares and the Japanese equivalent of "Huh?" If you travel to a foreign country and wish to carry on meaningful dialog with the people you meet, it's your responsibility to learn their language. They have no incentive to learn yours.

Using the spoken language that we employ on a daily basis as an example makes the point in a very clear manner. Most of us have had the experience of meeting someone from another land and being frustrated by the fact that we had no way to carry on a conversation with them. However, when we all share the same spoken language and work at the same company, it's not so obvious that we even have communications obstacles.

By understanding that your audience will not hear what you're saying if you use the technical jargon specific to your particular job or skill set, you've created the opportunity for a solution. All you have to do is limit your conversation to a subset of your tribe's language that's common to the other tribes.

First, take a look at the information you were about to present. Is the level of detail you're offering really necessary, or is it just the way you're used to talking?

By taking the time to understand the other person's world and translate your desires into a perspective that's meaningful to them, you've created an opportunity to not only get your point across, but you'll have built a tighter bond with your people. Having endured countless other meetings by managers in suits who spoke in vague corporate terms, your workers will be talking at lunch about how great it is to finally have a manager who understands what they're doing. This small step can increase the enthusiasm of the people you're speaking to in a very significant manner.

One additional technique that you'll find effective is the written word. When you want to make a point, it can often be disrupted by others who ask questions and interrupt with thoughts of their own. Memos, letters, and email offer no such opportunity for disruption. You can present your case completely and comprehensively. They'll read from the beginning to the end, and you're thus able to walk them down the path that you have in mind without distraction.

However, it's important to bear in mind that email and other forms of written correspondence are much easier to ignore than a real, live human being standing right outside your office door. Nonetheless, there's a time and a place for all tactics, and, when you need your thoughts conveyed in a complete manner to be most effective, never overlook the power of the written word.

Even so, the same rules apply, whether the communications are written or oral. If you want someone to understand what you're talking about, and furthermore to become enthusiastic about supporting it, you must speak a language that they can relate to. If you go the extra step and learn to speak in their native language, you'll gain additional benefits by showing that you respect and care about them enough to have made the effort. Combined, these steps can lead you to your most effective presentations and conversations ever.

THINK IN TERMS OF THEIR BENEFIT.

The observations we just made about the value of going that extra step to learn the other person's language represent just one example of an important overriding principle: if you want people to become enthusiastic about your agenda and rally to your cause, you'll get much farther down the road by thinking from their perspective than you will by being self-centered and considering only your own wants and needs. As shocking as this may be to you, nobody cares about your needs. They're too busy thinking about their own. It's another predictable—and therefore very useful—facet of human nature.

However, focus on what's in it for the other guy, and you'll have his attention every time, without fail. Even if he's a kind-hearted soul who would have helped you just because he's nice anyway, you'll still get his attention by appealing to his own personal gain. As an added bonus, you'll carry the day with people who couldn't possibly care less about anyone but themselves. Having a single, unified tactic that will work in all cases is an efficient and dependable way to build your overall strategy.

Consequently, your first step in promoting your own interests should be to consider the people whom your plan will involve. These are the people whom you need to support, the people who authorize your ideas, and any groups or individuals who might resist the plans due to competing initiatives or tribal warfare. Put forth the effort to understand who all of the players are and what goals and priorities drive each of them. The more you know of their personal agendas, what they're looking to accomplish both in the company and in their private lives, the better position you're in to find a creative solution.

Next, consider the specific goals you have in mind as an overlay, and see how it interacts with their desires. If you succeed in getting what you want, does that cause trouble for some of them? Knowing these things shows you exactly where people will fight you, and why. By extension, and more importantly, it shows you not only how to avoid a conflict, but how to gain enthusiastic supporters.

Now, based on what you've seen in terms of the threats you pose and the potential benefits that you might offer to those around you, it's time to make some choices and consider your tactics. First, take a look at your own desires. Take the time to prioritize all of your targets in order of their importance to you. This will show you if you could concede or forego any items to make your idea more attractive to others without costing you anything important. Compromise can be a very powerful tool.

By giving true and sincere consideration to the well being of others, you also gain one other subtle but powerful benefit. Regardless of the specific gains that you promote to others and how much they truly care about them, one thing will come shining through every time. Your audience will see that you obviously took the time to consider them, understand their goals, and care about their feelings. People like that sort of thing.

Very few will jump up and down making a big deal about this, but it will have a very strong effect on each individual—and on a very fundamental level—whether they realize it or not. Humans are social creatures. It makes us feel good when others in the herd show us attention, kindness, and consideration. It makes us feel important and valued by others. In fact, many people go out of their way to be the recipient of such feelings.

If you think of other people and how they can personally benefit from your ideas, you will be manipulating them at a very low level, giving them powerful motivations to go along with your plan. We normally think of manipulation as a bad thing, but, when you're leading them from their current position to one where they're in even better shape, that's a positive thing, made all the more so because you've also achieved your objectives.

PERFECT YOUR TIMING.

Anyone who has braved the cold stage and hot spotlight to present themselves to an indifferent crowd in the role of a standup comedian will tell you that, without a doubt, timing is everything. They may also be able to share some great tips for removing tomato stains from your clothing, but that's a separate issue. What the standup comic knows that most people promoting their agenda fail to consider is that the perfect line will fall on deaf ears if delivered at an inopportune moment.

The first and most obvious thing you should consider when approaching anyone to further your agenda is the current state of affairs as it pertains to your idea or initiative. For example, if you're trying to increase departmental productivity, you may have a great idea for some bonuses and incentives that you're sure will spur people on to new heights. Because this requires spending money, you're always going to be competing with other people who are after a cut of the same budget. However, even if you can completely justify your idea and it's the hands-down winner, that's not going to matter in the slightest if your company just went through a series of massive layoffs. Above and beyond the fact that your budget has probably already evaporated, think of how your boss would look if he approved bonuses at a time like this. A couple of months later, after the pain of the moment has passed, you'll get a much more receptive ear.

Another situational consideration is that of your audience's current standing. Let's say that your company is doing fine, and there were no layoffs. In fact, things look so rosy that your manager just made a few departmental expenditures that were considered to be a bit frivolous by his superiors, enough so that he was called on the carpet and given a strong reprimand for his fiscal irresponsibility. While his posterior is still smoking from the encounter, it's going to be a pretty good bet that he'll be a little gun shy about spending money for a paperclip, let alone going along with your bonus ideas. Once again, though, this will pass. In a week or two, the bruised ego will heal, and he'll then hear your ideas based on their merit instead of considering them from an emotional point of view and wondering if they'll just cause him to get chewed out again.

You can approach someone with a great idea, knowing full well that the timing as far as the company is concerned will never be better, and still fall flat on your face if the person you're trying to win over is in a bad or unreasonable mood. It doesn't matter what the reason for that mood is, either. Unhappy people are cranky, contentious, and difficult to deal with. If you should encounter such a situation, the next move is clear: walk away. Come back later in the week, when they've regained their normal balance and perspective. If you approach them any sooner, the answer is very likely to be *no*.

And don't even mention it to them briefly with the thought of planting a seed in their mind for later. If you do, then next week when you sit down to talk about it, they'll have a negative feeling in the pit of their stomach about your plan because that was their reaction when you first mentioned it. The fact that they would have had a bad reaction to someone offering them a gourmet dinner for free at that time will be completely forgotten. They'll just have a bad feeling about it, and it will influence their later reactions to your presentation. These are subconscious feelings, and people rarely bother to analyze such things.

What you want to do is just the opposite: approach them when they seem to be in a normal frame of mind, or, better still, when they seem to be in a particularly good mood. Believe it or not, an average emotional setting is actually better in many cases than catching them in some sort of euphoric state because you don't have to worry about a backlash effect. Sometimes, people will agree to things when they're in a really good mood that they might have considered more carefully at another time. This means that, when their emotions settle back down, they're going to reconsider their decision, and you may have to fight the battle a second time. If you catch them in their business-as-usual state, you can be fairly confident that they'll stick with whatever they commit to.

ASK FOR MORE THAN YOU WANT.

This next trick is so fundamental and pervasive in the marketplace that it almost seems too obvious to mention. It's the tactic of suggested retail prices. We're assaulted with this method of marketing literally every single day of our lives, to the extent that our senses become dulled to the approach. On American television, we're bombarded with offers of products that normally sell for $100 but are available today through this special offer for just $19.95. TV advertising is *extremely* expensive. They wouldn't keep using this angle if it didn't work. You'd think that, because we'd seen it so often, we wouldn't fall for it, but we do, time and time again. Not just the sheep that can be herded into buying anything, but even reasonable and intelligent human beings. Why?

Part of the reason is as old as marketing itself. If you tell people what they want to hear, they'll believe it. Anyone with any common sense realizes that, if a product normally sells for five times the offered price, it's financial suicide to sell it for a fifth of that as the reduced price doesn't likely even cover the cost of manufacturing. Nonetheless, people get caught up in the excitement of the sales pitch, and they really, really want to believe that they're getting a great deal. Therefore, even though the price is, and has always been, $19.95, they'll walk away feeling like they saved $80.05 and made out like a bandit.

There's also a bargaining aspect to consider when you state your initial requests. I've lost track of how many times I've seen people go after a new contract, customer, or even a job and, in the first round of negotiations, ask for no more than the minimum that they needed to make the effort profitable. Typically, the customer bargains, and, when it's all said and done, they end up working cheap. Really cheap. All because, in the beginning, they didn't ask for more than they wanted.

Fear accounts for a part of this: people are basically afraid that, if they ask for too much, the other person will balk and immediately say "no." If that's the case, then the idea you're selling wasn't very compelling to begin with. If someone is going to say "no" and slam the door in your face just because you asked for the moon, other issues beyond the price are involved here. Therefore, you have to take a deep breath and ask for more than you think you can get, and say it like you truly expect to get it.

One of my clients is a small consulting firm that bills by the hour for its services. The principal is very good at what he does, and has not only a good reputation in the industry but also a bit of fame. Even so, every time he contacts me about a set of negotiations, I'm astounded at how little he's prepared to ask for in return for the job he's doing.

Consequently, I continually urge my client on each bid to propose a much higher price than what he's comfortable with. He never gets the amount I suggest, for the customer always bargains. However, when the deal is closed, he always gets more than he was originally planning on asking for. Furthermore, buyers always assume that they get what they pay for, and in his case it's true. They paid higher-than-average rates, and his firm did an excellent job. The customers are not only delighted and come back to do business with him again, but they often take pride in paying the higher fees. Clearly, it's a company that settles for nothing but the best.

No matter what you're asking for, the most important thing to consider is that any transaction is a process of bargaining, whether it's with careers or customers. If you don't ask for more than you want then you have no room to compromise, come down a little, and make the deal. Never ask for your rock-bottom requirements up front. Always pad it with more than what you want. If you get more than you needed, it's a nice bonus. At worst, you'll get what you absolutely must have, and the other party will feel clever for having bargained hard with you and beaten your price down. You get what you want, and the other person feels good about the deal. Everybody wins.

~~~~~~~~~~~~~~~~~~◎~~~~~~~~~~~~~~~

GIVE THEM A REASON TO ACT NOW.

Often, people will have their plan completely organized and make a stunning proposal, only to be greeted with a response of, "we'll think about it and get back to you." This is typically a very subtle way of saying "no." Most of the time, if people put off making a decision, it's because you didn't make the sale. It's over. You just don't realize that it's over.

You'll also find that this is a tactic frequently used by people who have difficulties with confrontation. If, for whatever reason, they're not comfortable telling you "no" to your face, they'll simply put off the decision. That way, there's no immediate pressure from you because they didn't really say "no," and their hope is that, if they ignore you for long enough after that, or continue to put you off, you'll eventually go away. None of which helps you accomplish your objectives. How do you overcome this potential obstacle? After all, asking for a little time to think things over is rarely an unreasonable request.

The secret to motivating people and encouraging them to make an immediate decision in your favor comes back to a theme that we've continually encountered as we look at ways to unify the tribes and build a stronger empire. It's the age-old question: *what's in it for them?*

People are not going to leap into action because you have a need. They're going to get excited and active because *they* have a desire. Therefore, you need to show them why it's in *their* best interests to act now. Simply put, you must offer them some sort of incentive that makes it worth their while to act now and not later. In sales parlance, this is known as *creating urgency*.

This is another of those tactics that are almost invisible to us because we see them so often that we're conditioned to think that way. I've seen the most intelligent and rational people scoff at television ads that speak in urgent tones about a limited-time offer on the latest $19.95 gizmo, and then insist that they be given the day off work to go buy a new car because the newspaper says it's a one-day-only sale. No matter how logically you try to explain it, they will refuse to understand that it's the same approach in both cases.

A close relative to the limited-time offer is the limited supply. The first sales job I ever had involved a pitch in which we were instructed to tell customers that yes, it was an excellent deal on the product at hand, but unfortunately we only had three boxes left. We knew that we had a live one when they asked how many were in a box.

Of course, we had a warehouse full of product, and the quantities per box were completely irrelevant. Based on what we'd learned about the customer and how much we thought they might buy, we would say that the box held anywhere from three to one hundred of whatever we were selling, always following our previous rule of asking for more than we expected to get. The typical successful response was along the lines of "twelve in a box?! There's no way I can use thirty-six of these things! I'll sure take a box, though."

Whether they needed the product right now or not, they were motivated to place the order because, when those three boxes were gone, the price would go back up to normal. They had to buy *now* if they wanted the special deal, because, at these prices, they were going fast.

This leads to the next method of creating urgency: competition. When someone would waffle on the commitment, saying that they'd think about it and get back to us later, we would become suddenly nonchalant, explaining that we understood and it really didn't matter because another customer was supposed to call back in a few minutes to take all three boxes. Now, with the prospect of someone else snatching their deal out from under them, they would suddenly change their mind and place the order before they lost the opportunity.

Naturally, the specific techniques I've listed thus far are but a few examples of the many ways that you can create urgency, and you'll have to apply these principles to your own specific situations. The most important thing to remember is that it doesn't matter how great your ideas are: if you don't give the person a reason to act *now,* you'll still be sitting there twiddling your thumbs and waiting for a decision when the cows come home.

BE PREPARED FOR OBJECTIONS.

N o matter how carefully you prepare, when it gets down to making a case for your plans, there's a very good chance that the person you're speaking with will throw out a couple of reasons why they don't want to go along with the program. In the sales business, these are called objections, and they're overcome with rebuttals. Sometimes your presentation or hall meeting will go flawlessly, and you'll win without a fight. However, if you're not prepared to survive and prevail in a scrap each time you present your ideas, they'll eventually carry you home on your shield.

The first and most important thing you can do to be ready for resistance is to take some time and think from the other person's perspective. Be the bad guy. Be brutally honest and think of every flaw in your plan. Write each one down as it comes to you. Really. Get a pen. We'll wait.

You will never be able to build a comprehensive set of rebuttals that works 100% of the time. You'll always encounter that one wise guy who comes up with something you didn't consider, and you'll be forced to think on your feet. Even so, the reason that structured and successful sales organizations maintain highly detailed lists of the most common objections and train their staff in overcoming them is because, most of the time, it's sufficient to win the day.

Now that you've got a list of highly detailed insights that show just exactly how insane your little hare-brained scheme was, it's time to get creative. Climb back over the fence and once again view things from your original perspective. Yes, your idea is still brilliant. Furthermore, the only reason that anyone would raise an objection is a blatant lack of understanding.

All of which, of course, brings us back to your initial list of objections. Now that you have a list of every possible flaw that you can find in your plan, and you understand the spirit in which they must be answered, you're ready to get to work. For each objection, find a way to put a positive spin on it. Is their opinion simply misinformed? Explain the part that they missed. Are they pointing out a small problem that is overshadowed by much larger benefits? Put the two side by side so that they can see for themselves that it still winds up with a net profit. Do they not see the need for your solution? You didn't paint the problem vividly enough. Try again, and this time make the monsters big and scary. In a similar manner, walk through every item on your list and, using logic, sound reasoning, and an obvious consideration of their own well-being, use each negative as an excuse to explain why they must act, and *now*.

When you're done creating your list of every possible objection that could be raised, you should have an answer for each one you've listed. Next, you need to compress the wording of your rebuttals down to just a few sentences. Lengthy replies lose people's attention. Now, practice with a friend. Make your pitch, have them throw out objections, and practice your comebacks. Allow for the flexibility of natural speaking. It's good to memorize your rebuttals, but, if you insist on delivering them exactly as you've written them down, you'll eventually find yourself in a position where they don't fit exactly and you'll look foolish. Burn the *idea* of the rebuttal into your brain, and be prepared to use it. That's what's important.

One last tip. Always start your rebuttal by agreeing with and validating their objection. People like it when you agree with them. By acknowledging that they had a reasonable thought, you're building bridges instead of creating conflict. Furthermore, the more legitimate their objection, the more powerful your rebuttal because it solves a significant problem for all to see.

No battle plan ever survives contact with the enemy. Be prepared for people to object to your plan. This is the single biggest difference between the people who are successful in promoting their agenda and the people who have brilliant ideas but get slam-dunked in every meeting. When you're prepared for every obstacle, the only possible outcome is victory.

〰〰〰〰〰〰〰〰〰◎〰〰〰〰〰〰〰〰〰

GET AN AGREEMENT.

I've met some very convincing and charismatic people in my day. Some folks just naturally have the gift of gab and could charm the birds out of the trees with little effort. Every word from their lips seems golden. Their reasoning and timing is impeccable, and soon the entire room is nodding their heads in agreement. To anyone looking on from the outside, it would seem a foregone conclusion that this person will undoubtedly get their way. And, yet, when the room empties and everyone goes their separate ways, he leaves without the decisive victory he sought. It wasn't that anyone objected to his plans. They just never agreed. If they don't say "yes," you lose.

So what went wrong? This is an extremely common mistake even among the people who sell things for a living. They give stellar performances, have the audience weeping with joy, build enough enthusiasm to power a small city, and then forget to ask for a decision. Because they asked for nothing, that's exactly what happens.

Having shown people the problem, how it affects them personally, and how your idea will provide an excellent solution, you have to cross that last bridge and help your audience make the transition from understanding to acting. They won't do it alone, no matter how obvious the need for action may be. You have to lead them by the hand and get them to make a commitment. Before you can declare victory, people have to orally, and sometimes in writing, say that, yes, they'll do exactly what you propose, and they'll do it now. Anything short of that will accomplish nothing. But how do you get them to make this pledge? You *ask* them.

This, in the language of the professional salesman, is known as *closing*, as it's short for "closing the deal." Consequently, your request that they make a commitment is known as a *closing question*. These are sometimes involved or subtle statements, but there's one closing question that you have known intuitively since you were a small child. It's a one-word query: "Okay?"

Even though it may strike you as very simplistic, this is an extremely robust technique because it relies on the gut instincts of human nature. It's not merely the word that does wonders, however.

Telling someone what you want to do and then asking "Okay?" *firmly*, as a question, and with the attitude that you clearly expect them to agree, will get you many commitments. This vocal trick can be applied in a variety of ways, and you'll instinctively hear the effect when you practice. You do practice, right? Good. Just checking.

Sometimes, you'll want to get a series of small agreements as you go along just to get them used to saying "yes" so that, when the time for a decision comes, it'll come naturally. If you intersperse phrases such as "You know what I mean?", "Right?", "You with me?", and other similar phrases, people will actually nod their heads in agreement with you. When you get down to your final "Okay?", they won't know what to do with their heads other than to nod them up and down.

No matter what you're asking of someone, they won't make a commitment unless you ask for one. Don't be afraid to use human nature to your advantage. Above all, however, always remember that, if you don't have a good plan, all the closing questions in the world aren't going to help you. Make sure that what you've put together is effective and that it has legitimate benefits. Then just ask them to agree, okay?

BELIEVE!

Our last technique is not a technique at all, and yet nothing in all we've covered thus far will work without it. It's so incredibly simple as to need very little explanation, and most of the discussion required is necessary only to make you understand what an absolutely crucial component this is to your presentation. No matter what you're proposing or who your audience is, the most fundamental rule to follow is a very straightforward one. You've gotta believe.

But believe in what? That magic pixies are going to come in the night to solve all of your problems while you sleep? Sorry. It doesn't work that way. A career as a pixie is a union gig, and they don't work nights. No, what you must believe is that you will succeed, that people will say "yes" when you ask them for a commitment. Does that seem like something so obvious that even a grade school student doesn't need it explained to them? Let's examine this.

If, deep down in your gut, you don't believe that you're going to succeed, that subconscious conviction is going to come out in your personality and interaction with others. You've met many people in your life who exhibit this in an extreme enough way to illustrate the point. It's the guy who, no matter what you say, shakes his head and sighs that, no, things will just never work out for him.

Of course, chances are good that you don't exhibit these tendencies to such a degree. However, you also don't need a calculator to show you that, if you feel only half as strongly that you'll fail as our unfortunate example, then your chances for success will still be reduced by, you guessed it, half. Who wants to go into battle with those kinds of odds? Not me.

Let's consider the opposite extreme. This is the person who's always smiling, always seems happy, and is always optimistic that, yes, he's going to succeed. Everything will work out just fine. He's got a bounce in his step, and, even when he encounters difficulties, his attitude is not one of unhappiness at his misfortune. Instead, you'll hear him musing out loud, saying, "Hmmm, now how do I solve *this* problem?" Careful attention to his attitude and vocal inflections will make it clear that he knows he's going to solve the problem, the only question is how.

So, let's do a little simple and realistic math here. Obviously, it's highly unlikely that our positive friend here will succeed 100% of the time throughout the duration of his life. Our negative friend, though, believing he will fail, may very well come close to a 100% failure rate. No matter what the actual percentages are, however, it should be clear that, given identical situations, one person will tally up an impressive list of successes, and the other will fail time and time again. And here's the thing to note. *Neither of them will be surprised at the results.*

There are two other aspects of believing in your inevitable success that you can see in the real world: confidence and charisma. Someone who truly believes in their abilities and strides down the hall without a shadow of doubt will often have other people right behind them. People follow confidence.

That quality, and that quality alone, is enough to rally people to your cause. Even if your ideas are bad and destined to fail, if you present them with conviction many people will follow you right off the edge of the cliff without giving it a second thought. It's human nature.

If, on the other hand, you do your homework and have a solid and realistic plan, and you walk up to people with unshakeable confidence in the outcome, you're going to experience more than just a single success. You'll get the snowball effect. As you lead, whether it's from the front or the middle, your successes will draw the attention of others. Everybody wants to be on the winning team, and, because of that, you'll draw more and more support. Because this increased support gives you greater power to make things happen, you'll have ever more confidence in the outcome. When you talk, people will listen. When you recommend, they will concur. And, when you lead, even if it's from within the ranks, they will follow.

All because you believe.

PERSUASION

Never forget that you're dealing with people.

- ◉ Make a friend.
- ◉ Leave your emotions at the door.
- ◉ Speak the other person's language.
- ◉ Think in terms of their benefit.
- ◉ Perfect your timing.
- ◉ Ask for more than you want.
- ◉ Give them a reason to act now.
- ◉ Be prepared for objections.
- ◉ Get an agreement.
- ◉ Believe!

VII | Strategy

Teach tactical skills to every person in the empire.

M ost companies are run from the top down, which is the classic organization followed in the old business model. The concept is very simple and easy to grasp: the people who hold the highest positions in a firm are obviously really smart and educated and thus more capable of charting a course and guiding the company than the lowly, uneducated masses who do the actual labor. As you might imagine by now, this perspective has several flaws.

The people who have the least amount of input regarding the company's overall direction and strategy in the marketplace are those who have the most practical view of the empire. Your frontline workers—the ones whose opinions many casually disregard—are precisely the people who are out there actually coping with the day-to-day situations as your company does business. No matter how good the plan sounds in the boardroom, the frontline workers are the ones who confront reality and either make it happen or suffer the consequences of unrealistic direction from on high.

They're also the ones peering out of the trenches and staring the enemy in the face. Who better to inform you of what tactics are working, what ones aren't, and what practical new steps to take? To be their most effective in the heat of battle, these people need the skills and ability to plan, scheme, strategize, and think on their feet. If they don't have it, your competitors will overrun them.

However, your workers aren't the only ones who need tactical training. Just because some individuals have a position in middle or upper management doesn't guarantee that they are brilliant strategists. They may be very good at what they do and possess many other valuable qualities, but that doesn't mean that they'll know what to do in a crisis, nor does it ensure that they have the long- or short-range planning skills to avoid the crisis in the first place. Chances are good that it's just not what they were hired for.

Consequently, at every level of your company, you have people who desperately need training in the art of war. They're not getting it, and, because of this deficiency, the empire suffers. If everyone in your company gave daily thought and consideration to improving their abilities in strategic matters, you would be so fierce and unstoppable in the marketplace that your competitors would all be asking you to buy them out rather than face you in battle. No matter what the job, ways can always be found to improve and build a better, more productive tomorrow. To do this, you need strategy.

REALIZE THAT BUSINESS IS WAR.

Remember that companies are all competing for revenue and turf. Your competitors want your market share, your income, your customer base, and even the best of your people. Only so many consumer dollars are available for your particular product or service, and your company isn't the only one who wants it. If you don't have a clear picture of this and the threat to your well-being that it implies, you will be totally unprepared for the curves that others in the marketplace throw you.

If you don't appreciate the fact that others perceive you as a threat, you will not bother building adequate defenses. When they strike at you to eliminate this threat to their own prosperity, you will never see it coming and you will make an easy target. It's worth mentioning that living as a target is not an entirely pleasant way to spend your days. Therefore, you absolutely must realize that you are locked in a fierce struggle with your competitors and must prepare appropriately or be destroyed. And it's always worth reiterating that, if your company is demolished, you, the individual, will be out of a job.

Of course, business is a martial exercise on many other fronts as well. For you to bring your very best efforts to the company as a whole, you have to survive many internal threats that have nothing whatsoever to do with your true enemy, the competition. Throughout your enterprise, tribes both large and small are competing for budgets, projects, and control. Sometimes they're clearly recognizable as individual departments or workgroups, but, other times, it's a collection of people who have together to promote their particular agenda.

The warfare doesn't end at the tribal level, though. Even within your group, people vie for power and position. There are promotions to fight for, juicy job assignments to struggle over, not to mention raises, bonuses, and even such seemingly trivial bits of plunder as a corner office or an assigned parking space. No matter what it is, if it's a perk, people will compete for it.

Furthermore, it doesn't matter if you want to play the game. You're in it whether you like it or not. At the personal, tribal, and company levels, these skirmishes are a part of your daily life. There's an old joke about engineers and architects, undoubtedly put forward by the former: engineers build weapons systems, and architects build targets. If your position happens to be a target in any way, shape, or form, you can ignore that fact all you like, but you still won't be immune to your adversaries' weapons.

The only way that you'll ever be able to devise effective defenses and strategies for conquest is to first realize that you're in a battle zone. That knowledge gives you the proper context for your actions, along with a reasonably high degree of motivation. There's nothing like the sound of an arrow whizzing toward your head to make you realize that, yes, now would be a great time to duck.

Whether you work in manual labor, the back office, customer service, middle management, or even as the CEO, your job effectiveness will not be at its peak if you don't analyze your daily situations, define the problems, and come up with new strategies to cope with the obstacles you encounter. You will never even consider doing this, however, until you first recognize that your everyday existence is set amidst a constantly changing backdrop of aggression from others, at several different levels.

Armed with practical insight and a realistic assessment of your environment, you'll know exactly what steps need to be taken and will be highly motivated to do so. In short, there's no point building a strategy unless you have something to accomplish. Realizing that business is war and that arrows are uncomfortable to sit on give you all the reasons in the world to improve your tactical skills.

KNOW YOUR ENEMY.

Divisions, departments, and groups of people—both those officially organized and those loosely confederated—will frequently pursue their own agendas without regard to the health and well-being of the company itself. Their prevalent attitude is to look out for their personal interests exclusively and at all costs, and to let the company take care of itself. These groups will hoard resources, manipulate circumstances to build power, and are often very subtle and secretive in their workings. Still, no matter how practiced they are in the ways of cloak and dagger, you will know them by their spirit and their actions, regardless of what they say to the contrary.

When evaluating such groups, ask yourself a few simple questions. No matter how many fine words they may use, what are the consequences of their actions? Do they profit at the expense of other departments or individuals? What about the output of their labors? Does it benefit them or the company as a whole? Do they live true to their word, or do they always have a reason or excuse when others suffer because of their actions? By considering such things, it's easy for even the most innocent soul to see that these groups do not have the good of the many in mind. As such, even though they may be productive to a degree, they remain a threat to the empire.

Having identified the various pockets of trouble in your area, your next step is to study them carefully. What are their goals and agenda? Where will it take them? Who stands between them and what they want? As you paint an ever-clearer picture of what their desires are and what steps they need to take to achieve them, you'll have a very reliable roadmap that will show you where they are likely to strike next and what their objectives will be. Many times, this is the most important information you could have in your own camp, as it tells you by inference what your next steps should be to prevent the damage they're about to inflict on others.

Keeping a record of their antics will also serve you well. History tends to repeat itself, and people will naturally employ similar tactics over and over again, for no other reason than the finite extent of our tactical skills. If you want to predict the future, keep accurate records of the past, for the wheel will always come around again.

I strongly encourage you to keep a personal journal in which you detail such observations and any conclusions that you're able to draw from them. And never, ever, keep it at work. As melodramatic as it may sound, if it should fall into the wrong hands, you're completely vulnerable. Even more so if you're never aware that it's been read. When it comes to strategy and battle tactics, I trust neither man nor machine. My journals are kept in cheap, run-of-the-mill spiral notebooks that I buy at the grocery store. Computers crash; paper doesn't. And these notebooks also never leave my home, under any circumstances. And, yes, in fact, they are stored close to my collection of swords and assorted weaponry, but I'm sure that's just a coincidence.

It's also important to see where your enemies present the greatest threat to you, your group, and the company at large. Even though you want to consider the good of the company as your highest priority, remember that, if they're successful in attacking you personally, you may not be around to protect the company. People lose jobs to tribal warfare every day, so don't be the next victim. If you become a casualty, you're useless to the empire.

Determining where they pose the most danger is a similar exercise to observing their weaknesses. What weapons do they use? How do they use them? What types of targets do they strike? Do they work individually or as a unit? If you know how they're armed and what their methods of attack are, you'll know how to defend yourself.

Once again, your journal will serve you well. Over the course of time, there will be many battles, and they will not win them all. Take special note of who has been effective against them, and how they achieved the success. Even if you have an enemy who learns and adapts quickly, the history of their failures will lead you to the next effective tactics against them.

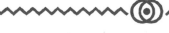

BUILD STRONG ALLIANCES.

No one stands alone—not for very long, at least. You may be the single most brilliant person in your company, but, without the support and protection of others, you will eventually fall prey to tribal warfare. One of the oldest rules of the animal kingdom applies equally to the business world: there is strength and safety in numbers.

When people think about building alliances, the first and most natural step that they take is to start networking with other like-minded people in their department. This is, without a doubt, an excellent first step. The more strength you can build in your own tribe, the stronger a force you will be for the overall good of the empire. But why stop there?

If you truly want to extend your reach and build a powerful base from which to work, stretch out. Get to know the people who work in all the other departments of your company. It will probably seem obvious to you that the more people you can align yourself with, the stronger your position will be. What may not be as clear, however, is the reason that you would want to have anything at all to do with people who work in departments far removed from your own.

Becoming familiar with other aspects of your company's operations will give you a much better view of the big picture. If you're a vice president, you are naturally expected to think at a high and abstract level. However, just as the guy working on the assembly line in the manufacturing department isn't going to have much insight into this year's profit-and-loss statement, you haven't got a clue what really goes on down there on the shop floor. Unless you have friends in the right places, that is.

Building these alliances, regardless of the person or department, is easier than you may think. If you take the time to understand other people's goals and priorities, doing so will put you in an excellent position to know what you bring to the party. You must think in terms of their benefit. Look deep into your own skills, contacts, and environment, and make a list of all the things that you could do to help them.

Next, look for opportunities for casual conversation and interaction so that you can start building a friendship, for the best alliances are always built on this most valuable attribute of society. As you spend time talking with your new friends, listen to what their problems are and where their weaknesses lie. Knowing what they need, you then offer your aid and resources wherever you can, expecting nothing in return. This last thought is an important one. If people think you're being nice to them only because you want something from them, it immediately cheapens the relationship and breeds mistrust.

However, human nature being what it is, if you don't offer a good reason for your offer of help, they'll fill in the blanks for themselves, and it will rarely reflect on you in a flattering way. So, because you need to offer a reasonable explanation for your benevolence, simply tell the truth. Shocking, isn't it? Nonetheless, the true reason you're helping them is a concept that you also want to reinforce in their own mind: that there's strength and safety in numbers. Explain to them that you think highly of their work and you therefore feel that, by joining forces, you'll all be stronger for the experience. That's believable, and, better still, it's *true*.

In all that you do, simply assume the union with your new comrades. Let them see it as evident from your actions and attitudes that you consider them an ally and intend to move forward with their best interests in mind. Although there's a time and a place to explicitly ask someone for a commitment to an alliance, you'll find that you can frequently build strong bonds just by acting as though they already exist. Of course, you don't want to present vulnerabilities or expose critical information until you've seen indications in their own actions and attitudes that they're willing to do the same for you. That's just common sense. However, aside from normal caution in exposing your weaknesses, you'll find that the single easiest method of building a strong and powerful alliance is to simply treat others as a friend.

CULTIVATE AN INFORMATION NETWORK.

An important aspect of the alliances you build is the cumulative knowledge base and information network that results. Advance notice and inside information are some of the strongest advantages you'll have in any struggle. Just as you never want to give warning of your plans before you put them into action, your opponents feel the very same way. The reason for this is a matter of obvious practicality: if you know what your adversaries are up to, you can be prepared and thwart their initiatives while promoting your own.

As you build friends and create unions, you'll have an ever-increasing stream of tips, insights, and knowledge at your disposal. Naturally, it's easiest to think of individuals when building this network. It's much easier to communicate with one person than it is with a hundred. If you have a touch of cloak and dagger in you, you can even think in terms of cultivating spies who roam the empire in search of useful tidbits that help your cause. In general, the smaller the number, all the way down to the individual, the greater the stealth that can be employed.

Still, building alliances among tribes has some natural benefits as well, for in the end that's what we're reaching for. The various departments, social cliques, and other groups that people in your company fall into will represent a great many opportunities for networking. Wherever you find a group, you will find an agenda that's being promoted. Just as we discussed previously, an easy way to get the ball rolling is to volunteer some useful information that you're privy to facilitate the exchange and flow of information. The great thing about aligning your tribes with others is the increase in cumulative knowledge. The more people in your far-flung network, the better the chance that someone's going to hear something you'll want to know.

No matter whom you may be talking with, one of the easiest ways to get them to share their expertise and knowledge is to simply show an honest and sincere interest in them and the details of their life. Another little jewel of human nature is that most everyone enjoys talking about themselves. There's nothing wrong with this, nor is there anything wrong with using this fact to broaden your network. You make others feel good by treating them with interest and respect, and you improve your cause by learning from them. Everybody wins.

In most cases, you won't have a way to physically reward those informants who bring you juicy tidbits or hidden insights. Often, the reciprocal relationship is all that you have the power to give. Nonetheless, always be on the lookout for ways to reward people who do good things for you, even if you must occasionally dip into your own pocket to do so. Something as simple as buying lunch for a friend and valued confidant can work wonders in building a relationship. As has often been said about holiday gift giving, the thought behind the action is the most valuable gift of all. These people are important to you and can help you a great deal. Showing your gratitude in a tangible way will always be well received.

Most importantly, you should always be on the lookout yourself for new and timely information that will benefit your allies. It's only natural for us to approach our day-to-day endeavors from a self-centered perspective, and, in this context, that's not a negative thing. If you don't look out for yourself, your competitors will demolish you. How much good will you be to others at that point?

However, this is just the default way of looking at things. If you add to that self-centered perspective an ever-present desire to ferret out crucial facts for those who are your friends, or that you hope will soon be counted among them, you'll realize that you encounter a wealth of knowledge out there on a daily basis. Although much of it will be widely known by your allies, you will from time to time bump into time-critical or sensitive information that your friends would never know about were it not for you. You were always surrounded by these details, but, because you weren't interested in them from your own perspective, you never noticed. Once you start looking, though, you'll be amazed at what you can find that will benefit others. Sharing these discoveries with them builds powerful bonds and fuels the bonfires of a united empire.

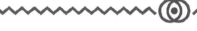

THINK SEVERAL STEPS AHEAD.

No matter what your plans are and how you go about executing them, you're going to continually encounter the unexpected. Some of your ideas will work brilliantly, and others will fall a little short of expectations when faced with the cold, hard light of reality. Most importantly, you must never forget that, anytime you make a plan, the enemy gets a vote. All of this adds up to a single, inescapable conclusion: each initiative you embark upon has more than one possible outcome.

The fundamental concept to consider in this regard is that there are no actions without consequences. The consequences may not always be obvious, and they may not always be visible, but, without question, each and every action you take will in fact generate consequences. Many, many more than you would expect, unless you really sit down and think about it.

The key to seeing the consequences to your actions lies a step beyond this. For every move you're prepared to make, stop and think about the situation from your adversary's perspective. If you were in his shoes, what are the different ways that you might respond? You can probably think of several. Now realize that what you've just done is to consider the problem in terms of how *you* would handle it if you were in his position. The perspective gained will still be useful in planning, but by itself it's not sufficient.

You must now add to those possible consequences a list of responses that he might make according to how *he* thinks. This will build a collection of moves that he might make, based not only on your perspective but on his as well. To this, add one more set of possibilities. Everyone has their influences. Close attention will have revealed to you that a select group of people frequently advises him on strategy and tactics. Through observation and meticulous note-taking, you'll also come to understand how they think. Once again, consider the threats you pose and the openings you've created from their perspective, and add the ways that they might respond to your list of possible consequences.

The important thing to keep in mind is that you must, and I mean absolutely *must*, think about the consequences of your actions and how the enemy can use them to your disadvantage. In doing so, it's also advisable to make long-term plans loose and keep your detailed plans limited to very short-term initiatives. You won't be able to keep track of the complexities for every step in a large-scale plan, and you will therefore become sloppy and careless about the consequences. It is at that point that the enemy will breach your defenses, burn your ranch, and steal your cattle. The cows will not be impressed with your tactical skills.

Therefore, be thorough in your short-term plans, but always maintain a sense of flexibility. If you keep a dynamic element to your plans, you'll be prepared to react quickly when the need arises, as it frequently will.

Lastly, you must realize that plans are not written in stone. As you put your initiatives into play, you must make it a standard practice to take another look at your strategy with each new development. In most cases, you'll proceed according to plan. However, sometimes your enemy will do something extremely clever that knocks your initiative completely off the tracks. Because you've been constantly analyzing the changing situation, though, you'll be prepared to quickly alter your tactics at the first sign of trouble. He who fails to continually reexamine his plan in the heat of battle will eventually run straight into a wall because he didn't change course. But you're always thinking ahead, and you'll be ready when this happens to your opponents and will therefore seize the moment.

ALWAYS HAVE A BACKUP PLAN.

In addition to being aware of all possible reactions, it's important to maintain an alternate route for every initiative you embark upon. In fact, it's best to have as many contingencies as possible at every step of the way. Daily life is full of unexpected little adventures, both large and small. In fact, I'll declare that that's one of the few constants in life that you can count on no matter what.

One of the oft-contested points of redundant systems, spare parts, and detailed backup plans is the fact that all this effort is typically wasted. Disaster never strikes, and so this time, money, and effort was all for nothing. In fact, many people will try to commandeer these resources for just that reason. To make matters worse, should disaster actually strike, they won't be the people to take the heat. You will, though, because it was your responsibility to make sure that the world kept turning as it should.

For the people doing the planning, it's actually their greatest hope that their backup scheme will never come into play, even if they're perfectly prepared. There is always an element of risk in switching from plan A to plan B at the last instant. It's better that you should avoid such excitement in your life. Nonetheless, if you don't have a plan B, you're in for a very bad experience should the unexpected strike. If you have one and you put it into action, no one will care how long those resources sat idle before they saved the day. And, of course, should this happen, you'll make note of it in your journal as further justification for your control of all the equipment that's required for your backup plan.

Therefore, if you want to build a robust and long-lasting empire that will provide for you and your family for many years to come, you must constantly be thinking in terms of a backup plan for everything you do, no matter what your job. Make it a habit to continually look for the critical failure points in every action or process with which you're involved, and then come up with a plan to put out the fire should it flare up—and preferably in such a smooth and seamless manner that no one ever realizes there was a glitch to begin with.

Along those lines, you should hang another motto on your walls: *Always keep a spare.* Of course, it's not feasible to have a physical backup for every piece of equipment or bit of supplies in your domain, but you should endeavor to build your stock of spares as much as you possibly can. It will always give you an advantage in battle, for few people are diligent about this.

In the heat of the fight, when an important part goes bad or a critical supply runs out, you can be sure that it will happen after business hours or on a weekend, making it impossible to get a replacement for hours or even days. When your competitors encounter this, you'll see nothing but a stream of perfectly justifiable excuses on why things have come to a screeching halt. You, on the other hand, will continue to improve your reputation as the one who can always be counted on when you simply slap in your spare part, fire up your operation, and continue.

Make it a reflex to ask yourself at every turn, "What happens if something goes wrong?" More importantly, have an answer for this question. If you strive to have a backup plan no matter what you're involved in, you will achieve a much higher overall success rate than will those who do not. Not only is this level of preparation good for the empire, it aids your personal cause. You'll come to know the great power in trust and having a good reputation. Eventually, people will come to depend upon you when the issue at hand really matters, for you will be the one who achieved your goals even when things didn't go exactly as planned.

NEVER GIVE WARNING.

When we were kids playing games, it was often part of our rules that we had to give "fair warning" before we attacked. Even as adults, we can see that this is often a part of what's expected in a civilized society. International convention dictates that, before hostilities begin, nations are supposed to first publicly and officially declare war against each other.

Actually, I've never understood this mentality. The notion of giving fair warning before attack is just plain silly from a tactical point of view.

Why on earth would I want to announce to my opponent that I'm about to strike so that he can mount defenses against me? In the rough and tumble world of business, this is a mistake that you never want to make.

One of the first things that you should add to your way of approaching strategy is the old adage from World War II that loose lips sink ships. Simply put, it means that the more you casually blab about your affairs, the more opportunities you give the enemy to figure out what you're doing and plan an effective attack against you. It might sound overly dramatic, but you should keep all of your conversations regarding any plan you're contemplating on a strictly need-to-know basis. Discuss the specific details only with the people who require that information to perform their part. If someone truly needs to know the high-level concepts or critical inside information, that's fine, too. Otherwise, to put it bluntly, keep your mouth shut. You might soon be riding on the ship that gets sunk.

Furthermore, you must impress the need for discretion upon each person who will be the holder of any knowledge. If someone's attitude doesn't convince you that they can be trusted to treat your information with the care that is required, don't tell them. If you can't use someone else for the job and absolutely must tell them a few important details to get the task done, then make sure you reveal only the bare minimum. Additionally, if you can doctor in any way what you tell them by adding a little disinformation, it could help if they do in fact pass along closely guarded secrets. That way, even if they do talk, what the enemy gets may well cause them more confusion than anything else. Know who you can and cannot trust, and treat them accordingly.

We've discussed the tactic of lacing an untrustworthy person's knowledge with false information to protect your plans. Another approach is to use this method explicitly and as a form of attack against your competition. Using people whom you know can't keep a secret, pass along as if in greatest confidence that you plan on moving in a specific direction with all your might. Urge them to keep this confidential, knowing inwardly that they couldn't if their life depended on it.

Then, as your adversaries throw the full weight of their effort into defending where they've heard you're attacking, you hit them from the exact opposite direction. This, of course, was your plan all along. Had you spread your disinformation by telling them directly, you wouldn't have succeeded because they don't trust you and would question anything that you said. However, because they heard it through the grapevine, perhaps via someone they consider to be a reliable informant, the information will carry enough weight to influence their course of action. By the time they figure out that they've been had, it will be far too late. But then, that's the entire reason for never giving warning, isn't it?

IMPROVE YOUR SKILLS DAILY.

Within this thought lies the key to creating tremendous change within your organization. No matter what you do for a living, if you're like most people you may very well go in to work each day with the mistaken impression that your job skills are the only valuable and important thing that you need to deliver. Consequently, as a conscientious and ambitious worker, you will doubtless put in considerable effort over the years to become increasingly better at what you do. However, as I hope is becoming evident by now, the ability to swing a sword is only half the battle.

One of the biggest reasons that the Roman army was victorious over others and built a huge empire is that it fought not just with swords, but with strategy. The discipline, organization, and tactical skill of the Romans enabled them to win many battles against fierce and capable opponents that would have otherwise been lost. It should be no different in your empire.

Should you have excellent job skills and deliver the results for which you were hired and get paid for? Absolutely. But that alone will not win your battles, nor will it strengthen your empire. To accomplish this, you must, like the Romans, employ superior strategy in your maneuvers. Therefore, you must take your strategic skills every bit as seriously as your job skills and dedicate yourself with the same passion and enthusiasm to attaining excellence in this area as well.

Once you've realized how important it is to spend as much time and effort on your tactical skills as you do on your job skills, it's time to consider what to do next. This begins with an honest and frank assessment of your strengths and weaknesses. Assuming you have your trusty notebook handy, it's time to take pen in hand once more and start jotting down some observations.

This is not a five-minute exercise, by the way. No matter what your vocation is, few people would assume that you could summarize everything there is to know about your job in a quick session. Along those lines, assessing your strengths and weaknesses in the arena of strategy and tactics will be an ongoing project. At a minimum, you should dedicate some time each week to sit down with your favorite beverage and contemplate these matters, updating your notes as you go.

The point of this exercise should be easy to understand: you can't figure out how to get there until you know where you're going. In other words, how can you possibly enhance your strengths and improve your weaknesses without knowing what they are? This may sound too obvious to mention, but very few people sit down and seriously consider these things. When you do, you'll have a clear tactical advantage.

Once you have a clear path to follow in terms of improving your skills, the next thing you should do is hit the bookstore or the library, where you'll find a tremendous wealth of information and instruction on every topic under the sun. It's all yours for the taking, and the only requirement for this education is the ability to read.

In our discussion of strategy, much of the emphasis has been on your personal improvement. The other thing that is worth mentioning here is that, just as you're constantly looking for ways to improve these skills, you must each day muse on how you might improve and benefit the empire as a whole. Remember, the fate of the empire affects you in a very personal manner, even when the link between cause and effect is a subtle or complex one. As long as you make it a serious part of your life to reach for improvement in these areas on a daily basis, you will come out a winner in the overwhelming majority of your engagements.

SOCIALIZE FREQUENTLY TO BRAINSTORM.

It's not uncommon for us to socialize with some of the people we work with. In fact, our job is one of the primary places where we find new relationships because we spend such a large portion of our waking hours there. Building the bonds of a strong individual relationship is always a good thing, and our work-oriented friends often fall into this category. We're going to take that one step further. Instead of picking and choosing individuals to build social ties with, we're going to bond with the group as a whole. The people who play together rock the business world together.

Why do we need to take the professional relationships we have with each other and turn them into family? There is a very practical reason for this, and it will yield tangible results that reach far into the future. When the work relationships are personal, the job becomes personal. And, when that happens, the good of the empire itself becomes important to each of us on a very intimate level.

To unite the tribes, you must first unite your own tribe. Having done that, you help others unite their individual groups as well, which moves you toward the unity of all tribes. You need fuel for this endeavor, and you'll find that the less officious and formal the setting, the more good times and high spirits you'll have. Therefore, as you start a movement toward more all-inclusive gatherings after hours, keep it casual and relaxed. It can be as simple as people meeting at individual homes, ordering a few pizzas, turning up the music, and just enjoying the company of kindred spirits.

But why have frequent social gatherings of this kind? Your company has functions for all the important holidays and internal events. What's to gain by spending frequent weekend or weeknight time with the people from the office? The answer is that we're going to mix business and pleasure. These are not just normal cookouts or drinks after hours; these are strategy parties.

You've been working hard to improve your skills in the area of general tactical operations, and the point of all this effort has been to achieve new goals, both as an individual and a department. However, as everyone knows, individuals have blind spots. Additionally, each of us has a different personality and set of traits, which can bring a much wider diversity of talents to the party. In this case, I mean that in a very literal sense.

One of the reasons that most departments don't work effectively as a unit in strategic terms is that everyone is simply too busy working every day to do any brainstorming. There's barely enough time in the workday to be productive as it is. Standing around laughing, joking, dreaming, and scheming would probably be frowned upon in most environments. By taking it out of the office and gathering on a frequent and possibly even regular basis, you have the time to finally pool your collective skills.

Suddenly, your tribe takes on a strategic life of its own. Instead of a loose collection of individuals trying to cope with problems as they arise on the job, the next time you act, it will be in concert with one another. Now that you've taken the time to actually talk, you can formulate plans of attack and overcome obstacles one after another. Where there was once a building with a lot of individuals, there is now a huge chessboard, with your team plotting brilliant strategies.

Not only do informal social gatherings give you the time and the place to brainstorm, they also provide an environment for you to share your skills and tactics with others. Each person has an appreciative audience with whom to share the latest successes and exploits. Every new technique learned by one individual becomes an enhancement to each person. Consider this: if you had a dozen people in your gathering, and each one brought only one new thing that they had learned to the party, you would each walk away with eleven new skills or pieces of information.

Because everyone came to have a good time, this is also a friendly and supportive environment that allows each person to share their weaknesses. In doing so, the entire group can then rush in to fill the void, protecting and strengthening each person where they need it most. Before you know it, your tribe and your empire will become like a suit of chain-mail armor, perfect in every way and offering no weak links for the enemy to exploit. This is how you build an invincible empire.

SHARE EVERYTHING YOU LEARN.

So, now you're great, powerful, clever, and wise. A master strategist, your tactical skills are the envy of your peers, and your adversaries have nightmares about facing you in battle. But don't get cocky, and don't get comfortable. It's still not enough.

No matter how hard you work to improve your personal abilities, you have not done your part for the good of the empire until you've shared it with others. You must make it a driving personal quest to help, inspire, and motivate each and every person you can come in contact with. Not just the people you casually bump into in your average day, either. To be truly effective, to light a fire that will eventually warm a nation, you must create opportunities to meet new people, even if only briefly. As you practice and improve on your skills as a source of knowledge and inspiration, you'll find that you can make a difference in someone's life in as little as a ten-minute encounter.

Therefore, you have to do something that goes against animal instinct. People have a tendency to hoard information, skills, knowledge, and tactical tricks so that they personally appear more powerful. They fear sharing their knowledge, for they believe that doing so will mean that they are no longer as important or valuable.

Cast aside your fears for a moment and consider the alternative. Instead of hoarding your knowledge and insights, what if you shared them freely and frequently? In the beginning, you might be the only person in the group who understood the importance of strategy, and would therefore obviously be the only person with any skills in this area. However, because you went out of your way to stress the critical need for these abilities and then shared every single thing you knew, others would eventually become stronger and more capable. A part of what you must teach others is that they, in turn, must teach. This means that your group becomes a hotbed of activity and an ever-increasing pool of power.

Because you've now poured every bit of your wisdom and skills into others and they have done the same, your group is an awesome and invincible force, for every asset has been multiplied not only by the sheer number of people you have, but exponentially by their interaction and synergy as well. This is true, but does it make you less important? With the group being so powerful, are you no longer the person everyone turns to? If that were true, then it would be understandable from an emotional point of view, if not a practical one, why you might want to withhold information to bolster your position in your tribe.

You were the one who inspired them to begin with. You saw a vision that they hadn't considered. You've shared that vision now, and they're stronger because of it. However, as they took the time and effort to strengthen themselves, you continued to do the same thing. You are not any less important now that others are more able, because you've become more capable yourself in the same period of time. Therefore, the only thing that's changed is that, where once you were a source of inspiration to a weak and vulnerable tribe, now you inspire a united and powerful tribe. You're still a big fish, but it's a much deeper pond.

Look for every opportunity you can find in your daily life to mentor others. Teach them what you've learned. Show them how it can affect them personally and make their lives better. Make it a game to see who can come up with the next new effective tactic to share with the group. Celebrate and honor those who are eager to learn, which will make it all the more appealing for people who are new to the movement to join in.

Take it upon yourself to be the spark that lights the bonfire and consider yourself successful each time one of your people decides to feel the same way. You're not just sharing tactical skills; you're starting a movement. Approach it with the same fire and zeal that you would if you were raising a nation, and teach others to do the same. Do this, and your future will be full of heady days, indeed.

STRATEGY

Teach tactical skills to every person in the empire.

- Realize that business is war.
- Know your enemy.
- Build strong alliances.
- Cultivate an information network.
- Think several steps ahead.
- Always have a backup plan.
- Never give warning.
- Improve your skills daily.
- Socialize frequently to brainstorm.
- Share everything you learn.

VIII ⸹ Brilliance

Encourage innovation by destroying
all obstacles to new ideas.

Regardless of your industry, you'll never gain the competitive edge over others in the marketplace by doing things the same way as everyone else does them. You need to stand out from the herd, finding some way in which to distinguish yourself, so that your potential customers can clearly see that you're the obvious choice for their business. Without that, who the customer chooses to do business with is just potluck. That's not exactly something you want to bet the farm on.

The first challenge in building a company that can be innovative lies in finding insightful, motivated, and creative people. Without such people, you have no innovation. However, even if you've been fortunate enough to staff every position in the entire company with such bright sparks, that's no guarantee that you'll get the kind of brilliance that you need to outshine all others in the field.

One of the greatest stumbling blocks that a business ever encounters on the road to glory is placed there by the company itself. In most companies, bureaucracy, politics, and petty ambition create an atmosphere that promotes the quest for an individual career at the expense of the empire. Additionally, people often become lazy and complacent. And for these reasons they will be unenthusiastic about any plan that requires more effort on their part.

Therefore, inertia sets in, and your departments become stagnant pools. This stagnated state then becomes the standard by which everyone is compared. For fear of political reprisal or out of a desire to avoid extra work, your people will not only be less than innovative, but they'll actively resist it. Until you change this tepid atmosphere, you will never have neither brilliance nor the decisive edge that it could give you over the predators that stalk you in the business world.

FOSTER DISDAIN FOR THE STATUS QUO.

Many companies, and most particularly the larger ones, have an almost tangible sense in every work area that warns against making waves. In fact, if you are one of those brave souls who forge ahead regardless and try to achieve great things for the company, you may even be reprimanded and told that you're "rocking the boat" when what you should really be is a "team player." For those of you unfamiliar with the phrase, at least when used in this context, it means that you should sit down, shut up, and avoid doing anything out of the ordinary.

But realize that, any time you try to promote a new idea, you're threatening the status quo. Of course, this is rather the point of being innovative, but many people don't see it this way. And they don't see it this way because they have a significant investment in the way things are, and they will fight very hard to keep it that way. This resistance usually starts by political maneuvering that results in higher authorities sitting you down and explaining to you, sometimes sternly, that you're out of bounds. If you're passionate and believe strongly in your idea, you may persist in the following days. This can and often does lead to additional reprimands and sometimes even being fired. Being fired? For trying to benefit the company? How can this be?

It's easy enough to understand, really. People often spend most of their time creating their little power base in whatever job that they have. This may involve having control over a group of people or other resources, but it may also be other expressions of power, such as creative authority or company perks like corner offices and reserved parking spaces. No matter what the benefits are, most people understand that, as long as things continue just like they are today, they're probably pretty safe in their ability to hold on to them. The minute that a change is introduced, though, uncertainty enters the picture.

To overcome this fear, you must first show the individual the benefits of striving for excellence. People need to understand that there's a better life to be lived in a company that's abuzz with excitement, creativity, and profitability, and you need to show them that these benefits justify and outweigh the risks and fears involved. You can't realistically expect people to take risks unless there's something in it for them.

You want to change this and build a new social structure in your organization. Where there was once a group of people who edged nervously away from the outspoken voices for change, you want to create an atmosphere in which people make fun of those who cling to the railing instead of rocking the boat. By winning battle after battle, resulting in higher quality and better productivity for the empire, you'll have the weight of momentum on your side.

People get excited when they're winning, and you can leverage that. With each passing achievement, continually reinforce the personality you want your group to adopt by telling them how great they are, pointing out their accomplishments, and building esprit de corps. Also, and very importantly, always remind them of the benefits that they've been receiving because they had the courage to buck the status quo and go for it.

When people feel that they're part of an elite unit that can do the impossible, the fear of change drops away and is replaced by the pride of purpose. The status quo will no longer be good enough, for you will have instilled in your people a new way of looking at things. You will have also proven the truth of your vision with success after success. Because nobody wants to be left out, this attitude will soon spread throughout the empire, and you will find yourself working for an entire company of people who will settle for nothing less than being the best of the best.

FORGET HOW OTHERS HAVE DONE IT.

Now that we've created an environment in which people are once again free to be brilliant, it's time to get down to the business of being clever. Everyone is looking for that next killer idea. How is it that we'll succeed in finding it when everyone else just keeps ending up with the same tired old solution, time after time?

The first thing you have to do is clear your mind. I say that like it's an easy thing, knowing full well that it's not. No matter what the issue or task at hand, we're constantly bombarded each day with how things are currently done. It surrounds us and permeates our very being. It is often the only reference point that we have.

Of course, inspiration plays a very large part in the process, and can do some things to help bring you closer to that creative spark. Surprisingly, the most productive thing that you can do to move your new project forward is the very first thing that you should do with any new endeavor: absolutely nothing. If that seems a little counterintuitive, perhaps I should explain. What I mean specifically is that, to forget about the way things have always been done before, you must start with a clean slate.

However, most of us are under continual pressures on the job and therefore tend to go straight from one task to the next without so much as a cup of coffee in between. Some consider this a good work ethic because we don't waste time standing around taking breaks when we could be doing work. This is, of course, short-term thinking. Not only does it impede the creative process, it's a sure-fire ticket to burnout, if not sooner than most assuredly later.

If you need to clear your head but can't sit idly at your desk without incurring the wrath of smaller minds, find other places to do your brain-storming. Take a walk. Go to lunch. Lounge about in the break room. It doesn't matter what the location is as long as it gives you time to think, free from the clutter of the daily grind.

If you work in such a restrictive environment that you'll catch blazes if you even leave your post, or are not at least seen working with others at their post, then some diversionary tactics are called for. Whatever you happen to do for a living, arrange your work area with the objects of your trade at hand, as if you were actually doing something with them. Now it will seem to the entire world that you're bustling about doing mindless busywork. However, at this point, you can simply ignore the environment and get down to the true creative work at hand. This doesn't take place on your desk. It takes place in your mind.

Deceptive? Absolutely. Unethical? Not in the slightest. You were not hired to be busy. You were hired to produce results. These are two completely distinct and different concepts. Think of it as your obligation and responsibility to remember what you were hired for even when leaders of lesser ability don't.

Remember, brilliance comes from inspiration and unrestricted thinking. Forget about the rules, and forget about how things have been done in the past. Take a little time to yourself, clear your mind, and let your imagination run wild. The benefits of what you achieve by doing so will far outweigh the amount of time that you spent staring off into the distance.

AVOID CLEVERNESS THAT BRINGS NO BENEFIT.

Many industries—such as engineering, software development, and product design—have an important thing in common when it comes to the creative aspect of the job: clever people. Because human nature is ever the foil of productivity, it's not difficult to see right away that this could easily lead to trouble.

Any time you find people who have entered a profession that they're passionate about, it's a foregone conclusion that they enjoy their work. Although we normally like to encourage that sort of thing, the problem arises when we get into the implementation of any given design or plan.

No matter what part you play, you must continually remind yourself that businesses exist to make money. That'll help you keep the proper perspective about what's brilliant and what may be clever but not terribly helpful. If you want to reap the long-term benefits of a prosperous empire, you must sometimes subjugate your personal desires to the good of the group. A simple sanity check that you can employ in this regard is to ask yourself with each new idea what value it brings to the group and to the empire as a whole. If it passes this test, it may be an idea worth fighting for. If it doesn't pass, let it go and move on to your next great idea.

The notion of eliminating complexities that don't bring with them tangible benefits applies not just to product development and design, but to any aspect of the plan that you may be working on. For example, if you happen to be a part of an effort to better organize office communications, you're going to find a huge amount of technology in the marketplace that you can apply to the problem at hand. However, just because you can do something doesn't mean that you should. In a small office with just a few people, telephone calls and email may be just one step away from overkill because the four people in the office can all simply look over their shoulders and talk to each other.

Nonetheless, it can be intoxicating to look at all the cool things that you can do with just a few extra pieces of office equipment and software. In fact, if the marketing department for these various products did their job properly, the list of features will seem so compelling that you can't imagine living without them. Many people have fallen prey to this line of thinking, only to find that what was once a simple phone call or email now involves numerous pieces of technology that waste more time than they save.

Inevitably, of course, some gadget will be temperamental, and other parts of the system won't play nice with the new version of software you just bought. Before you know it, you're spending almost half of your days installing, configuring, and troubleshooting your "labor-saving devices." Anyone who works within kicking distance of a computer has seen this at one point or another. Adding cleverness did not add to your productivity.

One other truth relates to the complexities in any organization. As time goes on, things will always become more, not less, complicated. That's because each passing generation of employees will feel the need to put their personal stamp on things. If someone holds the position of managing procedures, they often feel that, unless they're adding or altering rules, they're not doing their job. It is the bold and innovative employee, therefore, who trims rather than adds.

Whether it's technology, job skills, company procedures, or any of the myriad other areas in which humans can show how clever they are, try to remember that, frequently, as my musician friends are fond of saying, less is more. If your new idea will bring tangible and practical value to the organization, then let nothing stand in your way. However, if you can't see a real and unambiguous benefit to the empire, then learn to leave well enough alone.

BE OPEN TO NEW IDEAS FROM ANYONE.

In addition to the many tribes that populate the empire, a deeply ingrained sense of class-consciousness is also at play in almost every company on the planet. The dividing lines are too numerous to list comprehensively, but some of them are all too familiar to us all. In most parts of the world, women in business are taken less seriously and treated with much less respect than are men. Racial groups form another set of artificial classes. Although the cultures and races that are looked down upon vary from country to country, the resulting loss to the empire is always the same.

But it's not just the age-old boundaries of gender, race, and culture that divide people in the workplace. As if there's not enough stupidity to go around, we also categorize people by the kind of job that they have. Additionally, the amount of money that people make is yet another artificial indication of whether or not they're someone worth talking to. These are but a few of the prejudices and stereotypes that populate workplaces in virtually every corner of the world.

When you come in to work, your attitudes and the way you interact with others affect the overall health and well-being of the empire. In the professional world, whether you're a welder in a shipyard or the president of an international corporation, results are all that matter. Businesses exist to make a profit. Stereotypes limit your options and rob you of potential resources, thus diminishing your ability to be productive. Therefore, it's in your best interests to leave your biases and prejudices in the parking lot when you come in to work each morning. It's nothing more than a practical matter.

Why? Because we're reaching for excellence and innovation. A brilliant idea from the custodian is still a brilliant idea. Once a new concept or plan has made the journey from the person's mind to paper, computer, voice, or any other medium of communication, that idea becomes an entity of its own. It will rise or fall based on its merits and who can profit by it, and the only people who will care where it came from are the people who want to take credit for it.

It's very difficult to leave your preconceived notions at the door. When you talk to people, you're judging the content of what they say based on who's saying it. If that same information were sent to you via email from someone in a different part of the world you'd never met face to face, you would be unable to do that. You'd come much closer to judging the content of the email on its own merit. In short, we have a hard time divorcing the message from the messenger. That's a very costly shortcoming.

It takes continual self-discipline, but this shortcoming can, and must, be overcome. When you reach the point of hearing the content and nothing else, you'll suddenly have an entire world of new resources open up to you. Now, because you're not limiting your sources of inspiration and information, they can come from anywhere. Furthermore, as word spreads that you're open to brilliance no matter where it comes from, people who once stayed in the shadows because they felt shunned will now step out in the open and tentatively offer their ideas.

Now that you realize that your company is full of wild and wonderful ideas, perspectives from off the beaten path, and exciting new innovations, don't just stand there. Go out and meet them. Make it a point to stop and talk to people all around your company. Have real conversations with them, treat them with respect and consideration, and make new friends. There's no telling what you'll learn.

People are sometimes surprised when they see me treat the guy serving me a taco with the same respect and interest as I do the one next in line who's wearing an expensive business suit. It's true that the guy in the suit may have an MBA, but I'll bet he doesn't know squat about tacos. On top of that, how do I know that the guy behind the counter isn't slinging fast food while he's in college studying nuclear physics? Because I don't limit myself with false class assumptions, I may learn a lot about the nuclear power industry from the man cooking my lunch, and then pick up some great investment tips from the MBA while munching on a taco. All because I assume that everyone is an interesting and valuable human being until proven otherwise.

〜〜〜〜〜〜〜〜〜〜〜◎〜〜〜〜〜〜〜〜〜〜〜

CELEBRATE THE POWER OF GROUP CREATIVITY.

A magical thing happens when people combine their talents. The easiest way to understand it is to think in terms of one thing leading to another, although that hardly does the experience justice. Better still, just think back to experiences from your own life, for you've seen this time and again.

A group of people is gathered to participate in a common interest. One of them shares a great new idea with everyone. Enthusiasm builds as the members consider and discuss all the positive attributes of the idea. Because of this building excitement, another person has an inspiration related to the first idea and throws it out for all to hear.

Once again, everyone is happy and enthused at the prospect of yet another great idea, and the overall level of energy builds. However, because it was already elevated to begin with, group enthusiasm steps to an even higher level because the second idea began at a higher point than the first. This upward spiral can, and often does, continue long into the night. People laugh, joke, clap their hands, and raise their glasses to each other as the spirit of camaraderie builds and the pace and intensity of the discussion continue to rise.

This synergistic phenomenon illustrates an extremely important point that relates not just to people, but to our lives in general: we are all heavily influenced by our surroundings. Very few people are going to have their most inspirational moments when gathered in a somber and gloomy meeting, with everyone taking a turn at sharing visions of doom and gloom. It's depressing. At best, you'll have a tough time keeping your own spirits up. At worst, you can easily get sucked down into the mire with everyone else. The power of the group molds the spirit of the individual.

The very same concept is taught to sales and marketing professionals in every industry in the world. Enthusiasm is contagious. The next time you flip on the television, take note of how many commercials you see with people smiling and dancing about for joy, excited and enraptured by the wonderful experience of the product being sold.

We can easily make use of this, then, in our pursuit of brilliance. The ever-increasing enthusiasm of our planning sessions has no negative side effects. Everyone in the group is part of a winning team, and so any contribution that anyone offers in the thick of the excitement is something that they won't later regret. In fact, if you all approach your efforts on a daily basis with insight and dedication, the individual who offers creativity in the meeting will receive personal benefits after the fact. Meetings, even the good ones, don't last forever, which means that the excitement that occurs when your groups get together can diminish as well.

Fortunately, it doesn't have to be that way. In all of your day-to-day interactions, make it a point to continually remind each other of all the great ideas and innovations that the group has accomplished. Celebrate the individual who offered yet another valuable insight, and they will benefit personally through increased self-esteem.

But how do you kick-start this process? It's much easier than you may think. You must show excitement and enthusiasm even if you're not feeling it deep down inside at that very moment. Do this, and before long your enthusiasm will become real. Then, from your initial spark the fire of brilliance will grow.

As is so often the case, what works for the individual works on an even larger scale for the group. Not only do you want to exalt the people who participate in your efforts and contribute freely, the same applies to the unit as a whole. High morale is yet another rich source of power for your tribe and the empire, and esprit de corps can build it to ever-increasing levels. When the members of your tribe gather to discuss new ideas, solutions to problems, and bold new initiatives, the ensuing excitement will spur the group on.

Just imagine the power that this will reveal when all of the tribes unite to pool their collective enthusiasm. If you thought it was exciting and fun to be part of an intense and powerful tribe, it's nothing in comparison to raising your voice with countless others as part of an invincible empire.

~~~~~~~~~~~~~~~~~~~~~~~~~~~~(◉)~~~~~~~~~~~~~~~~~~~~~~~~~

LISTEN TO THE PEOPLE WHO DO THE WORK.

Companies are typically organized in a hierarchical manner so that you have a small number of people at the top making decisions for a large number of people below. This is good, logical organization, and armies have been taking this structure into battle for as long as people have been swinging sticks at each other. However, regardless of the organizational benefits, it comes with a certain degree of risk as well.

The higher you find yourself in the chain of command, the farther removed you are from the people on the front lines who must encounter the enemy. Any information that they may have—and any improved ways of doing things that they see from their extremely relevant point of view—may never reach you. It could be lost completely through confusion or miscommunication, intentionally kept from you by subordinates with their own agenda, or garbled beyond recognition after having passed through many interpretive sets of hands.

As the leader responsible for making decisions that affect these people, you may have absolutely no idea what their reality actually is. Whether you realize it, when you consider what goes on in the trenches, you're doing little more than guessing. How then can your decisions or initiatives have any hope of success?

Although this idea flies in the face of the old business model, in which educated and important leaders at the top of the company are the only ones who know best, the people who do the daily work know more about what's going on in your company than anyone in the building. They may not understand the big picture if you don't make it a point to inform and educate them on such matters, but they know exactly what works and what doesn't in every productive corner of the empire. Ignore them at your peril.

If you have not yet become too important to hear the better-informed voices of the working people in your enterprise, simply make it a priority to do so on a regular basis. In any event, you should take time out in your personal life, either each day or at most once a week, to reflect on who you are, how you act, and what attitudes you're currently experiencing.

Honest, frank, and sometimes brutal self-examination can be a very diffi-cult experience. Only the great ones—or those destined for greatness at what they do in life—have the courage and dedication to begin walking this path. The benefits for those who do, though, are immense.

I'm hoping that the questions you should ask yourself on a regular basis are fairly obvious at this point. How do you view and treat other people? Do you really listen and consider all points of view, regardless of whom they come from? Are you arrogant, egocentric, and self-important? Even these few examples are sufficient to illustrate how uncomfortable such self-examination can be. Parts of your ego will resist with all its available energy. You'll suddenly get the urge to get up and do anything else but sit there and think about these things, or your mind will conve-niently wander off to other topics. When you look in the mirror, you won't always like what you see, and that's no fun for any of us.

However, for those who persevere, the value they bring both to the empire, its people, and their own individual lives far outweighs the dis-comforts of the regular exercise. When you build a balanced self-image, combining true self-respect and acknowledged self-worth with an honest and realistic perspective of the value of others, you will stand out in many ways. Because you treat others with respect and show a sincere interest for their opinions, they'll like you and share their thoughts with you.

When leaders make it a point to listen to workers, and the people on the front lines communicate their expertise in a meaningful way to their leaders, a union is formed that can overcome any problem. It all starts by listening to your experts, the people who do the gritty, day-to-day work that moves your empire forward.

EDUCATE WORKERS ABOUT THE BIG PICTURE.

It's not necessary for the guy flipping burgers in one of your ubiquitous fast-food palaces to comprehend the details of your annual profit-and-loss statement. Chances are that he doesn't have an MBA, let alone any accounting degree. But then, if he handed you the spatula, you'd probably just burn the burgers. You each have different skill sets, and it doesn't really matter if you're a lousy cook, as long as you keep the company profitable enough to buy the buns.

Let's take a look at a working example. In this scenario, you're a major corporation selling cheeseburgers nationwide. They're plump. They're juicy. Each bun has the perfect number of sesame seeds. And your competition is kicking your buns all over the marketplace. Why? Because at your cheeseburger paradise you've always got long lines at your register and it seems like it takes forever for customers to get their order. People are impatient. Your burgers are good, but they're not *that* good.

Down at the competing burger joint, however, you'd think that they were wearing rocket packs. Their entire operation runs like the proverbially well-oiled machine, and their cooks deliver freshly grilled cheeseburgers (paradise optional) with great efficiency. Your kitchen, on the other hand, is a comparative exercise in disorder. Furthermore, your competitor's employees are on fire with enthusiasm and spirit. They truly seem to *care* about delivering excellence to their customers. Your people are apathetic, and that's on a good day.

Your corporate profits are plummeting as more people get fed up with your lackluster service and defect to the competition. The board of directors then informs your CEO that, if things aren't turned around soon, cheeseburgers won't be the only thing with grill marks on them. After extensive research, the main problem that seems to be costing you customers is your slow service. Clearly, something must be done. Consequently, an edict comes down from on high that customer service must be improved. Or else. Nothing more, nothing less. No explanations, no recommendations. Just a less-than-veiled threat and a dictate to "improve customer service."

Your managers at locations nationwide get the memo and just shake their heads. What exactly does "improve customer service" mean? With no clarification or direction, the managers are left to their own devices and make different decisions in different stores. One encourages the people at the counter to smile more. Another decides that the tables aren't being cleaned often enough. Still another decides to change the elevator music being played in the background. One manager gets it, and takes the appropriate action. He tells the guys in back slinging burgers, "Cook faster." The cooks, of course, just shrug their shoulders, continue to work at the same rate that they always have, and the customers continue to defect to the competition.

Most people want to get paid more, work fewer hours, and have a better time while they're doing it. That's a pretty universal constant. So, to truly reach the people in your kitchen, take a look at recent events in your own cheeseburger paradise and find some examples that will strike close to home. For instance, maybe you recently had to fire the dishwashers to reduce your payroll. Of course, the dishes still have to be washed, but now they pile up in a sink and the cooks have to go back every spare moment they get to wash them, making sure the fries don't burn in the meantime.

You now have an example that they can relate to. By showing them the chain of events from the decline in customers due to the slow service all the way up to the declining profits in the boardroom, and then back down to the resulting payroll cuts that eliminated their dishwashers, they will begin to understand cause and effect. They understand the difference that their personal efforts can make for the empire at large. And, most importantly, they also realize in a new way how the fate of the empire affects them personally. Because they see the big picture, they understand the importance of every action they take.

Even if your company never gets near a cheeseburger, your people have a tremendous effect on the health of the empire. Most of them have all the skills they need to change your world, but they'll never be properly motivated or truly effective until they can see their efforts integrating into the empire as a whole. Once they do, however, you'll be amazed at what they can accomplish.

CREATE AN INSPIRATIONAL ENVIRONMENT.

Most companies aren't abuzz with excitement and innovation because most people don't have an *adventure*; they have a *job*. Each day at the workplace is the same: dull, tedious, and boring. Whether it's the grind of manual labor or the mind-numbing tedium of bureaucracy, most work environments have no spark whatsoever. It's little wonder, then, that the people don't either.

One of the reasons for these dull places of business is the focus on getting the job done. This reason may seem a bit strange because most people think that that's exactly what they were hired for, but, like many such things, it's just not that simple. If all you want is people to get the job done, that's all you'll get. And not one ounce more. Doesn't really sound like a recipe for excellence, does it?

Do you want a staff so alive that sparks fly from their fingertips? Are you looking for people who deliver innovation, excellence, and brilliance? You're not going to get it as long as people feel as if they're slogging away in the salt mines. You need to create an atmosphere that sparkles with excitement. If you can make every day a great new adventure that people can't wait to join, then you'll have the beginnings of that creative spiral that becomes more and more energized with each passing week. In short, you need to find a way to make their jobs fun.

Does this mean that I want to talk about personal finance issues with a banker dressed in a clown suit, no matter how much fun he's having? Obviously not. There's a time and a place for everything. Nonetheless, if I walk into a financial institution where people are alive, happy, and obviously having a good time with what they're doing, I have a much better feeling about the quality of attention my money is going to get. Dull, staid, and lifeless people rarely deliver excellence.

Laughter is not the only way to create inspiration in the workplace, although it never hurts. People love to win, to achieve, and to accomplish things in life. Regardless of the particular output of your job and department, there's always a new record to set and a new goal to achieve. What's that, you say, you weren't keeping track? Then start! Create scenarios whereby people can be recognized for the job they do. It doesn't have to be a big event each time, either. Sometimes, a series of smaller achievements do much more to generate momentum for the group.

Back when I ran a sales consulting company, one of my clients took orders over the phone. It was a very boring environment. However, the owner of the company had a small ship's bell. I had him mount it on the wall next to the whiteboard where the daily sales numbers were written, and I told his people to ring the bell every time they made a sale. Suddenly, the entire office came alive! Even though they made a commission on their sales, the commission had never motivated them much in the past. Now, however, everyone just wanted to get up and ring that bell, particularly because I made sure that the rest of the room hooted and applauded every time someone did.

Furthermore, what was once a roomful of people who appeared very bored with their job was now an eight-hour, raucous party. People literally stood on top of their desks and danced a little jig when they made a particularly big sale, to the delight of the entire room. Everyone cheered the top producers. Everyone cheered the lowest producers. And that's not all. Instead of a collection of individuals, each person would now put their sales numbers up on the wall, add the total, and pronounce "We're really rocking now!" Not *I*, or *me*, but *we*. Without so much as an official announcement, the place suddenly had a collective consciousness. They united and became more powerful because of it.

Sales skyrocketed, of course, and they sold more in one quarter than they'd seen in the entire previous year. Best of all, everyone was having a blast and looked forward to coming in to work each day. Remember, happy people are the most productive people. Find ways to build an environment that will inspire them, keep them excited, and make them happy. You'll all laugh. All the way to the bank.

BE PREPARED TO OVERCOME FEAR OF CHANGE.

Humans have a herd instinct that's as old as the species itself. It's a primal thing, and it drives us in many ways. Although we are each individuals, and many of us cope with life fearlessly, that's not something that you can assume of each person. Therefore, it's wise to understand and recognize those things that frequently tend to make the herd nervous. Stampedes can get ugly. Of all the common anxieties to which humanity falls prey, one of the most common even today is the fear of change. Not surprisingly, frightened people are rarely at their most brilliant or productive.

Consequently, you must *expect* to encounter fear and resistance with each and every new idea that you propose, and, having anticipated it, you must have a plan for overcoming these problems. Part of your preparations for introducing change, therefore, should include some reconnaissance to determine what sort of things this group values the most. Is it power and control over turf? Perhaps instead they're more concerned with not having to work overtime. Job security is another common concern. And, of course, we should never forget the basics of human nature and the ego. People like to feel important. By researching and taking note of what their priorities are, you have the gateway to successfully introduce a new idea. You know what benefits to sell.

Your best bet for change in a reticent environment is an incremental one. It's even better still if you can slide change in so slowly and gradually that they don't even realize it's happening. At least not in the beginning. However, as time passes and you've successfully migrated them through various phases of transition, it's time to start building their confidence a little.

Making sure that you reach far back enough in time to not make them notice the change taking place at the moment, point out the improvements that they've accepted and implemented. Additionally, as you do this, make sure that they see the benefits that they personally received as they implemented your new procedures. As you have them slowly nodding their heads and realizing that, yes, they did accomplish some cool things and are now better off for it, subtly change the topic of your conversation from the changes that they've accepted to what an excellent, capable, and flexible group theirs is.

You already had them agreeing with you, so, when you start talking about how great they are, they're certainly not going to start disagreeing with you. Therefore, they will find themselves acknowledging what you say and supporting the notion that they are strong, fearless, flexible, and capable of taking on anything and prevailing.

You're not only building esprit de corps (which is always valuable), but you're also helping to change the collective self-image of the group. People who are afraid of change often feel inadequate and incapable deep inside, even if they won't even admit it to themselves. They're not, of course, but it doesn't really matter. It's true as long as that's what they believe. As you continually point out their accomplishments, compliment their spirit and ingenuity, and reaffirm what an outstanding and capable unit they are. They will eventually come to believe it for themselves. As well they should, for it will be true.

Change can be dictated from any level of management, but the greatest innovations always seem to come from within the ranks. After all, it's the frontline workers who understand the job enough to offer innovation in the first place. However, those who work in the ranks don't have the power or authority to demand change. Therefore, you must master the art of overcoming people's fear of change and their inherent resistance to new ways of doing things. Once you do, your brilliance can shine through for all to see.

ALWAYS LOOK TO THE NEXT GREAT ACHIEVEMENT.

The competition never sleeps. Of course, that probably explains the bags under their eyes, but it nonetheless means that you can never sit back and be content with the accomplishments of today, for tomorrow the enemy may well have an improvement of their own that renders yours obsolete. Thus, innovation must not only be a priority, but a perpetual one. The minute you slow down, your adversaries will overrun you.

A great idea today and no new thinking tomorrow leads to stagnation. Furthermore, much of the enjoyable benefits that your people receive by being part of an exciting and inspirational group will diminish when the newness fades, and that which was once bold and new becomes the tired old status quo. As a result, not only will you have footprints on your back from the competition, you won't be having any fun when it happens.

If you're thinking this means you can never rest, that's pretty much the size of it. Of course, if that were true in a literal sense you could never sustain improvements within the empire, for everybody needs a break every now and then. Otherwise, burnout happens, and you lose the edge forever. You always need a way to recharge the batteries. So how do you maintain a culture that never sleeps and yet rejuvenate the body and spirit?

In the glory days of the great Khans, they, like our modern business counterparts, would never rest. There was always another conquest, always another reason to move on to the next grazing area for the animals, and never a moment to just sit back and do nothing. And, yet, not only did they stay rejuvenated, they were strong and rested enough to conquer a large portion of the world. If they had bags under their eyes, no one was foolish enough to point it out.

Where did that energy come from? How could they live a nomadic lifestyle and actually strengthen in spirit rather than letting the constant change grind them down? As it turns out, there is a distinct difference between rest and rejuvenation. If you're under a great deal of stress and worry, you can sleep for twelve hours straight, but, when you wake up, you're still going to be stressed out and worn down. Rest didn't solve the problem.

On the other hand, in your distressed state, you can stay out until 4:00 A.M. with a group of friends taking in a movie, eating, seeing the sights, and talking and laughing with each other. When you get up the next day, your body may be physically tired, but you'll have much more energy and strength for the recuperative effect of social activities and distraction. In short, you were recharged by participating in things that you enjoyed. Just as group enthusiasm builds to ever-greater heights because the excitement of one person fuels that of the next, so too do any positive pastimes stoke our engines.

The Mongols didn't sit around thinking about how tired they were. They were having too much fun conquering the world. That's a rather invigorating pursuit, made all the more enjoyable by the fact that it is, by definition, a consecutive string of successes. As we've already seen, incremental achievements do great things to morale and enthusiasm, and these positive feelings do the work of recharging our bodies and spirits.

Consequently, if you manage things properly, you have a dual solution to the problem. The competition never sleeps, and so you must continually remain innovative to stay ahead of them. However, by keeping your people excited and enthusiastic about their continual string of successes, and the dreams of victories to come, you overcome the problems of fatigue.

Therefore, make brainstorming and creative problem-solving a daily effort in your group. Always ask "how could we do it better?" Moreover, always keep your attention turned toward the enemy. Beyond the obvious fact that it's unwise to turn your back on the enemy, let your troops have fun with the adventure of defeating them in battle after battle. Once your troops get caught up in the game of competing and conquering, they will naturally strive to create new and better ways of doing things so that they can beat their adversaries at every turn.

BRILLIANCE

Encourage innovation by destroying all obstacles to new ideas.

- ◎ Foster disdain for the status quo.
- ◎ Forget how others have done it.
- ◎ Avoid cleverness that brings no benefits.
- ◎ Be open to new ideas from anyone.
- ◎ Celebrate the power of group creativity.
- ◎ Listen to the people who do the work.
- ◎ Educate workers about the big picture.
- ◎ Create an inspirational environment.
- ◎ Be prepared to overcome fear of change.
- ◎ Always look to the next great achievement.

IX ⦚ Morale

Never underestimate the critical importance of emotions.

You can have the most brilliant people in the world and a plan of attack so incredibly effective that the enemy would simply give up if they knew what awaited them. Countless resources at your disposal and clear sailing ahead all may contribute to a notion that your initiative cannot fail. However, if you overlook the emotional state of your people, everything else becomes instantly irrelevant. You cannot lead a demoralized group into battle and prevail.

This fact applies not just to the frontline troops who have to carry out your plans, but to workers and leaders at each level of the empire. If your people—no matter what their jobs—are tired, dispirited, depressed, worn down, or in a negative and defeated state of mind, they will expect to fail. And they will not be disappointed. Alternatively, when everyone involved in your operations is alive with enthusiasm, confidence, and optimism, even a weak or mediocre plan can be transformed into a blinding success by the people who implement it.

No matter how things have always been done in the old business model, morale is not, and never has been, enhanced by handing out cheap plaques that cost less than the napkins at your last formal gathering. Empty words, canned speeches, and buzzword-laden platitudes will not sway the hearts and minds of your people. They're not stupid. If they were, you would have replaced them long ago.

Praise and accolades have to be real and sincere, or they're not only meaningless, they will simply have no effect on the morale of your troops. Nor is the maintaining of high spirits the exclusive responsibility of leaders. From the minimum-wage workers to the millionaire CEOs, each of you can, and must, assume a critical role in maintaining a positive emotional state for your people. It is the single most important consideration on the road to victory.

REMEMBER THAT THE PEOPLE ARE THE EMPIRE.

To get the most out of your efforts in life, you'll find that it's frequently useful to go back to the basics. Once we learn a skill and become involved in the intricacies of performing it, we will add one bit of finesse after another until we become experts at what we do. In the process, however, we often drift away from fundamental principals that are the very foundation upon which that finesse is built. With this in mind, the very first thing we need to do on a regular basis to improve morale is to remind ourselves of one crucial and all-important fact: the people *are* the empire.

Your people, from the most powerful leaders all the way out to the front lines, are not just folks who get up each morning, have a cup of coffee, and drive in to your business. They *are* your business. They greet the customers, produce the products, send the bills, solve the problems, and do every single thing that is required to make you a real, living, and breathing company.

History is replete with tales of the brave and fiery few warriors who held off an enemy that vastly outnumbered them, saving the day both for their comrades and their empire. Had they given in to despair, thrown their swords on the ground, and cried that all was lost, that would have been the reality of the moment. But they prevailed and returned home as heroes because they refused to give in to fear, and—more importantly still—they held on to their belief that they could defeat the enemy.

This is the stuff of legends, and it also happens every day, in companies around the world. Your empire is full of heroes who are capable of doing great and memorable deeds. All they need to bring these talents to life is the fire and passion of purpose, the belief that they can achieve the impossible, and the supporting cheers from those around them urging ever-greater achievements.

In every job throughout the company, everyone must give daily thought to the importance of morale. You must see it as your personal responsibility to keep spirits high with your every word and action.

When you see people who are sagging, it is your job to pump them up again. Five minutes ago, when someone else walked past the depressed receptionist, it was that persons' job. Five minutes from now, it will be someone else's job. At this moment, though, as you walk into the lobby on your way to your department, it's *your* job. And you absolutely must take it seriously.

Very often in life, you never realize the difference that you make in other people's lives by how you treat them. You also can't see the chain reaction that can occur and lead to terrible disasters or great things, a landslide all started by one small pebble, and that pebble is you.

How many times have you called a company to do business with them, and been so put off by their apathy or bad attitude that you simply ended the phone call and went on to a competitor? Price and service aren't the only things that people prize. Personally, although I'm always interested in saving a buck, I sometimes give my business to people who aren't the low bidder because their attitude impresses me and instills in me the confidence that they're going to take good care of me. Additionally, life is too short to deal with unpleasant people, and I try to avoid that experience whenever possible. When I make a call and get a bad attitude, I move on to the next company if there's any choice in the matter whatsoever. And there almost always is.

The people are the empire, and you are the walls that protect each other from the predators. It's up to each of you to make sure that every brick is strong.

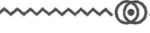

EMPHASIZE THE VICTORIES, NOT THE DEFEATS.

Another mistake common to the old business model centers on the things that are highlighted in the daily affairs of the empire. Encapsulated in the stern and demanding philosophy that people should just do their jobs because that's what they're paid for is the implicit management technique of ignoring the successes and shining every spotlight in the house on the failures.

254   THE PILLARS OF THE EMPIRE

From the logical perspective of the dry old school, this actually makes sense. After all, people are expected to do things properly. That's their job, so there's no need to waste any time talking about it when it happens. Besides, because things are working, there's no action that needs to be taken.

Failures are another matter. Again, from a purely logical point of view, if you ignore the things that are done properly and spend all your time fixing mistakes, you'll optimize the use of your time, having devoted it completely to solving problems.

In the black-and-white world of computers and robots, this logic is compelling. Waste no time on things that don't need attention, focus on eliminating problems, and your operation should be a model of efficiency. There's only one problem with this equation: robots don't have feelings. But people do. Robots also don't intentionally lose your critical paperwork because you hurt their feelings. People have been known to do such things.

Mistakes must be corrected. That much is obvious. However, to correct a mistake, you have to bring it to light. No matter what the job or problem, it's the equivalent of coming up to a person and saying, "You're wrong." At an emotional level, that's not a particularly comfortable experience. The fact that it's true doesn't make it any more palatable. Nonetheless, we're all grown-ups, so we can handle someone pointing out our shortcomings when they happen.

But what if that's all that you ever heard? What if the complete dialog you heard each day from the people you worked with was just a broken record telling you over and over that you were wrong? With nothing else to offset that, you're eventually going to feel like telling someone to take a flying leap. As an aside, that's typically a career-limiting move.

To maintain the balance, you need to occasionally remind people that they do excellent work. People make mistakes. It would be great if they didn't, but human nature appears unlikely to change anytime soon. However, people also do great things.

The way we alter the quality in our interactions with others is through the emphasis we place on each action. If we make it a habit to point out every good deed done, we're halfway home. When we get to the criticism aspect, the important thing to realize is that we don't have to make a big deal about it to get the point conveyed. Furthermore, whenever possible, if you can communication your criticisms as almost an afterthought, you will do much to minimize their effect.

For instance, if your local computer network went down and you're savvy enough to realize that it's because one of your peers ran a program with known issues, you could yell across the room that they shouldn't do anything that stupid again. Or, after the network comes back up, you could walk by their office and casually mention, "Oh, by the way, Joe, you know that xyz program? We found out that it's been trashing the network, so you might want to avoid it for the time being. It nailed a lot of us over the past few weeks before we figured out what the culprit was."

Then just keep right on walking. No drama, no finger pointing (no matter how much data you just lost because of his mistake), no big deal. Play it down. He'll get the message, won't make the same mistake, and also won't suffer any humiliation that would limit his effectiveness.

As we've discussed previously, you should look for every possible success you can find in day to day affairs so that you have an opportunity to tell others that they're great. We tend to believe what we frequently hear. If you downplay the mistakes and emphasize the victories at ever possible moment, people will come to believe that yes, in fact, they do a great job. This lifts their spirits, and makes it even more likely that they'll succeed again.

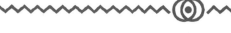

GLORIFY EVERY CONTRIBUTION.

While we're on the subject of pointing out the things that people do right, it's important that we be comprehensive in our approach. In every organization, some positions are just naturally going to get more attention than others. The day that our sales rep closes that million-dollar deal, the entire company will rattle the windows cheering the accomplishment. But how much do you cheer when someone fills out a customer service request to fix a client's problem? Or when you come in the next morning and see that your trash basket has been emptied?

Your company cannot succeed unless people, and a lot of people at that, *all* do their jobs properly. If any part of the operation suffers a breakdown along the way, it will disrupt the flow of money from the customer to your paycheck. And one disruption alone is enough to make the entire process break down.

But why should you care? Because you alone cannot guarantee that the customer's money travels all the way to your personal bank account. Because you have to trust the efforts of others in your company to do their part. Your ability to feed your family depends, in a very literal way, on how well other people do their jobs.

In looking at such a diverse and complex picture as a modern company, it might be tempting to just shrug your shoulders and declare that it's beyond your control. Fortunately, that couldn't be further from the truth. Not only are you capable of making a difference in your own job, you can have a positive and beneficial influence on every other operation with which you come in contact. That's because people perform every one of the operations that we've detailed so far.

Just as we've explored in so many other ways, the enthusiasm and emotional well-being of the people doing the work is a pivotal factor in how well that job will be done. Just as a moody receptionist can alienate a potential customer and blow a million-dollar deal, closing your store today because the only available clerk called in depressed and unable to work will limit your company's income.

When your company succeeds, you must adopt the attitude that a victory for all must also be a victory for the individual. You probably have awards ceremonies and the occasional celebrations when you land a new contract. However, when was the last time you made a big deal over the efforts of your support organizations, the people who push the paper so that your sales reps can bask in the glory?

At both the group and individual level, make it an important part of your day to seek out and commend all the people you can find who are just quietly going about their business of delivering the goods for your company, whatever those goods may be. When you celebrate the individual contributions of people throughout the empire, you build enthusiasm. Your praise and recognition will have an even greater effect than you might expect on many of these people simply because they've never even been acknowledged as playing any significant part in the achievements of the empire.

By showing gratitude and respect to those at every level of your company, you once again start spreading enthusiasm, the most contagious and beneficial phenomenon your company will ever encounter. And your people will love you for it.

KEEP THE GOALS BELIEVABLE.

There's nothing wrong with dreaming, and dreaming big. Personally, I don't know any other way to do it. It's important to remember, though, that not everyone has the same talents, passion, ambition, or drive as you do. Consequently, when you're setting goals, you're going to have to do so in a way that other people can believe in. If you don't, they'll simply roll their eyes and ignore you completely.

People are curious creatures. Like many animals, if a carrot is dangled in front of their nose, they'll try to reach it if they're hungry enough. However, if you hold it a mile away, hand them a pair of binoculars, and point to the carrot, they'll simply hand you back the binoculars and say, "So?" In other words, no one is going to expend any personal effort unless they believe there's a realistic possibility that their labors will be rewarded.

If you think about it, this explains many things you see in the corporate world. Over the years, I've witnessed incidents too numerous to recount in which people saw a problem, knew how to solve it, understood that it was important, and then simply shrugged their shoulders and went on about their business. Why on earth would people not do whatever they could to contribute to the health and well-being of the empire? For the same reason that we've encountered time and again: there's nothing in it for them personally if they do. You can be as idealistic as you like and wax philosophical for hours about how that just ain't right, but your passionate ramblings won't change a thing. It's human nature.

If we apply this aspect of nature to the topic of goal setting, it becomes immediately apparent why you must keep the goals realistic if you wish to enlist the enthusiasm and spirit of those you approach. The logic is simple. If they succeed in meeting the goal, there's something in it for them, even if it's just recognition. If they fail, they get nothing. Do the math. They're not going to waste all that time and effort if they believe that they'll find at the end of the rainbow only an empty promise and not a pot of gold.

It's important to make sure you know where your perspective is as well. From whose point of view are you thinking when you set these goals—yours or theirs? This is a very relevant question, for what you believe to be easy others may see as completely unrealistic. Because you're already motivated, your position is unimportant. You're trying to enlist the aid and efforts of others, so it's their way of looking at things that must be considered.

Consequently, you must first be sure that you understand their reality. If you just started this job last week and know nothing of their department, their politics, their goals, dreams, and desires, do your research before you approach them. It is only through a firm grasp of what they deal with on a daily basis that you can understand what benefits would be of value to them. And only armed with such tangible and relevant rewards can you hope to sway them.

The most important thing is to get your people to *believe*. If you set goals that they feel are reasonable and achievable, then you're giving them the chance to become winners once more, movers and shakers in the company who will be the envy of every other workgroup. Because you set a task before them that they felt in their hearts that they could accomplish, they'll stampede out of your office to prove that they're right.

REMOVE DRUDGERY WITH SPIRIT, FLAIR, AND ARTISTRY.

Maybe it's not realistic to expect every job in the world to suddenly become the stuff of Broadway musicals, with people spontaneously bursting into song and leaping about their work areas in carefully choreographed dance routines. And, frankly, on some Monday mornings, especially the ones that follow a particularly rowdy weekend, I'm not really sure I could handle that before my second cup of coffee anyway. Nonetheless, it is equally true that many jobs in the world don't have to be as dull, boring, and depressing as they currently are. Like so many other things, it really just comes down to attitude.

An Italian restaurant I used to frequent, another one of those corporate chain types, had the dining area set in one very large room, and against one wall were the grills, ovens, and cooks, all in plain sight. The specials of the day were written on a chalkboard near them, and there was a limited quantity of servings for each. When they were gone, they were gone, and the special was erased from the chalkboard so no one else would try to order it.

The cooks are the ones who know when they've run out, and cooks tend to enjoy running the show in general. When an item runs out, they don't just silently erase it. One of the cooks yells out at the top of his voice, "86 the anchovy lasagna!" (86 is restaurant slang for "get rid of it.")

The announcements would then prompt responses from across the restaurant, as servers, busboys, other cooks, and often even some of the customers chimed in, first echoing the command, "86 the anchovy lasagna!" but then frequently adding some wisecracks of their own to the fray, usually in a very bad, hammed-up, stereotypical Italian accent (it's *supposed* to be corny, folks). From "Whatsa matta? Did the little fishies swim away?" to "No, no, I bet Luigi took them fishing whena he got offa work!"

Of course, not only do the customers get a good laugh out of it, the workers are clearly having fun themselves. I don't know if you've ever bussed tables for a living (yep, I've done that, too), but I can assure you, anything to lighten up the shift is a good thing.

No matter what the task, find a way to take the dreariness out of the routine. You don't have to twirl knives like the Japanese steak house chefs do to have a good time. In fact, the last time I checked, twirling knives was frowned upon in most corporate environments. The important thing is to get creative and make the conscious decision to have a little fun with what you do. Loosen up! Learn to develop a sense of humor about what you're doing. It will also make the stressful times a little more bearable. There's no rule that says you can't take a matter seriously, give it the proper attention that it deserves, and make a joke at the same time.

One last thing I'd like to mention is something you should strive to avoid. Simply creating slogans and putting banners up on your walls is not going to change a thing without the action to back it up. In fact, when your workers come in one morning and see posters all over the walls with nifty little buzzwords and acronyms all declaring such things as "This is now a fun zone!" they're just going to shake their heads and do everything in their power to avoid being associated with your plan.

The best humor comes not from corporate mandates, but from the streets. In that Italian restaurant chain, it may well have been a corporate idea to shout out "86 the Special of the Day!" That's not too bad, but it's the people who will really bring it to life. A banner in the hallway with a stale corporate slogan isn't going to rally anyone. However, if it becomes a running joke that Luigi likes to fish using anchovies for bait because somebody took a spontaneous joke one night and ran with it, everyone will get a kick out of it.

But you can't legislate humor, spirit, or creativity. It just happens. What you can legislate, however, is a workplace environment in which people are free to explore the fun side of what they do without fear of reprimand. Forget the old business model. Get over yourself. And, most important of all, realize that the room full of people laughing, joking, and horsing around is outproducing the competition 10 to 1. Now *there's* something to laugh about.

REALIZE THAT ENTHUSIASM IS CONTAGIOUS.

I'm sure that more-educated minds could explain why enthusiasm is so highly contagious, but frankly I just don't care. All that matters to me is that it works. Out here on the streets, it doesn't really matter how well you can intellectualize a concept, or how trendy it might be. It either works, or it doesn't. In the latter case, it's discarded. Alternatively, we often look for other related approaches to duplicate the success. The nice thing about enthusiasm is that, not only does it improve productivity and quality, but it's self-replicating.

From the boardrooms to the back rooms, your company has many bright and capable people. These people going to offer you a continual stream of excellent ideas, and, as your plans move along, they're going to do their very best to tweak the process, fixing the problems, and enhancing the achievements. Their primary tool in these efforts is frequently their verbal skills, which becomes ever more true as you work your way up the chain of command. These are people who often make their contribution to the empire by presenting their ideas and perspectives to others. Unfortunately, a very high percentage of people in the workplace fail to recognize a truism that makes or breaks the support you get from others: *how you say it is as important as what you say.*

Logic alone is not enough. If you've ever had the pleasure of working with a group of people who were paid only when they accomplished something, the weekly results would amaze you. In a world full of workers who complain and moan because they don't make much money and life seems unlikely to ever change in that regard, here we have the exact opposite. There is literally no limit to how much money that they can make each week. If they want more money, they simply make more sales. No one will come along and say, "Sorry, but that's as much money as we're going to pay you this week." In fact, you'll find that leaders in sales organizations continually reinforce that they *want* people making big paychecks.

Therefore, the logical mind would conclude that all you need to do to motivate a sales force is to put the bare facts on the table: they can make as much money as they want. There is nothing else to say on the matter, because this information alone will make everyone so excited that they'll rip up the pavement and burn up the telephone lines in their efforts to rake in the cash. Of course, the logical mind would be dead wrong.

In fact, I've never been able to understand this myself from a personal point of view. Although I don't have a lot of college sheepskins on my wall, I nonetheless consider myself to possess at least moderate skills when it comes to logic and reason. Why on earth would people realize that they could make all the money their heart desired, and then sit back all day slacking off instead of working hard and succeeding? I just don't get it. Nonetheless, I know from years of personal experience that it happens. Logic isn't enough to motivate people. Good heavens, if money won't get people excited, what else will? You guessed it. *Enthusiasm.* That's why sales organizations constantly hold contests and other such motivational events.

The power of morale is the most incredible weapon that you can ever bring to bear on your adversaries. When you have a group of people who are excited and enthusiastic about the plan, passionately throwing themselves into their work and celebrating each other's achievements in a public manner, you're going to set records in your work that others can only dream about.

Furthermore, you're going to build your group to an ever-larger and more powerful force as others are drawn to the irresistible pull of your group enthusiasm. This is how you build a large and powerful tribe. This is also how you join together every tribe in the land, until one day you look up and find that you have united *all* the tribes, through the power of passion and enthusiasm, into an invincible empire.

ACTIVELY ELIMINATE NEGATIVITY.

No matter how persuasively you can speak nor how compelling your presentation, when you try to sway a group of people, particularly in an already downtrodden environment, you will always encounter detractors. A bad attitude is also contagious, although it's never as powerful a force as enthusiasm. Even so, a loud and pessimistic voice will slow you down and diminish your support among the people.

Let's take a look at some of the incremental ways that you can deal with the actively nasty personality who's dragging down the group. The first technique is to simply avoid the attack. If you're working with your peers or those who report to you and doing your best to instill hope and enthusiasm among the ranks, someone may very well sit in the back and mumble, "Oh, please, you've got to be kidding me." You could take that as an attack and strike back, but why risk the conflict, and the chance of hurting someone else, if you don't have to? Just ignore it and go on with what you're saying, and you will have avoided the entire problem.

Of course, your detractor may be more aggressive and instead speak up and say, "That all sounds like a lot of useless hype. That'll never work around here." Again, why fight if you don't have to? If avoiding him outright didn't work, you still don't have to demolish the guy. A simple deflection of his blow may well suffice. Sometimes it's enough to just chuckle and say, "Yeah, some days it feels like that around here, doesn't it? Anyway, as I was saying . . ."

Not everyone gives up on the first try. If he persists, you may have to acknowledge his aggression, responding in such a manner that you not only cast aside his strike but also leave him feeling vulnerable and exposed in the process. With luck, this will make him realize that, although you really don't want a conflict, it's hazardous to his corporate health to attack you further. If he boldly snorts, "This is all just a waste of time. I've got better things to do than listen to this nonsense," particularly if there are people of influence or power within earshot, it's time to make him realize the weakness of his position.

"Yes, Joe, I realize that you don't see the value in this right now, but of course what I'm trying to do is help us all improve our situation. I know that a lot of people here would really like to see things get better, right? [Look around the room to elicit nods of agreement.] And I'm sure you don't really want to stand in the way of everyone else improving their job, do you?" If he has any common sense, he'll note that not only have you defended your position but you've also subtly shown him that there may be more retaliation than he's prepared to deal with should he pursue matters further.

Nonetheless, aggressive people don't always have the best survival skills, and, if he continues, you may be forced to explicitly block his attack in a strong enough manner to set an example, both to him and to others who may have similarly foolish notions of attacking you. If you're going to block, make it a strong one.

"You know, Joe, I can see from your persistence in this line of questioning that, for some reason, you don't want to see us succeed. Whether you believe in our plan or not [now it's not *your* plan, but *our* plan], what you're doing is counterproductive and detrimental to the company as a whole. By continually making waves here and offering no constructive support, you're trying to keep us from doing a better job. Is that your intent? Is that what your superiors need to note about how you do your work? We're working hard here to improve things. If you can't contribute to that, you need to sit down and be quiet."

However, the very best defense of all is to simply make high spirits and enthusiasm the standard, normal way that everyone is expected to be. Faced with the awesome but subtle power of peer pressure, many of those who have been slow to join the conga line will reluctantly give it a try, just to keep from looking like a loser. Of course, the line immediately opens up and embraces them, and, before you know it, this person is truly having a good time. Once again, you have turned adversaries into allies.

UNDERSTAND THE IMPORTANCE OF TAKING BREAKS.

*B*urnout. In our day and age, it's a word that is becoming more and more familiar. We work hard and are dedicated to our cause. We're not afraid to put in the extra hours, go the extra mile, or lose the extra sleep. That's dedication. And with nothing to offset that intensity, that's also just plain dumb. You may have great endurance and be able to carry on like that for a prolonged period of time, but you can't hold out forever. Eventually, if you do, you're toast.

One of the first signs you'll see when burnout starts to rear its weary head is a marked effect on your morale. Remember, a tired people are invariably pessimistic. When we're worn out, the mountains seem very high, indeed. From a fresh and rested perspective, however, we often feel that we could attack Mount Everest with little more than a sturdy pair of sneakers.

Often, when we think about taking a break, we think purely in physical terms, such as sleep or the cessation of hard physical labor. These are necessary and obvious activities, or lack thereof. The state of your body will have a pronounced effect on your mental and emotional outlook. There will be times, however, when it will seem inappropriate to do the thing that would contribute to our productivity the most.

Most jobs have deadlines of one sort or another. Whether it's a manufacturing quota to meet, a job to finish for a customer, or a project schedule to release a new product to market, there will always be some form of pressure on us to produce, and to do so in a timely manner. Because of this, we're apt to feel obligated to work hard and without rest for the good of the cause. This might be a mandate from our leaders, or it may be peer pressure from other dedicated souls. Nonetheless, we all have our limits, and, once reached, personal productivity is guaranteed to plummet.

Particularly if you're in a leadership position, you need to understand this and keep an eye on your people. Correspondingly, if you're one of the workers, your contribution to the overall good includes making sure that your operation runs as effectively as it possibly can. Toward that end, it's up to you to keep an eye on your coworkers when they start to get a little crispy around the edges.

Whether due to a feeling of obligation, fear of reprisal, or just a strong work ethic, many people will jettison breaks in exchange for more hours of productivity. As I lean a bit toward the workaholic side of life myself, I'm familiar with this one in an up-close and personal manner. For some people, cultivating personal discipline in their lives may need to focus on being more ambitious or hard working in their endeavors. We each operate at a different intensity level. Others, however, need to acquire the common sense necessary to realize that, when your brain is fuzzy, your eyes bleary, and you can't remember where you left your coffee cup, you may not be doing your very best work. And, as you grind yourself further and further to a pulp, your attitude will suffer as a result.

If you know such people, the first thing you have to do is realize for yourself that overall quality and productivity are what's important, not the incidental details of how many hours people worked yesterday. Keeping that thought in the forefront of your mind, you must then act as a support mechanism (a safety valve might be a better analogy) for the overzealous souls within your domain. If you don't encourage or, when necessary, even require them to take a break, they won't. The work they do when they're mentally or physically exhausted doesn't help the cause. And the cause doesn't benefit if they push themselves to the point that they end up quitting, either. You just lose a great and normally productive worker.

You'll get much more done when you're sharp than you will wasting time in a worn-out state. You'll also get another productivity gain: you won't have to waste a few days redoing all your work when you come back. Best of all, with a fresh spirit and clear head, you'll be much more fun in the conga line.

SOCIALIZE FREQUENTLY AND SINCERELY.

The company that plays together stays together. It's vital that you work on a daily basis to improve the morale and high spirits in the workplace. When you go in to work tomorrow, stop and look around you. Think about who these people are, what they like to do, the things they laugh about, the kinds of food they eat, the movies they enjoy, the music they listen to. They aren't some group of corporate zombies. They're real, live people. Just like you.

Furthermore, given even half a chance, many of them would be wonderful additions to your circle of friends. You just have to decide to give them a chance and make an opening for them in your life. It doesn't even matter if work is the only time you see them. I have dear friends who live in different cities. The only time I see them is when I visit that city. The distance doesn't diminish the friendship in the slightest.

If you want to build morale, enthusiasm, and esprit de corps, the people who work together should play together. You'll always have more fun, of course, playing with your friends. And, if you work with the people you play with, work becomes much more fun and productive. Therefore, the secret to truly effective company social functions has nothing to do with the formalities of what, when, and where. It's all about people.

There are just a few steps that, if taken sincerely, can transform your tribe and your empire from detached workmates to a close-knit family. First, make a conscious decision that you're going to build true, lasting, and sincere friendships with every person in the company that you can make a connection with. Then, put forth the personal effort to make those connections. You already know how. You did it with your current friends, and you didn't have to go to college to learn how to do it. Do the same with the people you work with.

Be aware of the fact that you'll have to take the first steps, and you'll have to open the doors initially. Your approach will, by the necessities of human nature, vary from person to person. However, if you appreciate the fact that building better and more personal relationships with those around you will create a happier and stronger empire, you can communicate that to others as well. Just as you stretch out to make your coworkers your circle of friends, urge others to do the same, and explain why it's in their best interest to do so.

You're now ready to enter into another of the self-reinforcing cycles that we've encountered from time to time. You've decided to make your coworkers friends. Informal gatherings give you the perfect setting to do just that. However, as your make more and more friends, you're just naturally going to want to hang out and have fun with them. This calls for a party! As you can see, this will continue to build. You'll make more friends and therefore have more gatherings, where you'll make more friends.

So what exactly is a gathering? It doesn't matter. You can go out for dinner and drinks after work, meet at someone's backyard on a weekend for a cookout where everyone brings the kids, you name it. Is there a great new movie out that's all the rage? Gathering! A great new band playing across town? You guessed it, gathering! It just doesn't matter. Leverage the collective fun of your group. Everyone has things they like to do for fun. By exploring the antics of your friends at work, you'll open yourself up to great new experiences, and you'll have tons of great excuses to get together.

The luckiest people in the world are the ones who get paid to have fun working with their friends. They're also the most productive. When you decide to take advantage of this approach, you'll not only have the best company in town, you'll also have more friends than you know what to do with. Life doesn't get much better than that.

KNOW THAT YOURS IS SUPERIOR TO ALL OTHER EMPIRES.

Above all, the very foundation of company morale is the firm conviction that you are the best of the best. This is what you must work daily to reinforce in your people. Even if your competition is ahead of you in some areas, it doesn't matter. With the proper attitude, you and your people know that it's only a matter of time before your adversaries bite the dust because, ultimately, you are in fact superior to all other empires.

What truly matters, therefore, is that you tell your people that they are the best and convince them that it's in their personal self-interest to believe you, even if it doesn't appear to be true at the moment. Invoke simple logic. If you believe that you and your department are an absolute mess, how does that help the cause? What can that possibly do other than depress you? And, being depressed, how likely are you to improve or prevail in your efforts?

Alternatively, if you get up each morning and tell yourself that you belong to the elite, the advance guard who is going to lead your company on to bold and unimagined success, just imagine the effect that will have on your daily efforts. Pronouncing it to yourself each morning is powerful. Now imagine that, when you get to work, you're surrounded all day by people who reinforce that.

You will move from success to success. Each time something goes right, no matter how trivial, someone raises their coffee cup into the air and declares, "Yes! We are the elite!" only to be joined by a rousing response and raised cups from all the others. Driven by even more enthusiasm, everyone returns to their work with passion, creating yet another success to toast.

Does that sound silly to you? Then you've never seen the staggering power of a fired-up and united people, or what a sense of pride and purpose can do for even the smallest and weakest group. Such fledgling units have gone on to rule nations. What possible chance does your competition have against such a force?

So how do you get the ball rolling? Easy. *Look* for successes. Does that seem strange? It wouldn't be surprising if it did, for most companies have trained people to barely acknowledge the everyday moments when people do things right and instead to focus on the things that go wrong.

Once again, logic shows the most beneficial path. Problems need to be recognized so that they can be corrected. I'll give you that one. However, when you suggest to people that you should make a fuss over it when somebody does their job right, they're going to give you funny looks. After all, they'll reason, they're not doing anything special or out of the ordinary. It's just their job.

Technically, they're correct, but who cares? Once again, how does that contribute to your cause? In the beginning, when you're trying to turn around the attitude of a bunch of people who have either been through some tough times or are merely run into the ground from years of tedium, what possible motivation do you have to stick with the technically correct assessment of the situation? Absolutely none, of course. On the other hand, if every time one of your coworkers completes yet another task, no matter how routine, it gives you something positive to recognize and share with the group, it will soon become personal both for you and them.

That's what makes it so motivating. Once upon a time, you got up and went to your job working for someone's company. Now, however, it's *your* company, something you and your coworkers take pride in, leading to a sense of ownership.

Once you and your people realize that you *are* the empire, what the competition does to you in the marketplace also becomes a very personal thing. Once, you didn't really care whether or not the competition gained an edge in the market. Now, however, with the new sense of pride and purpose that your people feel, all can clearly see that the competition is their enemy.

They made a sale to one of your customers? How dare they! A popular business journal says the competition looks like the new leader in your field? Never! Why? Because you and your people know that you are superior to all other empires. And, with an attitude like that, if it's not true now, it soon will be. When spirits are high and everyone raises their voice together into a single shout, it will shake the very earth beneath you. That is the awesome power of human emotion.

MORALE

Never underestimate the critical importance of emotions.

- ◎ Remember that the people are the empire.
- ◎ Emphasize the victories, not the defeats.
- ◎ Glorify every contribution.
- ◎ Keep the goals believable.
- ◎ Remove drudgery with spirit, flair, and artistry.
- ◎ Realize that enthusiasm is contagious.
- ◎ Actively eliminate negativity.
- ◎ Understand the importance of taking breaks.
- ◎ Socialize frequently and sincerely.
- ◎ Know that yours is superior to all other empires.

X ≀ Unite!

Build a movement and become invincible.

I t is not enough for you to succeed personally. No matter how much you accomplish on your own, as an individual you are still weak, vulnerable, and powerless. No matter how strong your tribe may be, it can't stand alone either. Even a seemingly simple transaction such as selling a loaf of bread is actually an incredibly complex sequence of events that requires each tribe in the empire to perform well for the benefits to be enjoyed by all.

Therefore, even though you can gain tremendous personal benefits by studying and applying the Pillars of the Empire, if you stop there your achievements will be severely limited. Ultimately, working alone, your world will not change. Even if things appear to get better for a time, without the strength and support of your tribe and all others, your individual improvements will eventually be swept away by the slow but steady forces of inertia and the status quo.

Only by starting a movement within your company—tending the fires daily and helping them spread throughout the empire—will you gather enough strength and power to institute real and lasting change. If you want a better tomorrow for yourself and your family, you must accept that you need the support of others to secure it. You need people, in large numbers, flocking to your cause. But they will not appear at your doorstep by magic. It is up to you, personally, to bring the cause to them.

Whether you're a leader, a worker, or both, it is not someone else's job to build the movement any more than it is their responsibility to ensure that your family has food on the table. To build a better tomorrow, you must build a stronger empire today. Like any other journey, the road to prosperity, happiness, and rousing good times is traveled one step at a time. If you personally make it a priority to strengthen this movement within your company and spread it to the far corners of the empire in every way that you're able, you and your people will enjoy the greatest times of your lives.

DEDICATE YOURSELF
TO THE CAUSE.

As the old saying goes, Rome wasn't built in a day, and the Roman empire was a mighty one, indeed. At its height, the Romans enjoyed a standard of living that was unparalleled in human history. But it's important to note that the glory that became Rome was, in the beginning, just a small movement, a tiny collection of people against a vast and wide world. Forged through continual success, learning and improving from defeat, the empire that was to one day shake the very foundations of the world began life much like you and your people: a small group with vision, passion, and dedication set out on the road to greatness. And, like you, they traveled their path one step at a time.

The most important concept to be remembered from those early Roman days can be summarized by a single word: *dedication*. Those who build mighty empires don't spend a couple of hours a week, whenever they can squeeze it into their schedules, working toward their lofty goals. Instead, their quest becomes a part of their lives—a burning, driving passion that consumes them from the moment they wake until the last of their children has been tucked away for a safe night's sleep. They dedicate their spirit, their time, and, most importantly, their actions to achieve this one noble goal. Unite the people into a single, invincible empire, and let all within enjoy a standard of living never before imagined.

Building this movement and spreading it throughout the empire must be your highest and most sacred goal throughout each and every moment of your workday. This does not conflict with the specific duties you were hired to perform; it *enhances* them. A crucial part of building a glorious empire is delivering personal excellence. Dedicating yourself to a movement that inspires others to do the same guarantees that this glory will be achieved. Therefore, your highest personal priority must be to spread the word and strengthen the movement that will one day ensure an invincible empire. Don't forget that there is strength in numbers. But only you, and those whose lives you touch, can make that strength a reality.

Furthermore, you must on a daily basis tend to the details and effort of building a movement. You will never have a single day at work where you are not presented with numerous opportunities to share what you've learned, explain the benefits of unity to others, make friends, build alliances, and further promote the cause. These opportunities to build the movement, however, will not come to you. You must come to them.

From the moment you walk in the door each morning, every single person you pass is a potential ally. Look for and create openings to get to know them better. Having gained a new acquaintance, work over time to transform that into a friendship, sharing your vision of a stronger empire and encouraging them to join your efforts in promoting your movement.

When they see the personal benefits they can receive through the power of a united people, you'll find that they become as enthusiastic about the vision as you are. And, of course, you're speaking to them with a happy voice and a sparkle in your eye, because you know that this enthusiasm is contagious.

At this point, many of the people you've already spoken to are reading these words and wondering just how they can be such a powerful voice for change. Each person is an individual, with their own unique personality and strengths. Consequently, different people will have different styles.

Instead of shouting slogans across the office or standing on a table in the break room, just *talk* to people. You know, like you always do. Ask them about the things they'd like to see improve in the company. Get them to share their ideas on what a new, better world would look like. In return, share what you have learned, and show them how they can apply the Pillars of the Empire to their own jobs. Most importantly, let them see the benefits they can enjoy through a strong and united empire.

You'll find that, more often than not, they'll be grateful for any little tip, trick, or reference material that you can share that will make their day better. Suddenly, without being anyone other than who you normally are, you've strengthened friendships and alliances, and you've made the movement one person stronger.

Regardless of your personal style, then, you have the ability and opportunities each day to add momentum to the cause and to bring your people that much closer to a higher standard of living. Don't try to get there overnight. If you build your movement one small step at a time, you'll have momentum that you can count on for a long time to come.

EMPHASIZE YOUR COMMON BONDS.

With your new dedication to building a movement where you work, you'll find that one of the most useful and beneficial tools to have in your bag is once again basic human nature. Your company is not as strong today as it could be for many reasons, and one of the prevalent ones, of course, is a lack of unity. And, yet, that's a rather curious state of affairs from a logical point of view. Why would people get up each day and all go to work for the same company, and yet feel divided rather than a part of something bigger?

In fact, they *are* a part of something bigger. They just don't get it. They see what they've been trained to see since birth. Every day, in every way, society encourages us to notice what's different about others. Do you know what a barbarian is? No, don't bother reaching for the dictionary; it would only confuse the issue. The true meaning of *barbarian* is not some uncivilized bandit who raids your village and steals your livestock. The definition, which applies even today, is much more straightforward than that. What's a barbarian? *Anyone from out of town.*

Just because people are different doesn't mean that they can't become family. Is everyone in your family exactly the same? Not only do people not have to be the same as you for you to form close bonds with them, it's actually in your personal best interest to make alliances with as wide a collection of people as you can.

Back in the days of cavemen and wooly mammoths, knowing how to start a fire was a pretty handy skill. However, even though it kept you warm at night, it didn't do much for your empty stomach. What if every person in your tribe was just like you and could start a fire in a heartbeat, but wouldn't know how to hunt down dinner if, well, their lives depended on it? Just down the road from you, of course, is a tribe of hunters. They've got more wooly mammoth meat than all of you could eat in a season. But there's a problem: eating a raw mammoth is an unpleasant experience. But then, because they don't associate with barbarians, all they know how to do is hunt.

The obvious solution to this mutual problem is an alliance between the two tribes. Of course, the reason it's so very beneficial to the tribes concerned is due to the differences between them. Because of those different traits, two tribes combined are now stronger and more prosperous than either single tribe was separately.

But how do you start an alliance between different types of people? How do you convince the suspicious guards eyeing you from high atop the castle walls that, not only do you come in friendship, you don't even *like* sheep? All you have to do is reverse the equation. You've been trained all your life to notice differences. Subtract those from the person, and what you'll be left with are the things that are alike. If you need a calculator to do the math, go ahead and grab one. We'll wait.

Anytime you wish to form a new union, sit down before your first encounter and compile a list of all the things the two of you have in common. Furthermore, make a list of your common enemies. Nothing builds a bond like a mutual adversary. Most importantly, put the focus on the fact that, because of the things you have in common, you're really one people, not two. After pointing out that you therefore have the same basic human needs and that, due to your mutual enemies, you also have the same goals and ambitions and obstacles to overcome, you're free to build an alliance.

At this point, the sky's the limit. Share with them everything you've learned about the value of unity, and learn from them all that would benefit the cause. Then suggest that you move forward not as two tribes, but as one people, joined by the common sense of purpose and mutual benefit you'll all receive from the united empire you create together.

MAKE THE MOVEMENT ATTRACTIVE.

Your goal is to take what you've learned about building a strong and prosperous empire and spread that word throughout your company. With each success in this direction, your movement will become stronger and more capable of creating the kinds of change that you all want:

excellence in products and service, dominance in the marketplace, over-flowing company bank accounts from which individual benefits will flow. And friendship, camaraderie, fun, exciting days, and moving from one inspirational victory to the next. Does this sound like a great way to spend your days? The power of a large, company-wide movement will make it possible.

Best of all, you're once again looking at a phenomenon that can be self-perpetuating. The more attractive your movement is, the more your ranks will swell. The larger the movement, the greater the power. More power means continued success, bringing greater benefits to all. That, of course, just makes the movement more attractive.

From the moment you make that personal commitment, you can take an immediate step to start rallying others to your cause: you can start having fun. Sorry, were you expecting something difficult and tedious? You can do that, too, if you like, but the most important thing you can demonstrate to others in the beginning stages of your movement is that it's a great way to live your life. Misery may love company, but nobody ever comes to visit. Throw a party, and everyone on the block will show up, whether they were invited or not.

To gain support, swell your ranks, and build a powerful movement, you need people. If you don't have a track record to show yet, it doesn't matter. You can immediately turn your personal work area into an exciting, entertaining place. If I can turn a dirty, smelly, noisy factory job that literally tore skin from my fingers every night into a raucous hotbed of laughter, jokes, and competition, there's not any other kind of job that can't experience a similar transformation. We had fun because we decided to. In fact, we had fun because, in the beginning, I decided to. It's just not any more complicated than that.

People like to have fun, so they joined us. And so a movement was born that touched not just my little job but also many other departments. Incidentally, if you'll recall, we weren't even trying to encourage a movement. It just happened through the magical power of people having fun with what they were doing. Imagine how much better it will be when you make it a priority to start one.

Once you have their attention (and you will), your next step is to show them the personal benefits that lie in store for them when they join your efforts. You were smart enough to see this for yourself, so it should be easy for you to communicate it to them as well. Remember, the funda-mental motivating factor in just about anyone's life is their own personal

self-interest. Appeal to that and you will always get an enthusiastic response. After all, why wouldn't you? You're truly and sincerely trying to
make their life better.

The great thing about it is that you won't spend very much time at all
before you actually do have tangible results to show for your efforts. In
fact, you've been diligent about jotting these results down in your journal in a way that makes it easy for you to rattle them off to others, right?
Because of this, you now have not only the charismatic pull of people
having fun with what they do, but, once you have their attention, you
also have success stories. They say that nothing succeeds like success. Of
course what that means is that, when you're winning, everyone wants to
be a part of what you're doing, and all those extra people and their talents just make you a greater success.

BE GRACIOUS TO THE VANQUISHED.

In all of our discussions, we've been in and out of conflicts as we work
to unite the disparate and warring tribes of your company into a single, unified empire. By now it's obvious that, in the beginning, there will
be the occasional battle as the small-minded people of limited vision
compete for resources, threatening the long-term health and well-being
of the company. But the greatest victories are those that are won without
a fight because no casualties are left to mourn. However, at times you
must take up arms and put down a rebellious force for the greater good
of all concerned. How you handle this will have a far-reaching effect on
future support.

Just as we've seen previously when forced to defend the morale of the
group from a negative and destructive personality, it's important to use
only the force you need to remove a threat to your progress, and no
more. Whether you're an individual or a tribe, you do not want the
backlash of public resentment that invariably comes should you garner
a reputation as an insensitive bully. Fight when you must, and fight with

valor until you achieve victory. But do not fight out of anger, vengeance, or the petty desire to inflict harm on another.

Furthermore, people judge the victorious by their treatment of the vanquished. Once you have put a decisive end to a particular tribal squabble, your work is not done. In any corporate turf war, emotions will run high on both sides. That won't stop just because the fighting did. Remember, nobody likes to lose. Once the matter is settled, it's then time to tend to the feelings of the people who lost the conflict.

It is your job, no matter how difficult, to smooth the ruffled feathers and eliminate any vestiges of ill will. Not only is it your responsibility to make sure that no bad feelings remain between you and the opposing camp, you must also make sure that your people do the same. You'll sometimes find that it's just as difficult to get your own people to lay down their weapons as it is for your vanquished foe.

When the arrows start flying, people get hurt. And, when that happens to you or one of your friends, it becomes personal, and such personal feelings can turn into long-term grudges even when the battle is over. You simply cannot allow this to happen, and so you must use every means at your disposal—including the significant power of peer pressure among your own people—to make sure that everyone buries the hatchet and makes a commitment to get over it.

It's okay if it takes a reasonable period of time for everyone to cool off. It's unreasonable to expect people to walk straight from a vicious fight to an all-night dinner party with the opposition, whether they were on the winning or losing side. However, your people need to understand that they have a short and finite period to put it all behind them. You can't let this sort of thing drag on, or it will create ill will that serves no one.

You can win the hearts and minds of those you are forced to defeat in battle in another way as well. In addition to kindness and a desire to heal all wounds, remember this one simple tactic: if you want someone to become family, then treat them like family. When the fighting is over, consider sharing the spoils with the vanquished. That's the quickest way to make them feel like a part of your movement. Suddenly, you no longer have the victor and the defeated, but just one huge and powerful group.

One last step remains. You make sure that the word goes down on both sides to every last worker, reinforcing the spirit of unity. Even your most junior team member then moves forward and looks for opportunities to make friends in the other group. The following year, the lines between your tribes are blurry and no one cares. You're all having too much fun achieving your next victory, as allies rather than adversaries. The empire, and the personal power of each individual, has once again grown stronger.

BUILD STRENGTH BY TEACHING OTHERS.

In much of the Pillars, we've talked about the efforts to strengthen your group, and how your tribe can therefore benefit the empire. In addition to this perspective, we will now look beyond the confines of our own work area and help the empire by improving the quality of its structures. Of course, as ever, our building blocks are the most capable to be found: people. Consequently, if we want to improve the quality of the overall structure of the empire, we need to pay attention to the individual.

But why would we care about strengthening remote parts of the land, tribes, and individuals with whom we currently have no direct interaction? Surely this can wait until later, when we've expanded our local tribes to the point that they meet with our distant cousins, right?

In the old days, we slept at night within the confines of the castle walls for safety. If the enemy attacked while we slept, we were still safe because our walls were solid. However, if even a small opening in a wall could be exploited and widened, even if it were far away from where we slept, it wouldn't matter. The enemy would still pour in through that breach.

And, once they were inside, no one was safe. If you want security in life, each and every brick must be of the highest quality, no matter which wall it's used in. A threat to any defense is a threat to us all. Therefore, it is again in your own personal best interest to make sure that each and every brick you see is made as strong as possible, even if you'll never see that brick again.

This is very much like the difference between a small town and a large city. If you walk down the streets of a rural township, chances are that you actually know most people you see and can greet them in an individual manner based on what you know of their life. Some will be friends, others just acquaintances, but most will be familiar. Contrast this with a walk down a major thoroughfare in New York City. The sidewalks are literally packed at midday with people, all of them complete strangers. You wouldn't have the time to greet each one of them even if they were all friends. There's just too many. So, you put your blinders on and pretend that they don't exist. They do the same, and you are therefore able to be completely alone in one of the world's most populated cities.

However, as you make your way through the building each day at work, you can at least cut one or two from the herd. If you're an accountant standing in the break room having a cup of coffee and one of the warehouse workers walks in, you could put your blinders on and just ignore him as he would you. That's what usually happens. If instead you say "hello," and make any form of small talk, he'll stop, probably surprised, and respond. You learn his name and a little about who he is, and he does the same. A couple of days later, you're walking past the warehouse on your way to your car. He sees you, calls out your name, and asks how things are going.

You now have an acquaintance in a completely unrelated department. By making it a point to stop here and there when you meet, you start building that relationship toward a friendship. You've studied the Pillars and put many of them into practice, had quite a few successes, and refined your approach as time has passed. It's now becoming easy for you to see how to apply them to any tribe. Therefore, share what you've learned with the people you meet, and you'll find that you have not only new friends, but strong ones.

GAIN SUPPORT BY SPREADING AWARENESS.

If you want to make someone remember your point, you have to give it to them in a short and catchy manner. That embeds the idea into their brain and keeps it there. They will then follow through with whatever action is required to complete the thought when the time comes.

There's an additional consideration when you're looking to rally and motivate people, as we most certainly are. If you give someone a catchy phrase, they will remember it. However, it may not fire their passions and get them all worked up, which is really what we want. Therefore, drawing once again from days of old, we will utilize another time-tested technique: the battle cry.

If you pinned a printout to your wall that had several dense paragraphs of detailed information, no one would stop to read it. If, instead, you had something brief, it would get their attention. Change that to a battle cry, and for reasons that reach deep into the human psyche, they will be both curious and excited. On the inside, a little voice will say to them, "Hey, something's going on, and it sounds important!" It is. It's your future. Therefore, instead of printing out pages of mission statements and specific changes you want to accomplish to improve your department, focus instead on capturing their curiosity, passion, and interest.

As it happens, we already have a battle cry. It is, distilled down into a single sentence, the heart and soul of what we have been considering all along. When you're ready to get their attention and are excited about starting a movement in your own company, then regardless of your industry, here is both your banner and your battle cry:

Unite, and be invincible!

Simple, isn't it? And, yet, it is commanding. Hidden in this phrase is a power to stir the soul that's as old as humanity itself; it's both a call to action and a clear definition of the reward for doing so—and all in just a few words. It will turn heads, and people will stop and ask questions. And that's what you want.

Once you've got someone's attention, even for a moment, you have the opportunity to promote your agenda. You wouldn't have been able to stop people in the hallways with your ideas to improve the workplace. With the proper awareness campaign, however, you can get them to come to you. That's even better because, when you talk, they'll already be interested in what you have to say.

You can use this simple technique in many ways. Put your battle cry at the bottom of your standard email signature. Pin it on your cubicle wall, above the cartoons of the beloved engineer who has come to symbolize the plight of the corporate worker. Put it on your Web site, using it as a link to more information on your plans to build an invincible empire. You can even put it on the refrigerator in the break room, along with a pointer to where they can learn more. Use this attention-getting slogan as a device to lead people more deeply into your group and your plans. Show them what they can do, how they can join forces with you, how you can help them, and what the benefits are to all when you work for a strong and united empire. You want friends and allies, and you want them now. It's time to start a movement!

It is with this sense of enthusiasm and passion that you enter into your awareness campaign, spreading the word far and wide with the intention of gathering supporters, swelling the ranks, and building an overall sense of excitement about what you're doing.

But a battle cry does not win battles. People do. A slogan will not solve problems. What it will do is rally people to a central location. Along those lines, just reading this book isn't going to solve your problems. You have to take action and start a movement.

I've provided a variety of useful materials that you can download from our Web site (www.ShowProgramming.com) and that will aid you in your awareness campaign and help you build the alliances you need to start a powerful movement in your own company. You must build a massive awareness campaign to swell your ranks, but, above all, you must take the concepts in the Pillars of the empire and use them to create a solid, practical, and realistic plan of action that will work in your empire. Do this, and you will achieve stunning success.

~~~~~~~~~~~~~~~~~~~~~~~~~~~~((◎))~~~~~~~~~~~~~~~~~~~~~~~~~~~~

INSPIRE OTHERS TO ACT.

The basic components of a human being are consistent regardless of age, gender, nationality, or culture. The human creature is a highly complex one, but some basic components exist at a high level. For our purposes, we can think of them as the physical, mental, and emotional bodies. Better scientific terms may be available, but I'm more concerned with making the point than going to med school.

When you invoke logic, you can think of it as appealing to their mental body. When it's time for dinner, which is something that is a direct result of paydays, people are concerned primarily with their physical bodies. And, when you want to see any kind of reaction beyond the flat monotone of a robot, you'll want to interact with the emotional body. Furthermore, just to complicate things ever so slightly, people each seem to have a different proportion of strengths among these three bodies.

Some people are so mentally focused, sterile, and analytical that you couldn't excite them with the most primal stimulus available on earth. Others don't seem to care about much of anything but physical gratification, from the great restaurant down the street to the thrill of bungee jumping. Lastly, some people are so emotionally focused that you can't take a deep breath around them without setting off some kind of severe reaction involving their feelings. Of course, most people are therefore a complicated combination of these three strengths. If you can learn to discern this with just a brief bit of interaction, it's a serious edge in communications and promoting your agenda.

For our concern at this moment (getting people to act instead of just agree), we've already seen that mental rationalizations of the benefits are insufficient. Physical persuasion is equally irrelevant in this regard, no matter how much you'd like to gently tap your coworker on the head with a heavy object. This means, by process of elimination, that, when you want to motivate someone and get them off their seat and on their feet, you want emotional responses.

I have not studied the matter in college and so could not give you an accurate and technical explanation or justification, but years of experience have proven this to me over and over again: inspiration is an extremely emotional experience. When you want someone to do rocket science and solve a complex math problem, break out the mental capabilities. However, when you want a roomful of people to leap to their feet, rush out the door, and throw heart, body, and soul into the work of the day, you're going to have to touch them on an emotional level. That's the domain of excitement, and that's where the passions lie. Fortunately for us, we have just what we need for the occasion. Can you guess by now? Of course you can. *Enthusiasm!*

As you work so hard to build awareness and get everyone's attention, you must be prepared to give them practical direction once you have their attention. This means that you must have a plan in place, or at least the next couple of steps of one. Now that you've got them interested and agreeing with you, the last step is to get them to act. Just as you've done all along, you will simply present your ideas and propositions with passion and excitement. Have fun with it! If you're having fun and are clearly excited about the prospects for the future, they will be, too. Just as we're considering here, you must point out to them that understanding is good, but that they must act. Then, using the things you've learned from the Persuasion Pillar, you tell them what you need and persuade them to do it.

Most of all, whether you lead from the front or from the middle, you must *lead*! Remember, you don't have to be a charismatic, stand-on-the-soapbox sort to motivate your coworkers. You can lead from the middle by setting a shining example of unity and excellence, and especially through your constant and sincere enthusiasm for the cause. The power of even one dedicated, excited, and positive example can motivate countless people, who will then go on to inspire even more. Be who you are, and act in your own personal style, but make sure that you do all you can to serve as an inspiration to others. If you can move even ten people to action, you just became ten times as valuable to the empire.

BE RELENTLESS.

Many people encounter a new idea, get very excited about it, and then lose interest somewhere down the line. Is it because the idea wasn't compelling enough? No, it's just our old friend—human nature—come to call on us again. Just as people have a different combination of mental, physical, and emotional strengths, they also vary in their attention span and their ability to persist. But consistency is precisely what builds empires. You must throw yourself into the effort, and never let up.

Understand that, just as you struggle to maintain a steady effort week after week in building the empire, others must obviously contend with their own weaknesses. That means that you have to be a constant source of awareness, motivation, and inspiration to those around you. Don't give up the fight. And don't let your comrades give up the fight, either.

You must stand behind them, support them, encourage them, and push them on, just as you do yourself. To truly serve the people of your tribe and all others, you must also be relentless in your support of their activities. An added benefit to that is that we tend to receive the same as we give. When others see that you're as constant as the North Star in your encouragement and enthusiasm, you can bet that they will all rush to your side when you're having a low moment yourself. One for all. All for one.

Each morning, get up, grab your cup of coffee, and then sit down and make a list of what you can do today to expand the empire. No matter what projects are going on or how busy you are at work each week, there is never a day that passes without an opportunity for you to do something to bring your people together and strengthen the empire.

Make a promise to yourself right now that, every day—at the very, very least—you will always do at least one thing to unite the tribes and build an invincible empire. Just *one* thing. That doesn't sound like much, does it? And because it's a very small promise, it's one you can count on yourself to keep. Without a doubt, you will have days when you do much, much more than that. However, if you do just one thing each day to spread the word and unite your people, at the end of the year you will have made 365 contributions to the empire. And *that's* the power of consistency.

Another aspect of persistence is the spirit of never accepting defeat. If you fight enough battles, eventually you may lose one. Don't let that stop you. If you lose, gather your friends and come up with another angle and yet another plan of attack. And then hit the enemy again. Keep doing it until you are victorious. In fact, sometimes you'll win just because your adversaries finally realize that you just won't stop. They'll lay down their arms and just open the gates. *That's* the power of being relentless.

Remember this, too, as you're building alliances and rallying people beneath your banner. First unite your tribe. Then unite all tribes. But what if they say "no"? Easy. Just don't take "no" for an answer. When I ran a sales consulting company, I used to teach my client's salespeople that, if the customer didn't say "no" at least seven times, they didn't really mean it.

One day, I happened to walk past a sales rep. She was on the phone with a customer, and I knew instantly that he'd asked her, "How many times do I have to tell you no?" It was apparent to me because, to my surprise and delight, I heard her say, "Well, my boss told me that if you don't say no at least seven times you don't really mean it. So, as I was saying . . ." She got the sale. Why? Well, above and beyond pure chutz-pah that had both me and the customer rolling in the aisles with laughter, it was because she was relentless. She made it clear, in no un-certain terms, that the only option she was willing to accept was a "yes." And she got it.

Remember, it's excellent to be able to make a big splash here and there. However, what's most important—and what will ultimately move you and the empire to success—is consistent and continual effort.

START A CHAIN REACTION.

Personal effort can accomplish great things, but group efforts can do even more. However, both of these approaches will eventually reach the limits of their effectiveness. One person can do only so much. In a similar vein, the same can be said of a dozen, a hundred, or even a thousand. The path to true power, then, is to find a way to extend your reach beyond what you can personally affect.

You need your message to spread and propagate on its own. You need something that can grow, and continue to grow, for all the days to come. When you're teaching people the Pillars of the empire and moti-vating them to join with you in a unified effort, you need a chain reaction.

The mechanics of this are actually quite simple. When you've built awareness and have drawn people to you, they're going to want to be a part of what you're doing once they see how much fun you're having with your successes. In many endeavors, adding one more ally to the cause is the goal that was worked toward, and therefore this accomplishment ends the need for any further action. Adding that one person to your ranks will help. But what if he then added ten more people, and each of them did the same? It's easy to see how powerful this technique is in spreading your message across the empire.

But how do you accomplish such a thing? This is actually one of the easiest steps to take in your entire plan. When you're building alliances and motivating people to work together with you to improve your existing way of doing things, you typically have a pretty clear-cut picture of your objectives. Accordingly, you're able to communicate this to all who work with you to institute change. It can be as simple as telling people that the major initiative for the group at present is finding a way to improve customer response time by 10%. This gives them a tangible goal and directs them to take specific action. And, because of this, you get results.

What you must do is expand your thinking beyond the particular problems of the day. Yes, you need improved customer response time. Furthermore, after that's accomplished, something really needs to be done about how complex some of your procedures are. And, of course, after that there will be yet another goal to achieve or problem to solve. But where in all of this is your long-term thinking? Without a doubt, you are accomplishing great things both for your group and the empire, but putting out fires doesn't expand the nation.

The goal is not just to improve the quality of life for your group and give the empire a significant boost from your tribe. The ultimate goal is to unite all tribes, eliminating the feelings of separation, putting an end to turf wars, and attacking the competition as one unified force. It's going to take you some time to get there, and, to accomplish this, you must continually expand the movement until it sweeps through every tribe in the land.

To do this, you simply list this as one more goal to be accomplished by all who serve the cause, and you keep it a high priority. Consequently, when your people are at a gathering, laughing and joking over a backyard cookout and brainstorming over what their next great success will be, they will always have *two* goals, not just one.

The first will be spreading the word and recruiting new people to the cause. The second goal will be tending to the current goals for their tribe. Of course, as they build alliances and make new friends, they will pass these priorities along so that each and every person understands their responsibilities as twofold: they must make their contributions toward excellence, and they must continually expand the movement by reaching out to other people, helping them in their jobs, and teaching them all the tactics and concepts that they themselves have been taught.

In such a way, by constant propagation and growth, does the movement expand and the state of your company improve. Our entire purpose is to improve the lives of the individuals by improving the health and well being of the company. This is a noble and benevolent concept that harms none and benefits all. Furthermore, as this philosophy spreads, it grows stronger, thereby enabling all of you to do even greater things. Thus, it is your responsibility to the good of the many to do your part daily in spreading this ideal throughout the land, for with every new person you add to the movement the entire empire prospers.

~~~~~~~~~~~~~~~~~~~~~⊚~~~~~~~~~~~~~~~~~~~~~

DO IT NOW.

By definition, tomorrow never comes. Therefore, anything you put off until tomorrow will never happen. The problems and difficulties you face in your job today are real, and they affect you personally. And every day that goes by is one more day that you have to put up with it. I want a better tomorrow; it's true. But I also want a better today, and I'm willing to work for it. How about you?

The simple fact of the matter is that, if you don't act, nothing will change. Just as we spoke of inspiring others, you need to find the things that inspire you personally and motivate you to act. You can't act tomorrow. Putting it off until next week is meaningless. If you want to improve your life—and through that improve the lives of all around you—then there is one and only one clear path for you to take. You must act today. Not later. Not eventually. But *now*.

You are even now more prepared for the battlefield of the business world than any of your competitors will ever hope to be. In taking your first steps, you will immediately enjoy the fun of enthusiasm and the strength of numbers. However, many of the things that we've talked about have been, by necessity, of a conceptual nature. There's no possible way that one book can give highly detailed steps that will be comprehensive and specific to each company. That's because every situation, even within the same industry, is different. These concepts must be translated to your unique experience. Then, and only then, will they be relevant and effective.

Therefore, in our final chapter, we will look at the field manual that you will create to map these strategies into the real world in the context of your specific job, the people you work with, and the empire you serve. As we walk through the process of moving from the general to the specific, you will quickly see the first concrete steps that you can take to make real, physical, and tangible changes in your job. This is where the fun begins.

I love writing, mainly because I never try to be something I'm not. I've been the president of the company, the high-powered consultant, the speaker that got standing ovations, and all that other exciting stuff, but I'm also the guy who cleaned your offices at night after you went home. Yes, on top of everything else I've done, I've even been the janitor.

This variety of experience gives me some distinct advantages in life. First, it helps me maintain a sense of humor and perspective. That's why I enjoy the silly side of life so much, even when I'm working on books. However, it also makes me realize one very important thing, something that is an unshakeable part of my daily life. At the end of the day, it's all about people. You are the true power of the Empire.

And, so, no matter how much fun I try to have with my writing, at the end of the day it is my intention for this to be an extremely practical and useful book, something that you can take into battle, something that will help you achieve victory after victory. You're not done with it after the next chapter; if you close the cover after the last page and just put it in your bookshelf, then this was all for nothing. Your life will not change.

You cannot completely absorb or memorize all the things we've talked about throughout the Pillars of the Empire in one sitting, and you were never intended to. This book is a field manual. It's a reference guide for corporate strategy and battle tactics. I want you to wear this copy out. I may well give out a prize this time next year for whoever has the most tattered and battle-worn copy of this book on the planet. Keep an eye on our Web site; I've done stranger things to make my points.

The Pillars of the Empire can change your company and change your life. But they can do so only if you put them into practice, continually honing your techniques and improving your skills. That's why there's even room in the back of the book for notes. Scribble in the margins. Mark up the paragraphs with a highlighter. Dog-ear the sections that you frequently refer to. These are not sacred scrolls. This book is meant to work for a living, just like you.

UNITE!

Build a movement and become invincible.

◎ Dedicate yourself to the cause.

◎ Emphasize your common bonds.

◎ Make the movement attractive.

◎ Be gracious to the vanquished.

◎ Build strength by teaching others.

◎ Gain support by spreading awareness.

◎ Inspire others to act.

◎ Be relentless.

◎ Start a chain reaction.

◎ Do it now.

MAKING IT WORK

Your Field Manual

By now, you can fully appreciate the value of unity within your entire company and are no doubt already beginning to see the false barriers and divisiveness fall away as you look at your leaders and workers in a new light. You are not separate people or warring factions. Although you reside in many tribes throughout your land, you are truly all one people, members of the same empire.

Of course, even though you now see the vision of what this unity will bring, your company may presently be a long way from realizing these dreams. This means that you have work to do. At this point, you're also familiar with each major concept required to build a stronger company, as represented by the Pillars of the Empire. These Pillars, and the Stones from which they are built, are designed to guide you along the path toward a better and more prosperous future.

For those of us who live in the western world, we're used to getting our inspiration and instruction in plain language. We want explicit answers to our questions, and we want the solutions to our problems given to us in plain and simple language, leaving no room for ambiguity or interpretation. Many cultures in the eastern world, however, are accustomed to a more abstract approach to learning and growing. Their teachers and inspirational figures often speak in parables and metaphor, sometimes answering a question by telling a story in a way that seemingly has nothing to do with the listener's situation. It is up to the listener to comprehend the concept being taught and apply it to their own life. This is how some business professionals can read seemingly unrelated books on ancient swordsmen and the battle philosophies of ancient generals and apply them to modern commerce. Obviously, interpretation is required because it's typically considered impolite to show up at a board meeting and start swinging a sword, no matter how great the temptation.

As for myself, I like having an unfair advantage. Therefore, I see no need to limit myself to either approach. Finding tremendous value in both ways of thinking, I choose to use both and apply whatever may be convenient or appropriate to the particular problem at hand. Some of you in the back of the room may have just declared, "Hey. No fair! He's got two swords, and we only have one!" Fair? I never claimed to play fair. Business is war, and I don't like to lose. Live with honor, fight with valor, but take every unfair advantage you can get!

Consequently, it is has been my deepest desire throughout this book to make sure that, when you walk away, you'll have a sword in each hand. The competition only has one, you say? Too bad for them. To this end, throughout our considerations of the Pillars, I've used a lot of everyday examples that most people in the business world can relate to. Although I've chosen illustrations that would strike as close to home as possible, they will never completely mirror your own reality. Even so, there was much to learn from them, leaving you at this point already holding one good, sharp sword. Now, let's get you another one.

Realizing that not everyone is accustomed to taking a general concept and translating it into specific actions that will be meaningful in their own personal sphere of influence, in the sections that follow I'll walk you through how to do just that. It's not difficult, really. Like anything else, it's just a matter of learning another new approach. Once you've learned how to do this with the Pillars, by the way, you'll be even more capable than you may realize, for you'll then be able to go to the book store and by any book you like on some of the many topics I've suggested throughout these pages, and with this skill interpret them and make their concepts your own.

THE VALUE OF MEMORY

It's no accident that the Pillars have been designed in this fashion. You'll note that there are exactly ten Pillars. Furthermore, each Pillar is built from ten Stones. Additionally, you'll notice that each Pillar has a one-line summary to give you a sense of how you should apply that concept. They have been organized and arranged in this fashion to make it easy for you to remember them, and remember them you must.

Pilots make constant use of checklists. There are procedures before you take off, things to keep in mind as you fly, and, of course, yet another set of things to which you must attend after the tray tables have been returned to their locked and upright positions. That's a lot of stuff to remember, and you don't want to know what happens if a step is missed. These items are important, and so they use both checklists and other devices to help to make sure that all tasks are accomplished in the proper sequence.

But, frequently, when you're thirty thousand feet above the nearest smooth strip of concrete and an unexpected storm suddenly crops up and tosses you about like a bean bag on someone's knee, you don't always have the luxury of time to look things up. If you don't have the proper responses already embedded so deeply into your brain that they're reflexive, you may end up spilling a passenger's drink when you land. And you know how cranky they get about that sort of thing.

The same holds true with our Pillars. Each one has ten Stones because that's a number that humans just naturally relate to. Of course, the same applies to the number of Pillars themselves. In the beginning, as you start to put these principles into practice in your own organization, the preceding pages with the summaries will be the first to acquire the noble status of being dog-eared and battle worn. However, just like a pilot, you won't always have time to reach for reference books in the heat of the moment. Therefore, it's time for your first homework assignment. As quickly as you can, memorize the Pillars of the Empire. Start by listing all ten Pillars and their brief summaries. Then, move on to each individual Pillar, one at a time, committing to memory the ten Stones from which it is built.

Will there be a test later? I'm not telling. However, I don't know about you, but I've always struggled with homework. It's usually not that difficult to actually do. It's just that every time I sit down to do it, my guitar beckons me from across the room to stop the work I'm doing and have a little fun instead. If you're like most people, you've encountered a similar resistance to doing your homework from time to time. It's only natural. So, it's time for us to put one of the principles we've already learned into place: it's time for a party.

The whole point of what we've been learning is how to leverage the power of the group. That's why we want to unite in the first place! So, why should we send ourselves to our rooms and suffer through a lonely and dull learning experience when we can instead have fun with our friends? You've no doubt already talked to others about your cause. If there's not already a movement in your company, it's time to start one, and this is the perfect opportunity. Talk to your friends who are also studying the Pillars, pick someone's house, and order a few pizzas.

Then, spend the evening having some fun with each other as you commit the Pillars and their Stones to memory. Laughter is not only allowed, it's highly recommended. You can use flash cards. You can write them on a whiteboard. You can even turn them into a song if you like. It just doesn't matter. The only thing that's important is the idea that, as you test each other and memorize each one, you have fun with it. It would be very silly of me to sit here and tell you how to entertain yourselves. Every group is different with their own style and sense of mischief. Figuring out how to make a game of it is your first exercise. Do it well, and you'll not only benefit from knowing your battle strategies by heart, but you'll also start building morale and esprit de corps from your very first day. And remember, enthusiasm is contagious.

UNDERSTANDING THE PROBLEMS

Have you finished your memory party yet? Does everyone know the Pillars by heart? If not, don't be afraid to throw another party! In my opinion, you can never have too many. Most important of all, however, is to avoid overloading yourself. Don't hold just one gathering and try to accomplish all the exercises and goals we're covering here. It's just too much at once, and it will turn from a fun time filled with laughter and silliness to some tedious work seminar. No amount of pizza makes that worthwhile. So, take small bites and don't try to get there overnight.

Now, having thrown enough memory parties to get the job done and make sure that everyone has had their fill of pizza, it's time for the next step. Although you will continually use the concepts of the Pillars throughout your career, in the beginning you doubtless have a specific set of problems in your company or department that you'd like to solve first. What are they? Quickly now, and no fair looking at each other for help. Yes, that's what I thought. If you can't describe the problems that you're going to solve, and do so in mind-numbing detail, then you're not adequately prepared to forge a solution. The problem *drives* the solution, not the other way around. Once you know the detailed difficulties to overcome, then and only then can you put together a detailed battle plan to attack them.

So, let's put together an outline. You'll find that it's the best form in which to capture clear and organized information. At the highest level, you'll list all of your major problems. Beneath each of those, you'll break them down into deeper and deeper detail until you have not only an extremely clear picture of what the problems are, you also have them organized so well that, if you need to attack certain aspects at a time, you have all the information regarding that area right at your fingertips in a manner that's easy to comprehend.

This sounds like a quick and easy task, but, like so many things, the complexities are a bit deceptive, as you'll find once you start digging in and analyzing things. Let's take just a very brief look at an example. You're working a lot of overtime, and no one is happy about it. There's the problem that you need to solve. But is it really the problem? Why are you working overtime? Closer examination reveals it's because you're behind in production. Why? Are you just too lazy to get the job done in a timely manner? Heavens, no. Everyone is working their tails off.

It's actually two problems. First, you're understaffed. Second, the department that feeds you the work that you do is inconsistent. You'll sit around for hours with nothing to do, then suddenly be given eight hours of work all at once. Of course, the leaders can't authorize more people because you're clearly not understaffed. I mean, you sit around for hours doing nothing, right?

As always, this is contrived and extremely simplistic, but you can see how quickly the details can get deeper and deeper. Your primary weapon in this exercise is a tool that small children use to drive adults crazy at one point or another. For every single detail you consider, pretend you're a small child, and keep asking this simple question: "Why?" It's amazing how much information you can drag out of yourself with this technique.

You're going to have lots and lots of pages when you're done. If you have a laptop and word processor software that makes organizing outlines quick and easy, it'll make things much better for you, but, in the end, the important thing is the information, not the medium. Sound like a lot of work? It is. Furthermore, like anyone else, as you ask yourself questions and offer honest answers, you're going to discover two things.

First, sometimes you just don't know why things are the way they are. Second, you'll have blind spots. That's just human nature. Fortunately, there's an extremely effective method for coping with these deficiencies. Does anyone know what it is? Yep, you guessed it. It's time for another social event.

The power of group thought will compensate for the blind spots we each have. Also, even if you can't answer the "why" question, someone else probably can. Remember how we talked about the value of making friends and building alliances in other tribes? Here's a great way to foster those relationships and benefit at the same time. They'll see things differently from their tribe, and, between all the tribal members you invite to the party, you'll have a powerful perspective indeed.

At the same time, you absolutely *must* keep the atmosphere light and fun. It doesn't matter if it's someone juggling notebooks or everyone doing the conga line, find the things that your people consider fun and do them! If you're all laughing and joking while you're getting this task done, you'll not only be more productive, you'll have forged much stronger bonds among all of the tribes. Just be sure to order enough pizza. That's an important social consideration no matter which tribe you come from.

DEFINING YOUR GOALS

Where do you want to take the empire? What are your goals, dreams, and desires for your tribe? Once again, if you can't write them down in explicit detail, you can't be effective in putting together a plan.

There is absolutely nothing in this section that's different from the previous ones, other than the fact that, whereas before we were analyzing the problems, we're now considering our goals. The same benefits apply when you invite allies and friends from other tribes, and at the end of both gatherings you should have highly detailed and organized descriptions of every topic you've considered.

By the way, when you have these gatherings, get a single volunteer to be in charge of writing it all down. That can be a lot of work, so make sure that one person doesn't get stuck doing it every time you get together. When you're done, this person can distribute the information to everyone, and the entire group will have consistent notes from the experience.

Another word of caution: this can sometimes be sensitive information. Should your adversaries get hold of it, there's always the chance for trouble. Therefore, it's a good idea to keep this sort of stuff in your homes and not in your offices. Your home is secure; your office is not. Of course, be sure to follow any company guidelines regarding confidential or proprietary information as you do this. If you were to break the legal rules, that would just present another vulnerability to the group. So, don't be exceedingly paranoid, but don't be careless, either. You need these notes to be detailed and explicit if you're to solve your problems and accomplish your goals. Everyone will be much more frank and open if they know this information is secure.

APPLYING THE PILLARS

We now have two very detailed outlines: one with all the problems that you wish to resolve immediately, and the other containing the glory you would like to bring to the empire. It's time for solutions and specific, detailed plans of action. It is at this point that we employ the technique of translating the abstract to the concrete. We're going to apply the Pillars of the Empire to each item we wish to address, and thereby create strategies and plans with specific and detailed steps to take that will help us accomplish our goals.

First, collapse your outlines to the highest level and prioritize your tasks. You can mix the problems and goals together. It doesn't matter. All that's needed is that you rank them in terms of what's the most important. You won't accomplish all of these desires in one day, and, if you try to do too much at once, you'll do it all very poorly. Pick a problem and solve it. Pick a goal and achieve it. Sometimes, things will be related and you must deal with them at the same time. That's okay, too. Just get organized first in terms of what actions you're going to take in which specific order.

We will now take a structured and detailed approach to your highest-priority item. Looking not only at the problem or goal itself, but also the details generated beneath it, we will work our way, one at a time, through the Stones of each Pillar. For this, we now need to start an outline branch under the top level of this task, titled *Solution*. This is where we'll keep our notes on the steps to take.

Now begin work on the Pillars. Start with *Vision*. Consider the first Stone, "Picture the end result in fine detail." Looking at all the details of the task before you, ask yourself, what does this mean in the context of the task you're working on? How does it apply? Can you see the end result of your desires for this task? Can you see them in detail? Write those details down in the outline.

The next Stone you encounter is, "Plan like you're going to live forever." As you consider the task at hand, ask yourself, what are the long-term consequences? What if you were going to be there when the wheel came around? Accordingly, by applying this Stone, what changes or additions should you make to your plans to ensure that you're using long-term thinking?

In a similar manner, you will work through each Stone of the ten Pillars. When you are done, you will have gathered a comprehensive set of details and resources that you can apply to the task at hand. The Stones of each Pillar will generate a great deal of questions. Answering these questions is the key to your success, for it forces you to consider your plans from all of the important angles.

Furthermore, you'll find that you're training yourself to think in very practical terms regarding both your company and the real people you'll have to deal with in the course of your actions. And, of course, each time you do this exercise, you will improve your skills and as a result become better and better at it until you can not only do it quickly, but also have much more precision and insight as you do.

In applying each Pillar to the specific scenarios of the day, you will be doing more than just creating better plans. You will be teaching yourself to interpret high-level principals and apply their concepts to any task. You've been doing this all along, you know. From the very beginning, I've spoken of business as war. Any intelligent adult knows that real warfare involves acts of physical violence. And, yet, throughout your company each day, there is no killing or even fisticuffs. So, how, then, can business be war?

In a literal sense, of course, it's not. There are no guns, knives, bullets, or bombs. Just a lot of people vying for power and position. However, once you start thinking of the phrase, *business is war* as a metaphor, you're immediately able to apply the principles of warfare to a wide range of corporate activities. This is what they've been doing in the eastern world for a long time now. When you develop skills in these areas, as you will through working with the Pillars, you will one day be able to draw on a wide range of human literature, having the ability to apply the wisdom of the ages to your contemporary problems, all through the power of metaphor.

The following list contains just a few of the questions you'll find yourself asking as you apply the Pillars to a particular task. This is just a sampling to give you an idea of how to approach things. With the proper effort, each Pillar will prompt many more such thoughts, all highly relevant to what you're looking to accomplish.

◎ What resources are required to implement them?

◎ Who has the authority to approve your ideas?

◎ Do you need the cooperation of other groups to make this a success?

◎ What would be the direct benefit to the decision maker personally in implementing your idea?

◎ What would be the benefit to the supporting groups?

◎ What would be the benefit to the company?

◎ What allies might help you sway the decision?

◎ What's in it for them?

◎ How will you approach them?

◎ How would your idea benefit the peers you work with?

◎ What could they do to help get this idea implemented?

◎ What would be the best way to gain their support?

◎ What steps must be taken to make this idea a reality?

◎ What is the order of the steps?

- ◎ What are the consequences if this idea is implemented?
- ◎ Are you prepared for them?
- ◎ What's your backup plan if this idea doesn't get approved?
- ◎ What's your backup plan if this idea doesn't work?

As you can see, there's a lot of work to be done, but what should be equally clear is that, if you go to the trouble of doing this properly, your group and your solutions will overwhelm all opposition. Not only will your ideas be extremely well considered and cleverly planned, you have an additional advantage: because thinking through battle plans in this degree of detail is so much work, your adversaries almost never will do it. You will be fighting an unprepared opponent on the battlefield, and they will scatter in a confused and disoriented state before the might and precision of your plan.

You're now ready to sit down with your problems and goals and apply the Pillars to them. Obviously, you need as many good minds on the solution as you can get. You need to make sure that you have a wide variety of perspectives so that you don't leave holes in your plan that your enemies can exploit. You'll need the support of different groups of workers and leaders. And you need to get all of these resources together so that you can put together a plan of attack so powerful that no one will dare oppose it. It seems that there's only one thing to do in this case. Once again, socializing with others, you can mix business with pleasure and enjoy the best of both worlds.

YOUR JOURNALS

Throughout our conversations, we've made numerous references to writing things down and keeping personal notes. You should take this very seriously, for such note taking is a powerful tool for you to use over the course of your career.

Go down to the store and buy whatever kind of journaling tools work for you. There's a lot to choose from. Depending on your style, you can pick up what you need at the bookstore, stationery shop, or even the corner grocery store. That's where I get my stuff. I use cheap, spiral notebooks. I can find them anywhere, they fit nicely on a clipboard, and they don't take much space. Of course, they also illustrate the point that your journal doesn't have to be fancy or expensive. The information is what's important, not the quality of the paper.

There are two primary styles of keeping a journal. Some people make an entry every day, regardless of what happened or didn't. Others write only when there's something they want to note. Both methods are fine, so use what works for you personally.

When you make your entries, always record both the calendar date (with year) along with the day of the week. Although I don't personally maintain time of day, you may want to note that as well, depending on your situation. These details may seem unnecessary, but, over time, one of the values of your journal is that it will help you recognize *patterns*. You'll be surprised what patterns appear, and this information is one more thing to help you turn random events into something that appears to be repeating itself.

It's worth noting that we're talking about more than one journal. I strongly recommend three (and, for what it's worth, my style is to write only when I have something to note). The first journal is for your general notes. Anything goes, from observing other people's behavior, your own emotional tirades, trends and threats you see on the horizon, and, most importantly, all the wonderful little ideas and inspirations that come to you during the course of the day. You may be driving home and see a billboard completely unrelated to your business that nonetheless gives you a great new product idea. Write it down. You may have a sudden insight into what motivates a key player in your group. Put it in writing. Your general journal is for any and every thought that comes to mind, lest you forget it later. And, if you don't write it down, you will forget it.

The second journal, kept in a separate notebook, is labeled *Problems and Goals*. This is where you jot down the observations of the day and the bigger pictures to which they relate. Depending on your penchant for organization, these could be divided into two books, actually. You'll have a sense of whether you want to do that or not after you've been at it for a while. However, the output of this book is very valuable.

When you and your people have one of your frequent parties to discuss the general state of the empire, you'll bring this journal along so that you can raise the issues that you've made note of and get feedback from others. It is from these conversations that your next tasks are determined, leading you to build a new initiative and battle plan. Keeping this in a separate notebook means that it's easier to see the issues that should lead to action without having to weed through other details.

The third book is even more important. It's called *Success Stories*. Whether you prevail in a small, daily skirmish or in a huge battle that your group has been fighting for months, write it down! Speak freely in this journal about all the things that you and your people did right, all the brilliant ideas that people came up with, the inspired way that you handled those unforeseen and last-minute problems, and even stories of the wild and crazy things people did at the victory parties you threw afterward. You do throw victory parties, right? Good. Just checking.

Why would you bother with the paperwork when the battle has been won? Because you will always live to fight another day. When you see patterns in your Problems and Goals journal and muse that you've seen this before, your next step is to browse the pages of Success Stories. How did you solve this problem last time? I shouldn't have to tell you how powerful it is to be able to read all the details of how it happened. Of course, you may remember that you prevailed in a similar situation, but you'll always forget the details unless they're written down at the time it happened.

The other reason that this is an important journal to keep is straight out of one of the Pillars: *morale*. Battles can drag on. One hard day at work follows another. Sometimes things don't go right. You will, eventually, have times when you're worn down, worn out, and starting to question whether you're ever going to solve the particular problem you're grappling with. Your Success Stories journal gives you a powerful and much needed boost at such times. It will feed your spirit with inspiration, and that is the critical fuel that will carry you on from victory to victory. Therefore, each and every time you succeed, you absolutely must write it in your Success Stories.

Additionally, because this offers tactical information as well as inspiration, you need to write down which of the Pillars and Stones you used to achieve the victory. This information will be of obvious value when a similar problem occurs in the future. Even though the specifics may change and require different actual steps, you'll often find that you can streamline your response by going first to the Pillars and Stones that worked for you previously. Consequently, you need this information in your Success Stories journal, or you won't remember it when you need it.

As we've touched on so often, never, *ever* underestimate how important inspiration and motivation can be to your overall efforts. High spirits keep you on a roll, moving from success to success. Therefore, as you might have already guessed, there's yet another gathering to have!

Obviously, you'll have a celebration when you win a big victory. But what about those times when the going gets tough, and everyone seems bogged down and dispirited? Hope will diminish, spirits will sag, and people may begin to doubt that victory does in fact lie ahead. This can be devastating to your overall cause, and even to the movement in general. At such times, one of the best things you can do is hold a Success Stories party. Gather your people, call your highly popular pizza delivery guy, and make sure everyone brings their Success Story journals.

Start out just like you would any other kind of gathering. Forget about the world, forget about your troubles, and just howl at the moon a little. When people have lightened up a bit, it's story time. Even though you were all present at the last victory, everyone will tell the story a little differently. Take turns sharing your perspective on the glories and successes you've encountered thus far. Order doesn't matter. In fact, it doesn't even matter if you have a new friend over from a different tribe, and they tell stories of their own tribal victories that you never heard about. All that really matters is that, over the course of the evening, you will all laugh and cheer as you hear stories of brilliance, vision, and success. Your spirits will soar, and you'll greet your battles the next day with new life.

To that end, I strongly encourage you to visit our Web site, www.ShowProgramming.com, and share your success stories with us as well. By doing so, it allows us to make them available to the movement worldwide, providing a powerful resource for all who are working to build an invincible empire. You're free and encouraged to print out your favorite stories and share them with your group when you gather. Once again, the power of inspiration and enthusiasm will make you an unstoppable force for good in your company. Just as you need friends and allies in your own empire, you can look on this as drawing on new friends from empires the world over. As we share our successes, we all become stronger and more able to succeed yet again.

YOUR FREE COMPANION CD

In addition to serving as a meeting place for kindred spirits worldwide, you'll also find an ever-growing list of resources when you visit us on the Web. First, I've put together a free CD for you that highlights each of the Pillars of the Empire and other things that I hope will help to lift your spirits and better prepare you for your days. We've made it a normal audio CD so that you can listen to it in the car driving to work or anywhere else where a set of headphones is handy.

It turns out that the business realities of sticking the CD somewhere on the back cover would have driven up your cost for this book to an unreasonable extreme. None of us wanted to see that happen, so I instead offered to make it available from our Web site. When you visit, just tell us where to send it and we'll mail it to you. And, because mailing means a modest shipping cost, we've also made it available for download as a series of mp3 files well. Use either method or both, whichever is most convenient for your particular environment.

No matter how moving the written word, it's always been true that nothing moves the spirit like music and the human voice. That's why Shakespeare's plays are so much more fun at a theater than they are when you just read them. Consequently, you'll also find this CD to be an excellent tool when you're trying to get people's attention and build a movement in your company. Unlike our other products and services, the *Unite the Tribes* Companion CD and associated downloads are intended for you to copy and share for free with as many friends as you like. If it helps you to build an invincible empire in which quality, service, and profitability reign supreme, it ultimately strengthens us all.

ADDITIONAL RESOURCES

You'll also find a variety of other free resources at our Web site to accompany both this book and your efforts. And, of course, it's always good to hear from you. My email address is on our Web site. I draw much of my own inspiration for my writing, speaking, and other such mischief from the tales and success stories I hear from people just like you—the ones who go out there and actually change the world.

I also have the distinct pleasure of working with what I personally believe to be the best publisher in the business: Apress. My friends there exhibit the kinds of qualities that made me want to write this book in the first place. Not only can they react quickly and move from one excellent plan to the next without even breaking a sweat, each and every one of them are nice people. And, at the end of the day, just as in your empire, it's all about people. You'll find additional resources from Apress as well, from bulk discounts that help you order copies for all the people in your company to forums and information that help you achieve your goals. Not surprisingly, you can find them at www.apress.com.

I've been fortunate over the years to have had such a tremendous diversity in my careers. Even if I wasn't really crazy about the experience when I was the guy flipping the burgers or emptying the trash, I'm now incredibly grateful for it all. It has shown me the common bond that we all share, from the back rooms to the boardroom. More than anything else, though, working with people at every level of the empire has proven to me that, when you really need to achieve the impossible and create wonders beyond any the world has ever seen, there is nothing— and I mean *nothing*—that cannot be achieved through people's combined creativity, brilliance, enthusiasm, and power. Truly, the people are the empire.

Unite, and be invincible!

Index

NOTES

NOTES

NOTES

NOTES

forums.apress.com

FOR PROFESSIONALS BY PROFESSIONALS™

JOIN THE APRESS FORUMS AND BE PART OF OUR COMMUNITY. You'll find discussions that cover topics of interest to IT professionals, programmers, and enthusiasts just like you. If you post a query to one of our forums, you can expect that some of the best minds in the business—especially Apress authors, who all write with *The Expert's Voice*™—will chime in to help you. Why not aim to become one of our most valuable participants (MVPs) and win cool stuff? Here's a sampling of what you'll find:

DATABASES
Data drives everything.

Share information, exchange ideas, and discuss any database programming or administration issues.

PROGRAMMING/BUSINESS
Unfortunately, it is.

Talk about the Apress line of books that cover software methodology, best practices, and how programmers interact with the "suits."

INTERNET TECHNOLOGIES AND NETWORKING
Try living without plumbing (and eventually IPv6).

Talk about networking topics including protocols, design, administration, wireless, wired, storage, backup, certifications, trends, and new technologies.

WEB DEVELOPMENT/DESIGN
Ugly doesn't cut it anymore, and CGI is absurd.

Help is in sight for your site. Find design solutions for your projects and get ideas for building an interactive Web site.

JAVA
We've come a long way from the old Oak tree.

Hang out and discuss Java in whatever flavor you choose: J2SE, J2EE, J2ME, Jakarta, and so on.

SECURITY
Lots of bad guys out there—the good guys need help.

Discuss computer and network security issues here. Just don't let anyone else know the answers!

MAC OS X
All about the Zen of OS X.

OS X is both the present and the future for Mac apps. Make suggestions, offer up ideas, or boast about your new hardware.

TECHNOLOGY IN ACTION
Cool things. Fun things.

It's after hours. It's time to play. Whether you're into LEGO® MINDSTORMS™ or turning an old PC into a DVR, this is where technology turns into fun.

OPEN SOURCE
Source code is good; understanding (open) source is better.

Discuss open source technologies and related topics such as PHP, MySQL, Linux, Perl, Apache, Python, and more.

WINDOWS
No defenestration here.

Ask questions about all aspects of Windows programming, get help on Microsoft technologies covered in Apress books, or provide feedback on any Apress Windows book.

HOW TO PARTICIPATE:
Go to the Apress Forums site at **http://forums.apress.com/**.
Click the New User link.